THE
WAR ON CRIME

J. Edgar Hoover Versus the

John Dillinger Gang

Jeffrey K. Smith

ISBN: 1500804274
ISBN 13: 9781500804275

Note To Readers

More than once, I have been questioned about the absence of footnotes or endnotes in my non-fiction books. Simply answered—it is a matter of style. While recounting the lives and times of historical figures, I have chosen to present their stories in a narrative format. It is my goal to bring history alive, akin to a fast-paced novel. The chronology and accuracy of the events in this book and my other works of non-fiction are substantiated by extensive research, with the sources documented in the bibliography. Ultimately, I hope the readers will understand that fact is often stranger and more compelling than fiction.

The Federal Bureau of Investigation (FBI) was not so-named until 1935, after the majority of the events in this book had transpired. Prior to 1935, it was known as the Bureau or Division of Investigation. To minimize confusion, I have opted to use the term *Bureau*, when referring to the federal agency.

PROLOGUE

This is a story about cops and robbers, set against the backdrop of the Great Depression, a desperate time for many, when the boundaries between right and wrong were often blurred. It is the story of J. Edgar Hoover versus the John Dillinger Gang—the center pieces of the so-called *War on Crime*. When the dust settled, Hoover emerged as the nation's top cop—a position he would not yield until his death, nearly four decades later.

It was an era of bank heists. Between 1931 and 1934, bank robberies in the United States averaged two per day. Three-quarters of those robberies occurred in the Midwest; in Indiana, alone, there were 29 bank robberies in 1933.

Local law enforcement was woefully unprepared to combat the crime wave, and in many cases, lacked state police forces to provide support. Adding to their difficulties, lawmen were prohibited from chasing suspects across state lines.

The odds were tilted heavily in favor of the criminals. Most patrol cars lacked two-way radios, which would not become standard-issue until the 1940s. While police officers and deputy sheriffs could receive radio messages from headquarters, they could not transmit back to the station or to fellow patrolmen. Consequently, it was nearly impossible to coordinate chases or efficiently set up road blocks.

Worse yet, bank robbers were equipped with faster automobiles and superior firepower. Most police officers were assigned patrol cars powered by four or six cylinder engines. The lawmen's felonious counterparts drove Fords or Essex Terraplanes equipped with V-8 engines capable of accelerating to 90 miles per hour, which made it easy to outrun the good guys. Flush with stolen cash, the felons were free to purchase, if they chose not to steal, the newest and fastest automobiles. In one year alone, during the height of the Great Depression, John Dillinger bought more new cars than most Americans would purchase in the course of a lifetime.

The aptly-named *auto bandits* also benefited from the Federal Highway Act, passed shortly after the conclusion of World War I, which added 300,000 miles of paved highways to the American landscape. In 1924, Rand-McNally published its first national road map, which demarcated not only the major thoroughfares, but also state and local farm roads, allowing the robbers to precisely map out get-away routes.

Most police departments were lucky to have a handful of shotguns or hunting rifles to augment their standard side arms. In contrast, the bank robbers, often clad in bulletproof vests, were armed with automatic pistols and rifles, as well as frighteningly powerful Thompson submachine guns. First used in the World War I trenches, Tommy guns could accommodate either 20-round magazines or 50 to 100-round drums, loaded with .45 caliber bullets. When set on full automatic, the weapon was capable of firing 800 rounds per minute. Unlike pistols, submachine guns were classified as rifles, which did not require permits to carry. In an era absent background checks, customers could purchase Tommy guns at sporting goods and hardware stores, or via mail-order coupons in gun magazines, for around $175, each.

With plodding chase vehicles and inferior firepower, law enforcement agents were akin to the Keystone Cops. Processing crime scenes was also problematic, as few police departments possessed the skill and resources to dust vaults, cash drawers, door knobs, and steering wheels for finger prints.

If and when bank robbers were captured, it was difficult to keep them incarcerated. Prison overcrowding, coupled with discreet bribery of guards and wardens, facilitated unpublicized, but frequent escapes. Bribes paid to parole board members and corrupt politicians granted hardened criminals early paroles for alleged "good behavior."

The bank robbers also benefited from a host of facilitators. A number of Midwestern cities, like Chicago, Kansas City, and St. Louis, supplied fencers for stolen goods, money launderers, physicians who neglected to report gunshot wounds, lawyers who were as corrupt as their clients, police officers eager to accept bribes, tailors who designed jackets and trousers that accommodated concealed weapons, garage owners who kept get-away vehicles out of sight, and body shop specialists who discreetly repaired bullet-damaged vehicles.

Smaller cities and towns, known as "cooling-off joints," were readily accessible. Locales like Hot Springs, Arkansas, Joplin, Missouri, and St. Paul, Minnesota, served as temporary hideouts for bank robbers.

Most of the Depression-era bank robbers came from the lower Midwest and South. The infamous Bonnie and Clyde (Bonnie Parker and Clyde Barrow) were from Dallas. Charles Arthur "Pretty Boy" Floyd was a native of Oklahoma. George Barnes (alias Machine Gun Kelly) was a Tennessean, while Kate "Ma" Barker and her four sons were Missourians. The most notorious of them all, John Dillinger, came from Indiana.

Depression-era Americans, who could not afford to patronize entertainment venues, were fascinated by newspaper accounts of the bank robbers' exploits. Convincing an economically oppressed readership to part with a hard-earned nickel to purchase a daily newspaper, much less a dime for a weekend edition, led publishers to play loose with the facts and sensationalize the crimes.

A plethora of newspaper articles and movie theater newsreels provided the public with continuous updates about daring bank robberies, madcap chases, and bloody gun battles. Familiarity bred intimacy, humanizing the outlaws and allowing the general public to vicariously participate in bank heists, gunplay, and jail breaks.

The gangsters earned sympathy from many of their fellow countrymen. After the stock market crash of 1929, which precipitated the Great Depression, many jobless Americans saw their homes or farms drawn into foreclosure by banks. In the eyes of many small business owners and farmers, the banks were as much the enemy, if not more so, than the men who robbed them. Some who were deprived of their homes and livelihoods quietly cheered as the bank robbers extracted a measure of revenge against the heartless financial power brokers.

When John Dillinger began robbing banks in 1933, some 13,000,000 Americans were unemployed. Breadlines were commonplace throughout the country, while building entryways, park benches, and subway lobbies served as bedrooms for the homeless. Widespread despair reinforced the notion that banks had declared war against the common man. While hardly an unbiased observer, Dillinger gang member, Harry Pierpont, nonetheless echoed the cry of the common man: "Banks steal from the people."

"My conscience doesn't hurt me. I stole from the bankers. They stole from the people. All we did was help raise the insurance rates," Pierpont unashamedly proclaimed.

John Dillinger was the most celebrated of all the Depression-era bank robbers. A handsome and charismatic ladies' man, *Gentleman John* was also nicknamed the *Jackrabbit*—reflective of his agility when vaulting over bank counters. Unlike some of his blood thirsty counterparts, Dillinger was known to have killed only one person during his crime spree, making him appear more roguish than dangerous.

Beginning in the spring of 1933, Dillinger's binge of bank robberies, armory thefts, and jail breaks lasted for a little over a year. During that time, he was credited with stealing more than $500,000 in cash and bonds (equivalent to seven million modern-day dollars). Crisscrossing the Midwest, interspersed with vacations to Florida, Arkansas, and Arizona, Dillinger travelled an estimated 75,000 miles by automobile. Dillinger boasted that no jail could hold him, and proved his point on more than one occasion. All the while, the mischievous *Jackrabbit* taunted his pursuers with a series of phone calls, post cards, and letters.

An elusive Dillinger became the *Robin Hood* of his generation. In April of 1934, the *Indianapolis Star* newspaper portrayed him as all but invincible: "From pillar to post, the law has chased John Dillinger. The entire crime-fighting resources of the nation have united for months against one man, and he has continued to strike and vanish at will, with apparent immunity."

In the eyes of Bureau Director, J. Edgar Hoover, John Dillinger was anything but a Robin Hood-like hero. The humorless, tightly-wound Hoover viewed any measure of lawlessness as a threat to his organized world. Not yet secure in his position as the nation's top lawman and wary of exposing the fledgling Bureau's inexperience at fighting crime, Hoover was initially reluctant to wage war against the gangster element.

When the Bureau finally joined in the chase of the Dillinger Gang, Hoover demonized Dillinger and his cohorts as glorified, attention-seeking criminals, who must be extinguished. Consequently, Dillinger was designated as America's first *Public Enemy Number One*.

Much to Hoover's chagrin, Bureau agents stumbled and bumbled their way out of the starting blocks during the *War on Crime*. When the Bureau finally succeeded in tracking down and killing Dillinger, Hoover skillfully rewrote history, erasing earlier mishaps and episodes of incompetence. Dillinger's death, coupled with Hoover's mastery of public relations helped birth the now-legendary Federal Bureau of Investigation (FBI).

For the remaining 37 years of his life, J. Edgar Hoover wielded unprecedented power and influence from the throne he grandiosely, but aptly referred to as the *Seat of Government*.

CHAPTER ONE

Speed

The year 1895 dawned on an America consisting of 45 states and only 30 years distant from the end of the Civil War. At 7:30 a.m., on the very first day of that year, in Washington D.C., John Edgar Hoover was born.

J.E. or Edgar, as he was most often called, was the youngest of three surviving children born to 38-year-old Dickerson Naylor Hoover and Anna Marie (Annie) Scheitlin Hoover, who was four years younger than her husband. Edgar's brother and sister, Dickerson, Jr. and Lillian, were already teenagers. An older sister, three-year-old Sadie Marguerite, had died of diphtheria, 18 months prior to his birth.

Edgar's father, Dickerson, was employed by the federal government as an engraver for the U.S. Coast and Geodetic Survey—the agency responsible for charting America's waterways. His mother, Annie, had been a child of privilege, having attended St. Cecilia's School for Girls in Washington D.C., as well as a convent in Switzerland. Her grandfather had once served as the Swiss Counsel—Switzerland's highest ranking diplomatic post in the United States. Annie found it difficult to accept that her husband, a career public servant, could never generate the income and prestige befitting her proud lineage. Consequently, Annie pinned unfulfilled hopes and dreams on her youngest child. A niece later recalled that Annie "always expected that J.E. was going to be successful."

While Annie stood barely five feet tall, she nonetheless commanded respect within the Hoover household. Meticulous, responsible, pious, and image conscious, she was the matriarch of the family. From a young age, Edgar felt his mother's push to excel, as conveyed in a letter from Annie to her youngest son: "I was so glad to hear you were perfect in your spelling and arithmetic. Study hard, both your lessons and music, and try to be a very good boy."

As he absorbed Annie's lessons on life, Edgar became a quintessential mamma's boy. He would live with Annie in the family home until her death in 1938; at that point, he was a 43-year-old bachelor. Years later, Deputy Director of the FBI, Cartha DeLoach, perceptively noted that Annie was "the only person for whom he (Edgar) held a deep and abiding affection."

Edgar never established the same close relationship with his mild-mannered father. Dickerson, however, tried to bond with his youngest son, writing him affectionate letters whenever his job took him out of town. In one father-to-son missive, distinctly different from the letters Annie wrote, Dickerson encouraged Edgar to "take care of yourself and don't study too hard."

The two-story, wood-frame house, with its white stucco exterior and black shutters, at 413 Seward Square, just three blocks from the U.S. Capitol building, was the focal point of young Edgar's life. It was there that his prodigious memory became a source of amazement and pride to his doting mother; by age two, Edgar had learned the entire alphabet, and a year later, could already print words. Not surprisingly, in elementary and middle school, Edgar's grades were "good" or "excellent plus."

Naturally shy, Edgar never minded being alone, often spending long hours in his mother's shaded backyard flower garden occupied with books. When Edgar developed a persistent stuttering problem during elementary school, Annie took him for consultations with specialists, one of whom recommended that he speak rapidly to overcome his difficulties with articulation. From that point forward, Edgar spoke in a rapid, staccato fashion, earning the nickname *Speed*. Later in life, a court stenographer protested that he could transcribe 200 words per minute, but still could not keep up with Hoover, who spoke at least twice as fast.

Even though his parents did not mandate church attendance, both Annie and Dickerson regularly quizzed Edgar about his knowledge and understanding of scripture. Edgar started out attending a Lutheran church, but was later baptized as a Presbyterian, where he taught Sunday school and sang in the choir. It was there that Edgar found a substitute father figure—Presbyterian minister, Dr. Donald Campbell MacLeod. Edgar remembered the charismatic, energetic, and athletic pastor, who he met during a sandlot baseball game, as the "ideal of manhood." Later in life, Hoover reflected on his lasting impressions of MacLeod, which helped shape his own personality: "He was a vigorous, forthright Calvinist, whose rigorous sense of duty and clear-cut view of right and wrong did nothing to suppress his sense of humor or his joy in life."

Beginning in childhood, Edgar diligently recorded life events in a leather bound notebook labeled, *Mr. Edgar Hoover, Private*. Among his ledger entries were ratings of teachers and assessments of his academic performance. At age 13, he began keeping a diary, where he recorded mostly the mundane—his clothing sizes, daily weather conditions, money saved from performing odd jobs, and family births/deaths. On occasion, he wrote about novel experiences, like the time he witnessed the famed Orville Wright pilot his airplane from Washington D.C. to Alexandria, Virginia and back; in that diary entry, Edgar proudly noted that he was "the first outsider to shake Orville's hand."

At age 11, Edgar began publishing a neighborhood newspaper, entitled the *Weekly Review*. The masthead of the fledgling paper listed J.E. Hoover as *Editor and Printer*. Even though his 26-year-old brother, Dick, who was employed by the Steamship Inspection Service, helped with publication of the newspaper, Edgar credited him with the less prestigious title of *Typewriter*.

The *Weekly Review* was filled with neighborhood news and gossip, jokes, health tips, and brief biographies of historical figures. The newspaper also featured proverbs, which the young publisher found inspiriting, including: "Where there is a will, there is a way," and "Whatever is worth doing at all, is worth doing well."

An industrious Edgar took advantage of the fact that the local grocery store did not employ delivery boys. He soon offered to carry customers' groceries for a flat fee of 10 cents, "regardless of distance." Realizing he could maximize his profits by making more deliveries, *Speed* Hoover ran while carrying bags of groceries to their respective destinations. An entrepreneurial Hoover stationed himself outside the front entrance of Eastern Market from 7:00 a.m. to 7:00 p.m. on Saturdays, and after school, on weekdays.

Like most adolescents, Edgar was preoccupied with his appearance, and after developing a conspicuous Staphylococcus infection on his nose, he refused to venture out into the public. In an era before antibiotics, he repeatedly applied warm compresses until the boil ruptured, which left behind a permanent scar. Self-conscious about his squashed, bulldog-like nose, Edgar repeatedly told others the scar was the result of being struck by a baseball. While this may have been one of the first times that he altered facts to improve his personal or professional image, it would not be the last.

By the time he was 13 years old, Edgar's sister, Lillian, and brother, Dick, had married and moved out of the family home. Now that Edgar and his parents were the only ones left in the Hoover household, mother and youngest son drew even closer. In the fall of 1909, Edgar entered high school. While his older brother and sister had attended nearby Eastern High school, Edgar chose Central High School, located three miles from the family's Seward Square home. Eastern and Central were both public schools, but the latter offered industrious students the opportunity to take college preparatory courses, like chemistry, physics, Latin, French, and biology.

Though he was engaged by the challenging curriculum, Edgar still found time for extracurricular activities, including the library club, choir, and debate team. He later credited debate with teaching him "self-possession and mental control," while helping "to control my temper" and "free myself from sarcasm." During one debate contest, Edgar argued in favor of capital punishment, citing biblical references supporting the use of the death penalty in "Christian nations."

Eager to challenge both his mind and body, Edgar wanted to try out for junior varsity football, but the coach concluded that his 125-pound physique could not absorb the beating. Instead, he joined the track team; consistent with his nickname, *Speed* became a sprinter.

The Central High Corp of Cadets ultimately provided Edgar with his most satisfying extracurricular achievement. Founded in 1882, the Central High Corp was so esteemed that the famed John Phillip Sousa composed the group's marching anthem. The adolescent corpsmen prided themselves on their expertise in drill formations, successfully competing against area schools.

Edgar proudly wore his uniform to school on the twice-per-week drill practice days, as well as to Sunday church services. A photograph of 16-year-old Edgar, dressed in sharply creased gray pants, navy jacket, white gloves, and short-billed cap, clearly revealed his stern countenance and erect posture.

During his senior year of high school, Edgar was elected Captain of Company A, which placed him in command of six squads. Hoover and his charges were proudly selected to march in President Woodrow Wilson's March 4, 1913 inaugural parade. Captainship in the Cadet Corps convinced Edgar that he was well-suited to be a leader and motivator of men. As high school graduation neared, he wrote about the importance of camaraderie in his diary: "The year has been a most enjoyable one, for there is nothing more pleasant than to be associated with a company composed of officers and men who you feel are behind you, heart and soul. The saddest moment of the year was not when I saw the Adjutant turn toward his right, but when I realized that I must part with a group of fellows who had become a part of my life."

As might have been expected, Edgar was a diligent high school student, absent only four days over the course of four years. He proudly presented others with an embossed business card—*Edgar Hoover, Student, Central High School*. Classmate Francis Gray was struck by Hoover's ambition: "We called him *Speed* Hoover because he talked fast. He was so fast—talked fast—thought fast..."

While comfortable in the company of males, Edgar appeared oblivious to the opposite sex—a characteristic that would persist into his adult years. Edgar's niece later remembered that he was entirely devoted to academics and extracurricular activities: "Edgar never had any girlfriends."

Edgar's high school achievements came at a time when his home life was less than idyllic. As his son was distinguishing himself in academics, debate, and military drill, Dickerson Hoover was battling a progressively disabling mental illness. By the time Edgar was 16 years old, Dickerson had grown so withdrawn that when he returned home from work, he often ate no dinner, refused to speak with his wife and son, and isolated himself in the basement, reading classic literature and bottling homemade ginger ale. After his condition worsened, Dickerson forbid others from entering his basement sanctuary. Suffering from severe insomnia, fatigue, irritability, lack of motivation, and poor concentration, Dickerson was granted a leave of absence from work in 1912.

That same year, a concerned Annie consulted Dr. Jessie C. Coggins, Superintendent of the Laurel (Maryland) Sanatorium, located some 20 miles from Washington D.C., who arranged for Dickerson to be admitted to the psychiatric facility. During the several months that he was hospitalized, Dickerson received electroshock treatments, which proved largely ineffective.

While Annie and Dickerson, Jr. made regular visits to the sanatorium, Edgar refused to accompany them, steadfastly denying his father's illness. Edgar's niece, Margaret, struggled to understand her uncle's indifference: "I'm not sure, but I think he was ashamed." Another niece, Dorothy, was disappointed by his attitude: "My mother used to say Uncle Edgar wasn't very nice to his father when he was ill. He was ashamed of him. He couldn't tolerate the fact that granddaddy had mental illness. He never could tolerate anything that was imperfect."

While his father struggled to maintain his sanity, Edgar was nearing completion of his senior year in high school. Ranked number four in his graduating class based on his scholastic record, Edgar was nonetheless named valedictorian, as a result of his "academic achievement and moral character." The graduate's yearbook inscription proclaimed him to be "a gentleman of dauntless courage and stainless honor, and recognized Hoover as "one of the best Captains" of the Cadet Corps, and "some debater, too."

When the time came to chart a career course, Edgar was uncharacteristically nonchalant: "I don't really know why I chose law. You come to a crossroads, and you've got to go one way or the other." Even though he was offered a scholarship to the University of Virginia's law school, the financial aid award did not include room and board. Edgar's father, who had been discharged from the psychiatric hospital, was only well enough to work on a part-time basis. With the family's reduction in income, Edgar could not afford to attend law school in Virginia. Instead, he opted to attend the District of Columbia's George Washington University.

In the fall of 1913, J. Edgar Hoover was on the cusp of manhood. Energetic, disciplined, and ambitious, *Speed* was eager to make his mark on the world.

CHAPTER TWO

Johnnie

On June 22, 1903, eight and one-half years after the birth of J. Edgar Hoover, the man destined to become one of the most notorious criminals of the 20th century entered the world. John Herbert Dillinger was born in the Oak Cliff section of Indianapolis, Indiana, 14 years after his only biological sibling. Perhaps to more clearly distinguish father from son, the newborn was called *Johnnie*.

The outlaw-to-be's father, John Wilson Dillinger, whose ancestors lived in Germany and Prussia, was a well-liked and respected owner of a neighborhood grocery, and supplemented his middle-class income by leasing four rental houses. Mary Ellen "Mollie" Lancaster Dillinger had little time to make a lasting impact on her son Johnnie, succumbing to a stroke in February of 1907, four months before his fourth birthday.

In the wake of their mother's death, Johnnie's 18-year-old sister, Audrey, who had married at the tender age of 16, was forced into the role of mother to her little brother. Audrey ultimately gave birth to nine children of her own, one of whom died in infancy, and was unable to attend to the every whim of her attention-starved younger brother. While Johnnie and Audrey established a lasting bond, he later lamented his upbringing: "I only wish I had a mother to worry over me, but she died when I was three. I guess this is why I was such a bad boy—no mother to look after me."

Nine-year-old Johnnie's rebelliousness intensified when his father remarried in 1912. For the longest time, the younger Dillinger resented his step-mother, Elizabeth "Lizzie" Fields, who ultimately gave birth to a son and three daughters, giving Johnnie four younger half-siblings.

While consistently defying authority, Johnnie was a likeable, cheerful, fun-loving prankster, who later grew into a petty thief. Joining with a group of neighborhood boys, young Dillinger formed his first gang, who became known as the "Dirty Dozen." On one occasion, Johnnie and his mischievous pals tied one end of a rope to a neighbor's rose trellis and the other end to a streetcar. When confronted by his father, Johnnie showed no signs of remorse: "What if I did wreck his roses? The old bastard's mean, anyhow!"

Johnnie's pranks foretold greater misdeeds. A classmate remembered a costume Dillinger wore one Halloween, which proved eerily foretelling: "John came dressed in his father's derby hat, a turtleneck red jersey sweater, and a mask over his eyes and a gun in his hand."

Unsuccessful efforts were made to steer young Dillinger down the straight and narrow path to manhood. Audrey, who played the piano, tried to interest her younger brother in music, but soon found him far too restless and rambunctious. Instead, Dillinger and his Dirty Dozen companions earned a reputation for committing petty crimes, like thieving watermelons and stealing coal from the Pennsylvania Railroad train yard. Caught in the act of stealing coal, Johnnie was arrested by a railroad detective. During his arraignment in juvenile court, young Dillinger appeared largely unperturbed, smacking his chewing gum loudly. When the judge ordered him to remove his hat and dispose of the gum, Johnnie calmly and defiantly stuck the sticky wad atop his slouch cap.

"Your mind is crippled," the judge grumbled.

After his son was released by the court with a stern reprimand, Dillinger's father attempted to reform his first-born son. Desperate to keep Johnnie from engaging in further malicious behaviors, the elder Dillinger chained him to a wagon. John, Sr., a devout Christian who bragged that he never "spared the rod," proved to be an inconsistent disciplinarian, sometimes allowing his son to roam the streets of Indianapolis after dark, and other times, punitively locking him inside the house.

While attending Public School 38, Johnnie was indifferent to academics, accumulating mostly D and F grades. He continued to rebel against authority, running away from home several times. When John Sr. spanked him, a sullen Johnnie refused to cry. Concerning corporal punishment, Johnnie told his friend, Fred Brewer, that when he was one day rich and famous, John Sr. would regret having not been nicer to him.

In spite of his misdeeds, Johnnie had a charming side, one that he would exploit during his adult years. Audrey later reflected on the futility of parenting her younger brother: "I loved him so much; I couldn't see any faults in him." A Sunday school teacher, Ella Ellsbury, found the wayward youth equally alluring: "Johnnie was mischievous like the rest of them, but he was such a healthy, normal specimen of a boy that you couldn't help liking him. One thing about him I'll never forget—he always tipped his hat to me."

While Johnnie's misdeeds were mostly victimless, he could sometimes be cruel. After sneaking inside Drinkard's Veneer Mill, located next door to his father's store, young Dillinger and his pal, Fred Brewer, tied another boy to a carpenter's table and activated a buzz saw. Johnnie refused to turn off the menacing circular saw until the blade had made its way precariously close to the terrified child.

As he entered adolescence, Johnnie's mischief grew more reckless. After commandeering an unattended train engine, he crashed the locomotive into a series of coal cars. On another occasion, he swiped whiskey from box cars parked in the train yard, and later showed up at school intoxicated.

At age 16, Johnnie ended his academic career, as later recalled by his father: "He came to me the day before he was supposed to start at Arsenal Technical High School. 'I'm not going. I'm sick and tired of school, and I want a job. I not going, and that's that'!" When John Sr. informed his son that he would later regret his decision, Johnnie retorted: "That's my worry. I'm not going and I just thought you'd like to know."

The high school dropout went to work at a plywood veneer mill, where fellow employees were impressed with his skill at operating a saw. After a short while, he left the mill and was employed as a messenger for the Indianapolis Board of Trade. From there, Dillinger took a job at James P. Burcham's Reliance Specialty Company, a machine shop located in southwest Indianapolis. He was praised by his supervisor as being "very fast and accurate," as well as "sober, honest, and very industrious." Dillinger's work ethic, however, was inconsistent—after a three to four month stretch of employment, he would suddenly quit. Once he spent his accumulated earnings, Dillinger would return to work; because of his mechanical aptitude, Burcham invariably rehired Dillinger.

John Sr. eventually concluded that a small town atmosphere might have a less corrupting effect on his son. After selling his grocery store and rental properties, the elder Dillinger moved his family to a 60-acre farm in Mooresville, located 18 miles outside of Indianapolis. Mooresville, population 1,800, was the hometown of John Sr.'s second wife, and offered far fewer temptations than the city.

Not surprisingly, Johnnie had no interest in becoming a farmer. Instead, he commuted to his job at the machine shop in Indianapolis via the Interurban—an electric rail car that traveled to and from the capital city. Dillinger eventually saved enough money to purchase a motorcycle, followed by a Chevrolet coupe, bypassing the need to use public transportation.

Bored by farm life, Johnnie made no effort to assist in the requisite chores, as his father later recalled: "When he wasn't playing baseball for the Mooresville Athletic Club, he was generally out hunting. He was handy with a gun, and a dead shot." Much to John Sr.'s chagrin, his son also spent considerable time in Indianapolis pool halls frequented by older males with unsavory backgrounds.

While never a scholar, Dillinger enjoyed reading books about the Wild West, and was particularly fascinated by the notorious outlaw, Jesse James—a daring bank robber, who was known to be kind to women and children—behaviors Dillinger would emulate later in life. He was also drawn to gangster movies, admiring the toughness and swagger of the bad guys. Johnnie soon began wearing his hat rakishly tilted to one side and adopted the vernacular of the big screen outlaws.

Dillinger was enamored with the night life—drinking, carousing, and soliciting prostitutes. His relationships with women were most often fleeting, based on sexual gratification, rather than romance and commitment. Dillinger would later brag to a fellow prison inmate about his insatiable libido; too long without sex caused him to suffer from the uncomfortable sensation of an iron band "squeezing" his head.

In time, Dillinger developed a serious infatuation with his uncle's stepdaughter, Frances Marguerite Thornton. When the subject of marriage was broached, Dillinger's uncle objected, believing the couple was too young, and convinced his stepdaughter to end the relationship.

In July of 1923, when he was 20 years old, Dillinger's disregard for the law finally caught up with him. After stealing an automobile in Mooresville and driving to Indianapolis, Dillinger was confronted by a pair of police officers. In an unaccustomed state of panic, he not only provided the cops with an unimaginative alias, *Charles Dillinger*, but also readily admitted to stealing the vehicle. While being frisked, the self-professed car thief was discovered carrying a pistol. When one of the cops grabbed the suspect by the collar and dragged him toward a nearby police call box, Dillinger broke free and ran away. For the first but not the last time, Dillinger displayed a remarkable ability to dodge bullets; all seven shots fired by the policemen at the fleeing suspect missed their target.

Now a fugitive, Dillinger spent the night hidden in a barn, formulating escape plans. The very next day, he hurried to a recruiting station and impulsively enlisted in the Navy. Though Dillinger supplied the recruiters with his real name, he hoped to elude law enforcement by fabricating a false home address—*916 Bain Avenue*, in St. Louis.

The doctors who performed Dillinger's induction physical found him to be in good health, with 20/20 vision and excellent hearing. The examination report noted that the new recruit was five-foot seven-inches-tall and weighed 155 pounds, with brown hair, blue eyes, and a ruddy complexion.

Four days after he enlisted, Dillinger was shipped to the Great Lakes Training Station. After completing basic training on October 4, 1923, he was assigned to the battleship, *USS Utah*, anchored in Boston Harbor. As a Fireman Third Class, Dillinger's primary duty involved shoveling coal in the ship's massive boilers. After only three weeks of back-breaking labor, Dillinger went AWOL for a day. On November 7th, he was court martialed and sentenced to seven days in the brig and fined $18 (equivalent to one month's pay).

On November 9th, before his sentence had been served, Dillinger left his duty post without permission. As a result, a five-day solitary confinement was added to his existing sentence. The disciplinary actions only intensified Dillinger's defiance of authority, and on December 4th, he failed to return to the ship, following a 24-hour leave. After two weeks on AWOL status, the Navy classified Dillinger as a deserter, and posted a $50 bounty.

Dillinger's exact whereabouts between December 4th and the following March remain a mystery; it was later claimed that he was seen in Indianapolis, accompanied by an old girlfriend and a small child, leading to speculation that Dillinger may have fathered an illegitimate child. In March of 1934, he reappeared at his father's farm in Mooresville, explaining to family members that he had been *honorably discharged* from the Navy, secondary to a heart murmur. In a conversation with his father, Johnnie came closer to telling the truth, freely admitting that he detested military life, because there were "too many people ordering me around."

A month after he returned to Indiana, following a whirlwind courtship, Dillinger married 17-year-old Beryl Ethyl Hovius. The new bride, who hailed from the nearby town of Martinsville, falsely claimed to be 18 years old on the marriage license, bypassing the requirement for parental consent.

The newlyweds lived for a short while in Johnnie's bedroom at the Dillinger farm house. After a disagreement between father and son, the young couple moved in with the bride's parents in Martinsville, before finally renting an upstairs apartment (also in Martinsville).

Dillinger continued his pattern of irregular employment, starting and abruptly stopping jobs at a machine shop, furniture factory, and haberdashery. During his idle hours, he played sandlot baseball with a local team.

Anything but a model husband, Dillinger often left his young wife home at nights, while he frequented bars and pool halls, coming into contact with known or aspiring criminals. Not surprisingly, he found the lure of crime irresistible. In April of 1924, Dillinger and two accomplices stole 41 Buffingon Orpington chickens from Omer A. Zook, a local poultry farmer. After Dillinger's father compensated Zook for his losses, the farmer agreed to not press charges.

Even though he narrowly avoided a jail sentence, Dillinger remained un-repentant. He soon established a relationship with his first criminal mentor—31-year-old Edgar "Eddie" Singleton, a disreputable alcoholic, who reportedly had a prison record. Afflicted with syndactyly (webbed fingers), Singleton was hard to forget, and he tutored young Dillinger in the finer points of crime. During the summer of 1924, it is believed that Dillinger and Singleton robbed two gas stations in the Indianapolis area.

On Saturday evening, September 6, 1924, Dillinger staged a disastrous caper that would put his life on hold for nearly a decade. Along with Singleton,

Dillinger had been carefully monitoring the habits of a local grocer, Frank Morgan, who was known to carry the store's cash receipts home with him at the end of each day. Morgan also made it a habit to walk to John Smith's Barbershop every Saturday night for his regular trim.

Unbeknownst to Dillinger and Singleton, on the night of September 6th, Morgan had left the store's cash at home before making his weekly trip to the barber. While Singleton waited in the get-away car, a Model A Ford, Dillinger hid in the bushes waiting to ambush the grocer, armed with an iron bolt wrapped inside a handkerchief and an Iver Johnson .32 caliber pistol. Emerging from his hiding place, Dillinger struck Morgan twice in the head with his sling-bolt, knocking the grocer to the ground, but failing to render him unconscious. After Dillinger drew his pistol, Morgan fought to disarm him. During the ensuing struggle, the pistol discharged into the ground.

When Morgan shouted the Mason's *Grand Hailing Sign of Distress*, nearby lodge brothers rushed to aid him. A panicked Dillinger ran from the scene of the crime, only to find that Singleton had already fled in their get-away car. Abandoned by Singleton, Dillinger immediately sought refuge in a local pool hall.

Anxious and inexperienced, Dillinger did not use the opportunity to blend in with the other customers. Instead, he foolishly asked other patrons, most of whom were not yet aware of the attempted robbery, if they knew how badly Morgan had been hurt. Dillinger's suspicious-sounding inquiries, coupled with incriminating blood stains on his hat and pants, caused him to stand out among the crowd.

Later in the evening, Dillinger walked back to his father's farm, perhaps believing that he had narrowly escaped. His hopes were dashed the following morning, when two deputy sheriffs arrived at the farm with an arrest warrant.

Once incarcerated, Dillinger refused to confess. John Sr. soon met with the Marion County Prosecutor, who suggested the judge might be lenient if Dillinger admitted his guilt. A week after his son's arrest, John Sr. visited the jail: "Johnnie, if you did this thing, the only way is to own up to it. They'll go easy on you, and you can get a new start. You'll be okay, but you've got to tell them the truth." What John Sr. did not know was that the prosecutor actually had serious doubts about the strength of his case: "I took my grief to God. I got down on my knees and prayed for guidance."

Heeding his father's advice, Dillinger confessed to the crime, and also revealed that Eddie Singleton had been his accomplice. On September 15th, both defendants appeared in Judge Joseph Warford Williams' courtroom. When Singleton's attorney asked for a continuance, the judge immediately granted his request. Following the advice of his father and the prosecutor, Dillinger appeared in court without the benefit of legal counsel, pleading guilty to *conspiracy to commit a felony* and *assault with intent to rob*.

Contrary to Dillinger's expectations, Judge Williams showed no mercy, handing down prison sentences of to 2 to 14 years on the first count and 10 to 20 years on the second. Even though the sentences were concurrent, by law, the defendant would have to serve a minimum of 10 years in prison for a robbery that netted only $60. A bitter and devastated Dillinger believed that both his father and the legal system had betrayed him.

John, Sr. pled with Judge Williams to show leniency, but to no avail. The elder Dillinger was crestfallen, realizing he had been hoodwinked: "I should have got a good lawyer for Johnnie. I should not have let him face the music alone, depending on the glib promises of a politically motivated prosecutor. Can you imagine my feelings, when rumors reached me that there had been talk of turning Johnnie loose because of insufficient evidence, until I bulled in and persuaded him to plead guilty?" Dillinger's sister, Audrey, vividly recalled her father's dismay: "When we got the word, my dad just about keeled over. It liked to (have) killed him. I think he died of a broken heart. And, when John got that sentence, it just seemed like he went from bad to worse."

The day after his sentencing, Dillinger was transferred to the Pendleton Reformatory, located 25 miles northeast of Indianapolis. The newly-arrived inmate bitterly complained to the reformatory superintendent, A.F. Miles, that he had been tricked into a confession.

"I won't cause you any trouble, except to escape. I can beat your institution," a brazen Dillinger informed Miles.

"If you have a notion to escape, we'll play that game with you," Miles replied.

"I'll go right over the administration building," Dillinger boasted.

On October 25th, Eddie Singleton went on trial for his role in the robbery and assault of Frank Morgan. After deliberating for only 20 minutes, the jury found the defendant guilty of *conspiracy, accession,* and *assault*. Singleton received a 2 to 15-year prison sentence, accompanied by a $25 fine. When Dillinger learned about his partner's comparatively lenient sentence, he was incensed: "I'll be the meanest bastard you ever saw, when I get out."

Dillinger soon made good on his escape threat. After returning to testify in Singleton's trial, Dillinger was escorted back to the Pendleton Reformatory by Deputy Sheriff Russell Peterson. At the bus station in Indianapolis, Peterson, who felt sorry for the youthful offender, purchased Dillinger a soft drink and allowed him to sit at an outdoor picnic table. Suddenly and without warning, the inmate used his legs to overturn the table, knocking the deputy sheriff to the ground. Still in handcuffs, Dillinger sprinted away, dodging several pistol shots fired from Peterson's .25 caliber service revolver. In desperation, Dillinger ran into a blind alley, and was soon collared by Peterson.

Though angered by the prisoner's escape attempt, Deputy Peterson understood Dillinger's motivation: "I knew John's dad. I thought well of him. Besides, John was just a kid, and you can't take 10 years out of a kid's life."

Peterson was prescient; the decade that followed would leave John Dillinger permanently embittered.

CHAPTER THREE

The Director

While John Dillinger would spend the majority of his young adulthood incarcerated, J. Edgar Hoover embarked on a much different journey. In the fall of 1913, Hoover took the first steps toward becoming perhaps America's most famous lawman.

George Washington University, founded in 1831 and originally named Columbian College, allowed its law students to bypass the traditional undergraduate degree before attending law school; instead, students could enroll in a three-year bachelor of law program, after which time they could earn a one-year master of law degree.

With his father's declining health and limited ability to work, Hoover felt pressure to help provide for the family. Fortunately, George Washington University's law school accommodated *late afternoon students*, which allowed them to work day jobs.

On October 13th, Hoover was hired as a junior messenger at the Library of Congress. While earning a 30-dollar-per-month salary, he worked from 9:00 a.m. until 4:00 p.m., and then attended law school classes from 4:50 p.m. to 6:30 p.m. In the summer months, when the heat and humidity were oppressive, classes were held between 7:50 a.m. and 8:40 a.m., which still allowed Hoover to work a full day.

Attending school and working a full-time job, the next four years were a busy time for Hoover. He proved to be both a diligent student and employee. His study habits were particularly impressive; by the time he graduated,

Hoover had accumulated 26 notebooks, 100-200 pages each, filled with neatly transcribed lecture notes. Hoover's solitary ambition and work ethic caught the attention of a law school classmate: "He was slim, dark, and intense. He set off by himself against the wall, and always had the answers. None of us got to know him very well."

Like their undergraduate counterparts, law students at George Washington were allowed to join fraternities. Hoover, who enjoyed the care-fully-chosen company of ambitious men, pledged Kappa Alpha. Even though he continued to live at home, Hoover was chosen to serve as manager of the fraternity house. As expected, Hoover took that responsibility seriously; his fraternity brothers soon realized their strait-laced manager "took a dim and moral view of such chapter house capers, such as crap games, poker, and drinking bouts." Foreshadowing his future career, Hoover tried to enforce the law at the Kappa Alpha House.

"He located our contraband and destroyed it by sending it crashing to the concrete area way," fraternity brother, Dave Stephens, remembered.

"Speed chastised us with his morality," another KA recalled.

Not all of his fraternity brothers appreciated Hoover's stern piety. His detractors privately referred to him as "fatty pants."

In addition to what he learned in law school, Hoover received a valuable education about the inner workings of government bureaucracy while work-ing at the Library of Congress. At an annual salary of $360, he accumulated four years of experience as a civil service employee. Under the tutelage of its director, Herbert Putnam, who possessed excellent organizational abilities and skill at negotiating the byzantine layers of the federal government, the Library of Congress became a world class research institute. Putnam proved to be the perfect mentor, teaching Hoover sound administrative skills.

Hoover was awarded a bachelor of law degree in 1916, and a year later, earned his master of law degree. On July 3, 1917, Hoover received word that he had passed the bar examination. Three weeks later, he was admitted to practice before the Supreme Court of the District of Columbia.

Amidst the excitement of graduating from law school, Edgar was con-fronted with the progressive deterioration of his father's mental and physical health. In April of 1917, Dickerson's worsening depression and anxiety led to forced retirement. Even though he had been a government employee for 40 years, the elder Hoover received no severance or pension, and was crassly instructed to clear his desk out by the end of the week. The loss of his father's $2,000 per-year-salary forced Edgar to become the Hoover family's sole breadwinner. Taking note of his father's abrupt dismissal, Hoover was more pragmatic than bitter; anyone who demonstrated weakness would be trampled and forgotten, regardless of their loyalty and work ethic.

Annie Hoover, who thrived on appearances, found her husband's mental decline and job loss highly embarrassing. More than ever, she tied her hopes and dreams to her youngest son's promising future. As succinctly noted by biographer, Richard Hack, Annie formed a supportive partnership with Edgar: "Hoover's mother was his best friend, his confidant, his disciplinarian, and his rock. She alone knew how he liked his food prepared. She alone knew how to select his clothes, approve his friends, budget his money, and keep him well."

On July 26th, less than a month after passing the bar exam, Hoover was hired by the Department of Justice. Annie Hoover's influential cousin, Federal Judge William Hitz, likely played a key role in securing the new graduate his first job.

The Department of Justice, where Hoover would remain employed for the remainder of his life, traced its roots back to 1789, when Congress created the office of Attorney General. At that point in time, the investigation of crimes was delegated to local authorities, and the Attorney General's primary role was to serve as legal adviser to the President. It was not until June of 1870 that Congress established the Department of Justice (DOJ), whose mandate was the "detection and prosecution" of federal crimes. The scope of such offenses was narrow, including bankruptcy fraud, antitrust violations, peonage, and violation of neutrality laws. Infiltration of the Ku Klux Klan during the Reconstruction Era was among the Department of Justice's early and notable successes. Subsequent arrests and convictions of KKK members forced the white vigilantes into an extended period of hibernation.

For the first 38 years of its existence, the Department of Justice had no permanent investigators, and was forced to *borrow* agents from the Secret Service. In 1908, President Theodore Roosevelt first authorized the DOJ to employ its own detectives. A year later, the 34-man "special agent force" was placed under the supervision of the newly-christened Bureau of Investigation (BOI).

In June of 1910, Congress passed the White Slave Traffic Act (also known as the Mann Act), making it a federal crime to transport women across state lines for immoral purposes. As a result of its expanded responsibilities, the BOI nearly doubled its number of agents. Lawmakers, wary of establishing a national police force, were careful to limit BOI powers. Bureau agents were not authorized to carry weapons or make arrests; instead, they could make citizens' arrests, pending the arrival of local law enforcement agents or U.S. Marshalls, who would make the formal arrests.

In the summer of 1917, when J. Edgar Hoover reported to work at the Department of Justice headquarters, located at the capitol city's McPherson Square, the Bureau was an agency with a limited scope of powers. Hoover was hired as the less than prestigious *clerk in the files division*, at a starting salary of $990 per year.

That same year, when the United States entered World War I, all men between the ages of 21 and 31 were required to register for the draft. Twenty-two years old and in good health, Hoover would have been the ideal draftee, but his employment at the Department of Justice, which was considered crucial to national defense, allowed him to bypass military service.

Hoover made the most of his new job, working 12-hour days, including Sundays. His dedication soon caught the attention of higher-ups, and less than a year after being hired, Hoover was promoted to the rank of *attorney*, accompanied by an increase in annual salary to $1,800.

Hoover was assigned to the Alien Enemy Bureau (AEB), one of three entities within the Justice Department's War Emergency Division, which had been established at the onset of World War I to investigate potentially disloyal foreigners living in the United States. At that time, some 400,000 Germans were residing in the United States, and federal officials, on high alert, feared there might be spies among them. Operating under the authority vested by the 1917 Espionage Act, the AEB investigated 1,400 suspicious Germans—98 of them were actually arrested and another 1,172 were deemed potential arrestees.

Under the direction of War Emergency Division Director, John Lord O'Brian, Hoover investigated not only suspected German saboteurs and spies, but also other foreign radicals, who objected to America's involvement in the war. Hoover kept a close watch on those who were apt to commit offenses delineated by the Espionage Act, including opposition to the draft, propagation of dissension among members of the armed forces, and aid to foreign enemies.

Hoover, who proudly divided the world into two mutually exclusive camps, good and bad, took dead aim at foreign-born radicals. By late 1918, he had grown busy enough to hire his own secretary, Helen Gandy, who would remain by Hoover's side for the next 54 years. Now a rising star, Hoover tolerated no dissenters. When subordinates or peers questioned his opinions, Hoover responded with an annoyingly dismissive wave of his hand, as if he were literally brushing away their ideas.

After the armistice of November 1918, which ended World War I, Hoover was forced to shift his focus away from German spies and draft dodgers. The appointment of A. Mitchell Palmer as Attorney General in February of 1919 presented Hoover with an opportunity to target another rising menace. Palmer, who succeeded Thomas Gregory as head of the Department of Justice, was a prominent Democrat, harbored presidential ambitions, and realized that high-profile prosecutions made for good politics.

The Bolshevik Revolution of 1917, when Vladimir Lenin's communist regime violently overthrew the Russian monarchy, had a global ripple effect. Many Americans feared that Russian radicals living in the United States would attempt to foment a similar revolution. Consequently, individuals and groups advocating communism, socialism, fascism, and anarchism became targets of the Justice Department, marking the beginning of the aptly-named *Red Scare*.

Members of the radical left upped the ante when they launched acts of terrorism. On the night of June 2, 1919, nine bombs were ignited in various cities across the country, one of which exploded particularly close to home. At 11:00 p.m., a suicide bomber set off a nine-pound device near the front entrance to Attorney General Palmer's house. The powerful blast rocked the peaceful neighborhood, on a street that was home not only to Palmer, but also one former President (William Howard Taft) and three future Presidents (Warren G. Harding, Franklin D. Roosevelt, and Dwight D. Eisenhower).

Palmer, his wife, and teenage daughter were at home when the bomb exploded, but were not injured, in spite of extensive damage done to the house. Amidst the splintered wood, concrete fragments, and shards of glass, a note was discovered: "We have been dreaming of freedom; we have aspired to a better world, and you jailed us, you clubbed us, you deported us, you murdered us whenever you could...There will have to be bloodshed. We will not dodge; there will have to be murder; we will kill because it is necessary; there will have to be destruction; we will destroy to rid the world of your tyrannical institutions." The note was signed by *The Anarchist Fighters*.

The direct attack against his family was a personal affront to Palmer, who vowed to extract revenge against the Leninists and Anarchists. While he could not totally subvert the free speech of American citizens, immigrants did not share those same constitutional rights, and Palmer formulated a master plan to deport, en masse, those with un-American agendas.

The Attorney General soon established a kinship with the ambitious and workaholic Hoover. On July 1, 1919, Palmer promoted Hoover to head the task force targeting left-wing ideologues, which was christened as the *Radical Division*. Palmer charged Hoover with making "a study of subversive activities" and to make recommendations as to "what action can be taken in the field of prosecution." With his added responsibilities, Hoover's annual salary was increased to $3,000 per year, and he was instructed to report directly to the Attorney General, instead of the newly-hired Director of the Bureau of Investigation, William J. Flynn.

Drawing upon the skills he had learned at the Library of Congress, Hoover created a file card index listing the names of individuals professing left-wing political views; within a year, the file contained approximately 100,000 names. Focusing his efforts, Hoover compiled biographical summaries on nearly 60,000 people believed to be greatest threats to national security.

Hoover cross-referenced the indexed names, noting where individuals lived, their organizational memberships, and whether or not they wrote articles or editorials for any of the 500 radical publications the Bureau was actively monitoring. Years before the invention of the computer, Hoover's organizational abilities proved remarkable.

Among the Russian immigrants immediately capturing Hoover's attention were Emma Goldman and Alexander Berkman, who had founded the No-Conscription League, a haven for draft dodgers. Both Goldman and Berkman had been arrested in June of 1917 for violation of the Selective Service Act, and were sentenced to two-year prison terms. Hoover immediately set a plan in motion to deport Goldman and Berkman as soon as they were released from federal prison, certain their continued presence in the United States would "result in undue harm." Attorney General Palmer agreed, authorizing Hoover to utilize "all necessary manpower."

Just before Berkman's release from the federal penitentiary in Georgia, Hoover travelled south, hand-delivering the prisoner's deportation papers and interrogating him. Berkman proved to be an easy target. A long-standing anarchist, who was unrepentant in his attacks against capitalism, democracy, and the Wilson Administration, Berkman had previously served a separate prison term for attempting to murder Carnegie Steel Company executive, Henry Clay Frick.

Goldman, Berkman's one-time lover, who was incarcerated at the federal penitentiary in Jefferson City, Missouri, proved to be a sterner challenge for Hoover. A self-proclaimed anarchist, labor union advocate, and spell-binding orator, Goldman also promoted birth control and free love, all of which were repulsive to the straight-laced Hoover. Though widely ridiculed as *Red Emma* and the *Queen of the Reds*, the 50-year-old Goldman offered a strong argument against deportation; both her father and husband were U.S. citizens, and she had become a naturalized citizen by marriage.

The Immigration Act, passed in 1918, authorized the federal government to deport aliens who supported anarchism, advocated violent political reprisals, or belonged to organizations advocating the former. Hoover would have to convince the Immigration Department that Goldman had engaged in one or more of the prohibited activities. Cherry picking excerpts from Goldman's speeches and self-edited journal, *Mother Earth*, Hoover testified at her deportation hearing on October 27, 1919, linking her with the 1910 bombing of the offices of the *Los Angeles Times* and the 1901 assassination of President William McKinley. Hoover was almost certainly aware that Goldman had no direct involvement in either of those two infamous acts, but was of the opinion that the ends justified the means. Hoover's testimony proved persuasive; on November 25th, the Immigration Department ordered Berkman's deportation, and four days later, ordered the same for Goldman.

In his quest to rid the country of left-wing radicals, Hoover was decidedly opinionated and intolerant of opposing viewpoints. His interpretation of the evidence against an individual was all that mattered, and any ambiguities were ignored or dismissed with the wave of his hand.

Pan-African leader, Marcus Garvey, who Hoover labeled as a "notorious Negro agitator," also came under the scrutiny of the Department of Justice. Having been born and raised in segregated Washington D.C., Hoover was un-enlightened on the issue of race, and his prejudice changed little with the passage of time. In December of 1919, the BOI's first and only black agent, James Worley Jones, infiltrated Garvey's inner circle. Jones gathered enough information to enable the Bureau to sabotage Garvey's Black Star Line—a shipping operation that transported goods from black communities in North America to those in Africa and the Caribbean. The Black Star Line ultimately went bankrupt, tarnishing Garvey's image.

Hoover also investigated those who were bold enough to defend the rights of left wingers. Among those targets was lawyer and future Supreme Court Justice, Felix Frankfurter, who Hoover shrilly labeled as "the most dangerous man in the United States."

Attorney General Palmer, eager to punish radicals and fuel his political ambitions, took dead aim at the Federation of Russian Workers (FURW)—a trade union of Russian aliens, who had not applied for American citizenship. Not surprisingly, the FURW's 232 members were already listed in Hoover's card index.

At 8:00 p.m. on November 7, 1919, coinciding with the second anniversary of the Russian Revolution, Bureau agents raided the FURW headquarters on East 15th Street in Manhattan. The heavy-handed agents shattered windows, broke furniture, and physically assaulted union members. In the end, 211 individuals were held for questioning, without the benefit of legal counsel. By daybreak, 172 of them had been released, while the remaining 39 were taken by ferry to Ellis Island. Many were forced to sign confessions that they could not read, much less understand.

"We're going back to Russia—that's a free country," one of the immigrants groused, as he boarded the ferry.

Over the next several days, both in New York and other cities, additional arrests were made. The DOJ's targeted actions were further legitimized when Bureau agents uncovered a counterfeiting operation in Newark, and what was believed to be a bomb-making factory in Trenton. The discovery of inflammatory literature at one of the sites offered further justification of the raids; one pamphlet, written in Russian, encouraged workers to "convert small strikes into general ones, and convert the latter into an armed revolt of the laboring masses against capital and state." The pamphlet also urged workers to "mercilessly destroy all remains of governmental authority and class domination, liberating the prisoners, demolish prisons, and police offices." Once all the arrests were made and the evidence was reviewed, 246 of the immigrants were deemed dangerous enough to warrant deportation.

At 4:00 a.m. on December 21, 1919, Hoover stood on the chilly, wind-swept shores of Ellis Island when Emma Goldman, Alexander Berkman, and 246 immigrants (184 of whom were members of the FURW) were placed aboard the *USS Buford*, a naval war ship on loan to the Immigration Department. The deportees were bound for the communist mother land. In advance, Hoover had studied maps of Russia in preparation for the "vacation that a few of our anarchist friends will take shortly."

The mass deportations proved so popular that Attorney General Palmer tried to reward Hoover with an extended vacation. Hoover declined, unwilling to enjoy rest and relaxation until the country was free "of all radical low-life that threaten God-fearing Americans."

Hoover remained a workaholic. Still living at home with his mother and ailing father, he had little time for a social life. There was still no woman in Hoover's life, and his only close male friend was Thomas Baughman, a law school classmate and fraternity brother, who had been hired to work as a researcher in the DOJ's Radical Division. Handsome, athletic, and a decorated World War I artillery officer, Baughman was unmarried, and like Hoover, lived with his mother. Bound by their work and similar backgrounds, Hoover and Baughman often had dinner together and visited one another's homes.

Eager to make political hay, Attorney General Palmer ordered further raids, to be followed by mass deportations. Using names supplied from Hoover's files, the Acting Secretary of Labor, John Abercrombie, signed approximately 3,000 arrest warrants for targeted radicals. Secretary of Labor, William B. Wilson, who was on leave of absence to care for his terminally ill wife, seriously doubted that the majority of the individuals on Hoover's list warranted deportation, but the Acting Secretary apparently had no such qualms.

On January 2, 1920, one day after J. Edgar Hoover's 25th birthday, simultaneous raids were launched against communist party meetings in more than 30 cities across the country. The Bureau agents were instructed to use their "discretion as to the methods by which you should gain access to such places."

In a 24-hour period, more than 5,000 arrests were made, which in many cases, far exceeded the available jail space. In Detroit, 800 men were detained in a windowless corridor with one toilet and a single water fountain. A 300-bed prison in Boston overflowed with 600 arrestees, who were forced to endure the winter weather absent heaters; one of those suspects committed suicide by jumping out of a fourth floor window.

Bureau agents had difficulty matching the suspects' foreign names with their individual warrants; many of the names had alternative spellings and the writing on the foreign-born individuals' identification cards was often indecipherable. The frightened and confused detainees were not allowed to speak with their relatives and were denied legal counsel. Those who were able to prove that they were American citizens were released, as the violations spelled out in the Immigration Act of 1918 only applied to foreigners. In Detroit, 350 out of the 800 individuals initially detained were released after proving they were either American citizens or were immigrants with no ties to radical organizations.

Many of the immigrants who were ultimately released shared the sordid details of the so-called *Palmer Raids*, including the fact that some arrests were made without warrants, as well as the inhumane conditions in detention facilities. Hoover attempted to counter the negative press by promising reporters who wrote supportive stories about the raids access to the files of the accused—a clear violation of federal law. It is not known whether any such information was actually given to newsmen, but the mere suggestion was emblematic of what would become Hoover's ability to manipulate the press to print stories that supported, if not glorified, the actions of the Bureau.

At the deportation hearings, Hoover once again presented the government's case, arguing that the "Reds" should be loaded aboard "Soviet Arks" and deported as soon as possible. The lawyers representing the aliens countered with arguments that some of the arrests had been warrantless and many of their clients had been unable to understand the charges brought against them.

Acting Secretary of Labor, Louis F. Post, who had replaced the departing John Abercrombie (after the latter resigned his position to run for the U.S. Senate), refused to issue deportation orders for some 3,000 of the arrestees, and accused Attorney General Palmer of perpetrating "a great terroristic scare," while displaying "an absolute ignorance of American principles."

Palmer, who had been applauded for overseeing the first mass deportation, was suddenly placed on the defensive. The Attorney General, however, refused to back down: "I accept full responsibility for everything (my agents) did. If one or two of them, overzealous or perhaps outraged as patriotic American citizens—and all of them were—by the conduct of these aliens, stepped over the bounds and treated them a little roughly, or too roughly, I forgive them. I do not defend it, but I am not going to raise any row about it."

In the end, the negative publicity generated by the so-called *Palmer Raids* irrevocably damaged the Attorney General's once promising presidential aspirations. Maligned as the leader of a witch hunt, Palmer was rejected by delegates at the 1920 Democratic National Convention; instead, Ohio Governor, James M. Cox was nominated as the party's presidential candidate.

While Palmer took full responsibility for propagating the Red Scare, J. Edgar Hoover, who had been the Attorney General's chief facilitator, managed to emerge relatively unscathed. As the Wilson Administration neared its end, Palmer approved Hoover's recommendation to enlarge the Radical Division, which was renamed the General Intelligence Division (GID). In a memorandum, Hoover outlined the role of the GID in language only a bureaucrat could fully appreciate: "While the work of the General Intelligence Division was at first confined solely to investigations of the radical movement, it has now expanded to cover more general intelligence work, including not only radical activities in the United States and abroad, but also the studying of matters of an international nature, as well as economic and industrial disturbances incident thereto."

Hoover continued to expand his files, including not only dissidents, but also individuals who dared to question *his* philosophy concerning the communist menace. Consequently, GID investigators targeted left-thinking governmental officers, university presidents and professors, judges, and lawmakers. To protect his secret domain, Hoover used methods he learned at the Library of Congress to cross reference his filing system by subjects, rather than alphabetically. Only Hoover, and perhaps his loyal secretary, Helen Gandy, fully understood how to access the contents of those files.

Even though Attorney General Palmer was on his way out, Hoover proved to be a survivor. With his ever-expanding secret files, Hoover was well on his way toward establishing a base of power that would pave the way for continued career advancement within the Department of Justice.

The spring of 1921 was the beginning President Warren G. Harding's administration. It also marked the final days of Dickerson Hoover, who had been shuffled back and forth between the family home and the Laurel Sanatorium, in an unsuccessful effort to treat his chronic depression. Now pale and gaunt, Dickerson barely subsisted on soups and liquids. As before, Edgar refused to visit the psychiatric hospital, protesting that his father's near-catatonia "caused me considerable discomfort." When he was allowed to come home from the hospital, Dickerson mostly stared into space and rarely spoke. On occasion, when he was face-to-face with Edgar, Dickerson would burst into tears and wail loudly, much to the embarrassment and annoyance of his youngest son.

The end for Dickerson Hoover, Sr. finally came on March 30, 1921. The 64-year-old decedent's death certificate listed "melancholia" and "inanition" as the twin causes of his demise. In many respects, Dickerson's death was a source of relief to the image-conscious Anna and Edgar, who would no longer have to answer embarrassing questions about his mental health. Absent funeral services, Dickerson was quietly buried in the family plot at Congressional Cemetery.

After the death of his father, 26-year-old Edgar was left with Annie as his only housemate. While the bond between mother and son remained unbreakable, both possessed strong wills. The pair maintained a long-running battle about the window shades, which Annie preferred to keep closed; when Edgar returned home from work, he immediately opened them. The petty disagreements, however, paled in comparison to their unwavering devotion to one another.

"She ran a beautiful home for him, but he provided the wherewithal to run it beautifully. And, he was very good to her. He'd give her gifts, jewelry—some very nice jewelry..." Edgar's niece, Anna, remembered.

During the course of the Harding Administration, a series of scandals per-meated the executive branch of the government, including the Department of Justice. One of President Harding's biggest mistakes was the appointment of his campaign manager and long-time friend, Henry Daugherty, as Attorney General. Daugherty, nicknamed *Foxy*, was gifted at backroom political wheel-ing and dealing, without regard to ethics.

Daugherty perpetuated the cronyism by appointing his old friend, William J. Burns, as Director of the Bureau of Investigation. The former head of the Burns International Detective Agency and newly-designated head of the BOI had provided valuable assistance to Harding's presidential campaign, both as a trouble-shooter and an investigator of political enemies. Aware that Burn's administrative skills were suspect, Daugherty instructed him to appoint Hoover as his Assistant Director. The new Attorney General was impressed with Hoover's staunch anti-communism and was also aware that his secret files likely contained incriminating information that could be used against President Harding's political opponents. In spite of grave misgivings about his newly-appointed superiors, an ambitious Hoover readily accepted the promo-tion, which increased his annual salary to $4,000.

Daugherty's improprieties continued when he arranged a high-priority position in Harding Administration for his close friend and suspected male lover, Jess Smith. Daugherty and Smith lived together in a house on H Street, owned by Washington Post Editor, Edward B. McLean. Nicknamed the "love nest," the house was a rumored trysting spot for President Harding's extra-marital affairs.

While Smith was technically not an employee of the Department of Justice, he was allowed to keep an office there. Smith's proximity to the Bureau's se-cret files apparently allowed him to dispose of incriminating documents, in exchange for cash payments from those who wanted their names and alleged misdeeds erased from the official records.

Daugherty also hired his landlord as a BOI special agent. Based upon his token salary, McLean became one of the administration's notorious *dollar-per-year* employees. Daugherty made yet another controversial decision, when he hired Gaston Means as a BOI agent. Means, who had functioned as a double agent for England and Germany during World War I and had worked for the William Burns International Detective Agency, accepted a position at the Department of Justice. Under Daugherty's direction, Means readily accepted payoffs from Prohibition-era bootleggers seeking to escape federal prosecution. In later years, Means would reveal that he collected more than seven million dollars from such payoffs, which he split with Daugherty and Burns.

The corruption inside the Justice Department first came to light after Jess Smith learned that he was on the verge of being arrested for influence peddling. On May 30, 1923, Smith allegedly committed suicide, shooting himself in the head with a .32 caliber pistol. Rumors soon swirled that Smith might have been murdered to keep him from revealing what he knew about the wrong doings in the Harding Administration.

Hoover, who was aware of Smith's nefarious activities, had already opened a file on Daugherty's alleged lover. In the wake of Smith's death, BOI Director Burns ordered Hoover to turn the file over to him, which was then passed to the Attorney General, who most likely destroyed it.

The corruption during the Harding presidency was not confined to the Department of Justice. Secretary of the Interior, Albert B. Fall, was accused of leasing federal oil reserves at Elk Hill and Buena Vista, California, as well as Teapot Dome, Wyoming, to private companies, in exchange for cash payoffs. In what would become known as the *Teapot Dome Scandal*, Fall left behind an incriminating money trail marked by costly renovations to his New Mexico ranch that far exceeded his government salary. Once the press got wind of his alleged wrong-doings, Fall was forced to resign his Cabinet post (in March of 1923).

Attorney General Daugherty, who was close friends with Fall and did not want the public spotlight shined on his own misdeeds, ordered Hoover to investigate Montana Democratic Senators, Thomas J. Walsh and Burton K. Wheeler, hoping to uncover damaging skeletons in the lawmakers' closets.

Daugherty hoped the twin investigations would pressure Walsh and Wheeler to halt their planned congressional inquiry into the Teapot Dome Scandal.

The Montana lawmakers soon found themselves in the Bureau's crosshairs. Wheeler later recalled that federal agents "surrounded my house," and "constantly shadowed" he and his wife.

While Hoover followed the Attorney General's orders, he cleverly insisted that nothing about the investigation be placed in writing, making it more difficult to link his name to the politically-inspired espionage. In later years, Hoover rationalized his role in the investigations of Wheeler and Walsh, writing in third person: "He was a little like the soldier who follows his commander's order to kill. If the wrong man gets shot, the guy who pulled the trigger only has to point his finger toward his captain to escape responsibility."

It is not known exactly how much President Harding knew about the Teapot Dome Scandal. Harding died suddenly on August 2, 1923, while in San Francisco, during a tour of the western United States and Alaska. While the President's official cause of death was recorded as a heart attack, many considered the timing of his death suspicious. A few years later, Gaston Means authored a book alleging that Harding was poisoned by his wife after she learned about his extramarital affairs. Equally unsubstantiated rumors arose, accusing the Attorney General of poisoning the President; Daugherty, who was not a member of the presidential touring party, unexpectedly arrived in Seattle, shortly before Harding took ill, and spent several hours alone with the President.

Conspiracy theories aside, it appears likely that Harding first learned about the full extent of the corruption plaguing his administration shortly before his death. Secretary of Commerce, Herbert Hoover, who would later become President, believed that the devastating impact of the scandals led directly to Harding's demise: "People do not die from a broken heart, but people with bad hearts may reach the end much sooner from great worries." When he spoke at the dedication of Harding's tomb in Marion, Ohio, the Commerce Secretary defended the honor of the deceased ex-President: "Warren Harding had a dim realization that he had been betrayed by a few of the men he had trusted, by the men who he had believed were his devoted friends. It was later proved in the courts of the land that these men had betrayed not only the friendship and trust of their staunch and loyal friend, but they had betrayed their country."

When Calvin Coolidge ascended to the presidency after Harding's death, he was forced to deal with the scandals of his predecessor's administration. In October of 1923, undeterred by the Department of Justice's intimidating investigation of his past, Senator Thomas Walsh convened a special committee to investigate the Teapot Dome Scandal. Congressional investigators subsequently discovered that Secretary of the Interior Fall had received livestock and an estimated $500,000 in stocks and bonds as payoffs from the Pan American Petroleum Company and the Mammoth Oil Company.

Questioning the integrity of Attorney General Daugherty, President Coolidge named an independent counsel to prosecute Secretary Fall. A stubborn and unrepentant Daugherty not only refused to resign his cabinet office, but also attacked the Senate investigation. When the Attorney General testified in front of the committee, lawmakers accused him of directly interfering with the Teapot Dome investigation. The notoriously corrupt Gaston Means informed committee members that he had personally directed Bureau agents to covertly enter the offices of select Senators and search for potentially damaging information that might be used to keep them from investigating into Daugherty's misdeeds. In another shocking revelation, Means explained that the Attorney General was fully aware of his actions.

On March 28, 1924, President Coolidge fired the Attorney General. Daugherty managed to avoid a prison sentence, after two separate trials ended in hung juries. Secretary of the Interior Fall was not as fortunate—he was fined $100,000 and sentenced to a one-year prison term.

Coolidge quickly appointed Harlan F. Stone, Dean of the Columbia University School of Law, to succeed Daugherty as Attorney General. On May 5th of that same year, Stone informed William Burns that he could either resign his position as Director of the Bureau of Investigation, or be fired. When Burns was too shocked to offer a reply, Stone had him escorted from the building. That evening, Burns learned from a radio news report that he had *resigned*.

On May 10th, just a few days after Burns was discharged, Stone met with J. Edgar Hoover, who had carefully insulated himself from the Justice Department scandals. The new Attorney General appointed Hoover as *Acting*

Director of the Bureau of Investigation. Promotion to the full directorship would be contingent upon Hoover's job performance during an unspecified initial probationary period.

Over the years, Hoover recounted his initial encounter with Stone. According to Hoover, he informed Stone that he would accept the Bureau directorship under two conditions—all future appointments would be based on merit rather than political connections, and that he would answer only to the Attorney General.

The night of her son's appointment as Acting Director, Annie Hoover had the family cook prepare a special celebratory dinner. On his dinner plate, Edgar discovered a gift from his mother—a platinum band with a sapphire star and six diamonds. For the remainder of his life, Hoover proudly wore the ring; a lasting and concrete reminder of how much he had achieved by the tender age of 29. Just seven years after joining the Department of Justice, Hoover had proven that he was an achiever and a politically savvy survivor.

On May 13, 1924, five days after Hoover's promotion, Attorney General Stone sent the Acting Director a memorandum outlining his expectations for reforming the Bureau, which had been tainted by corruption. Stone provided Hoover with several directives: BOI investigations would be restricted to violations of federal law; a reduction in the number of personnel to meet the absolute needs of the Bureau; discharge of "incompetent" and "unreliable" employees; termination of dollar-per-year employees; and no new staff appointments, without the approval of the Attorney General.

Hoover, who was the sixth man to head the BOI, was eager to place his personal imprint on the agency and impress the Attorney General with his leadership skills. When he was named Acting Director, the Bureau employed 650 people, 441 of whom were special agents. Hoover immediately mandated performance evaluations and abolished seniority-based promotions. He also trimmed the employee roster, firing agents he deemed unqualified or incompetent. His criteria for discharging agents was not always objective; those "who looked like truck drivers" or "pinheads" were fired. Agents who did not measure up to Hoover's exacting standards were transferred to remote assignments. The Director attempted to exert control over the private lives of his employees, blocking marriages that did not meet his approval, attempting to end unhealthy marriages, and firing *double yolkers* (Hoover's term for agents engaging in extramarital affairs). Within a few months, Hoover had reduced the total number of Bureau agents from 441 to 402, while trimming the clerical work force from 216 to 99.

New criteria were established for entry-level agents—they must be between 25 and 35 years of age and possess degrees in either law or accounting. No favoritism would be extended to potential employees who were the friends or family members of Senators, Congressman, Judges, and Cabinet officers.

During the early years of Hoover's directorship, Bureau agents were almost exclusively white, male, and Protestant. There were few Jews and hardly any African Americans employed by the Bureau. When Hoover became Acting Director, the Bureau employed three female agents; within four weeks, two of them had been fired and the third had resigned. Hoover rarely hired Hispanics; he told others that "the average Mexican is a psychological liar," who harbors "visions probably of making money."

Ever the master organizer, Hoover used a map hung on the wall of his office to divide the country into 53 sections. Each section housed a field office, headed by a Special Agent in Charge (SAC). The SAC was responsible for supervising the other agents in that office. In some of the less populous regions, the SAC was the only agent assigned to that field office.

Hoover established clear, unwavering communication channels. Bureau agents were required to submit their investigative reports to the SAC. The SAC would then communicate the contents of those reports to one of the six Washington-based division heads appointed by Hoover.

Field offices were regularly subjected to inspections. Field agents dreaded the visits from Washington inspectors, referring to them as *Goon Squads*. Agents who committed minor offenses received letters of censure from Director Hoover. If their mistakes were deemed more serious, Hoover ordered their transfer to a more remote field office. Serious breaches of Bureau protocol resulted in *dismissal with prejudice*; if an agent was fired by the Bureau, he found it nearly impossible to land another job within the federal government.

Determined to keep anyone from embarrassing or sullying the reputation of the Bureau, Hoover insisted that all agents behave in a manner beyond reproach. In a memorandum, the Director reminded agents that Prohibition was the law of the land: "...I am determined to summarily dismiss from this Bureau any employee whom I find indulging in the use of intoxicants to any degree or extent, upon any occasion...I, myself, am refraining from the use of intoxicants...And, I am not, therefore, expecting any more of the field employees than I am of myself." True to his word, Hoover went so far as to remove his mother's sherry from the house.

Hoover's management style incorporated his quirky obsessions and compulsions. At Bureau headquarters, all window shades had to be adjusted to the same height; one employee, who lowered his shade too far, was chastised by the Director for giving the building "a messy look." Hoover routinely kept his office temperature cold, in an effort to ward off viruses and bacteria, and installed an ultra-violet light unit, designed to kill germs. During the summer months, a Bureau employee was assigned the specific task of swatting flies in the Director's office. If Hoover shook hands with someone who had moist palms, he immediately rushed to the washroom for a thorough scrubbing.

Office regulations at the Bureau were decidedly sexist. Hoover prohibited female employees from smoking; a habit he deemed undignified and unlady-like. Not until 1971, the year before his death, would Hoover allow female staff members to wear pants to work, instead of skirts or dresses.

In spite of his idiosyncratic and dictatorial policies, Hoover managed to transform the Bureau into a first rate investigative agency. He established formal training courses for new agents, and oversaw development of the Bureau's crime lab, where expert technicians analyzed evidence, including weapons, bullets, fibers, hairs, explosives, poisons, and handwriting.

Fingerprint analysis was still in its infancy in the mid-1920s, and most records were stored at Kansas' Leavenworth Penitentiary or the National Bureau of Criminal Identification (NBCI) in Chicago, the latter of which was part of the International Association of Chiefs of Police (IACP). In 1924, under Hoover's leadership, the Justice Department combined its existing fingerprint cards with the 800,000 sets of prints previously stored at Leavenworth and the NBCI, to form a centralized data base located at the Bureau's Washington headquarters.

While Hoover dreamed of collecting fingerprints from every American citizen, Congress nixed any such proposed legislation as reeking of totalitarianism. The Bureau, however, did collect fingerprints from all felons, thousands of federal employees, members of the armed forces, and all civilian workers involved in defense-industry contracting. By the time of Hoover's death in 1972, the Bureau's Identification Section had accumulated 159 million sets of fingerprints.

Hoover recognized the need to establish formal liaisons with state and local police forces. While the relationship between the feds and locals were often contentious, Hoover offered the services of the Bureau's crime laboratory to outside law enforcement agencies. He also oversaw publication of the *Law Enforcement Bulletin*, which contained a centralized wanted list for every state and local law enforcement agency in the country.

Attorney General Stone was impressed with Hoover's dedication and hard-work. Seven months after he named Hoover Acting Director of the Bureau, Stone appointed him to formal directorship, with a concomitant pay raise from $5,000 to $7,500 per year. For the next 48 years, spanning the administrations of eight different Presidents and 17 Attorneys General, the Bureau would be headed by J. Edgar Hoover.

Enjoying a rare celebration, Hoover and Frank Baughman took their mothers to New York City to see a musical. As always, Hoover almost exclusively preferred select male companionship. When Baughman married in 1929, a new figure appeared in Hoover's life. Clyde Tolson, a 30-year-old Missouri-born attorney, who had joined the Bureau in January of 1928, quickly became Hoover's shadow. Tolson had initially planned to work as a Bureau agent for one to two years, then return to Iowa where his parents resided, to practice law. A graduate of Hoover's alma mater, George Washington University, Tolson worked at Bureau Headquarters, before serving a stent at the Boston field office.

Hoover rewarded Tolson's hard work with a promotion to SAC of the Buffalo, New York office. After only five days in his new position, Tolson was summoned back to headquarters on an "emergency basis." The emergency likely had to do with Baughman's marriage, which left Hoover without a late-night work and dinner companion. In 1930, just two years after Tolson joined the Bureau, Hoover appointed him as one of two Associate Directors. Tolson would remain in that position for the next 42 years, until Hoover's death.

Hoover and Tolson were inseparable, eating lunch and dinner together nearly every day. They also accompanied one another on vacations and other social outings. Years later, after suffering a stroke, Tolson recuperated in the guest bedroom at Hoover's house. Many have speculated that Hoover and Tolson were lovers; including some Bureau employees, who nicknamed the pair, "J. Edna and Mother Tolson." Many others who worked closely with both Hoover and Tolson have vehemently denied that either man was homosexual. While both remained lifelong bachelors, Hoover rarely and discreetly enjoyed the companionship of females. On one occasion, he was seen leaving actress Dorothy Lamour's hotel in the early morning hours. When later questioned about whether or not she had a sexual relationship with Hoover, Lamour coyly replied: "I cannot deny it." Irrespective of sexual orientation, Tolson remained as Hoover's singular close friend.

While Hoover had established the Bureau as a world-class investigative agency, akin to the famed Scotland Yard, the agency's powers remained narrowly defined. Law enforcement was largely considered a function of state and local officials. Unarmed Bureau agents were still unable to make arrests, and their investigative powers were limited to violations of the Mann Act (prohibiting interstate prostitution) and Dyar Act (illegal transportation of stolen automobiles across state lines), as well as cases of bank and mail fraud, bribing or impersonating government officials, and theft of government property. As the decade of the 1920s came to a close, the Bureau was far-removed from its future glory days. Hoover, himself, had never fired a gun at a bad guy or even made an arrest.

Hoover longed to broaden the Bureau's powers and searched for high profile cases to spotlight the agency's investigative prowess. The first such opportunity occurred when a notorious car thief, Martin James Durkin, shot and killed Special Agent S. A. Shanahan on October 11, 1925. Shanahan was the first Bureau agent killed in the line of duty, which enraged Hoover: "We've got to get Durkin. If one of our agents is killed and the killer is permitted to get away, it will be open season on all our agents..."

For months, more than 200 Bureau agents pursued the murderous car thief through several states in the Midwest and Southwest. When Durkin was finally captured, he was tried in both state and federal courts, and sentenced to 35 years for murder and 15 years for transporting a stolen car across state lines.

Slowly but surely, Hoover elevated the Bureau's public profile. In his first annual report to Congress, Hoover initiated a lifelong pattern of wowing lawmakers with statistics, pointing out that Bureau agents had made arrests generating a total of 4,494 years in prison terms and $1,038,856.42 in fines, and had recovered more than 6.5 million dollars' worth of stolen cash and goods. Hoover's performance was praised by lawmakers and the press. At home, his proud mother began clipping laudatory newspaper articles and posting them in a scrapbook.

Hoover was well on his way to crafting the image of a tireless and incorruptible defender of justice. Though he had grown pudgy and would struggle with his weight for the remainder of his life, Hoover nonetheless cut a dashing figure in his pressed suits, conservative ties (never red, which represented communism), and spotlessly shined shoes. An around-the-clock watchdog, Hoover installed an extension, *Lincoln 3004*, which directly connected his bedside home phone to the Bureau night supervisor's office.

Another opportunity for the Bureau to attain nationwide recognition occurred on the night of March 1, 1932, when Charles Augustus Lindbergh, Jr., son of the famed aviator, was kidnapped from his parent's home, located just north of Princeton, New Jersey. At 11:00 p.m., Hoover was notified of the kidnapping by the Bureau's night supervisor. Unable to sleep, he tossed and turned until receiving a second call at 1:23 a.m., when he learned that Corporal Frank A. Kelly of the New Jersey State Police had discovered a ransom note demanding $50,000 and warning the Lindbergh family not to involve the police or make the contents of the letter public.

After receiving the second phone call, Hoover summoned his driver to transport him to Bureau headquarters. Even though kidnapping was not yet a federal crime, Hoover could not resist the urge to involve the Bureau in such a high profile case. The Director immediately telephoned the head of the New Jersey State Police, H. Norman Schwarzkopf (the father of the General bearing the same name, who later commanded United Nations' forces during the early 1990's Persian Gulf War), and offered Bureau assistance with the case. After being tersely rebuffed by Schwarzkopf, Hoover visited the White House the following morning and asked President Hoover to request that "all documents and material evidence" related to the kidnapping be forwarded to the Bureau. When New Jersey Governor, A. Henry Moore, sent a telegram to the President and the Governors of all the states east of the Mississippi River, asking them to send representatives to Trenton to help coordinate the investigation, the Bureau was able to join the case. President Hoover immediately designated the Bureau Director to serve as the federal government's representative.

When the task force convened on March 5th, Hoover was only one among hundreds of law enforcement agents present, which afforded the Bureau no special recognition. While in New Jersey, Hoover visited the Lindbergh's house, but was disappointed when the traumatized couple refused to speak with him. Lindbergh and his wife were decidedly unimpressed by Hoover, describing him as "a fussy little man."

Eager for the Bureau to play a prominent role in the high-profile case, Hoover assigned 26 agents to the kidnapping, commanded by Special Agent Thomas Sisk. Bureau agents interrogated potential suspects in New Jersey, New York, and Pennsylvania. Believing they had solved the case, a handful of agents raided an Italian couple's home, only to embarrassingly discover the baby in question was a girl.

The Lindbergh case was plagued by false leads and the family's secret payment of the $50,000 ransom. On May 12th, the baby's body was discovered buried in a shallow grave, less than a mile from his parent's house. In September of that same year, Bruno Richard Hauptmann was arrested and charged with kidnapping and murder, after attempting to use a gold certificate from the ransom money to purchase gasoline at a Bronx, New York service station. While Special Agent Sisk was present at the time of the arrest, the Bureau's involvement in the case had been limited, dwarfed by the New York and New Jersey State Police, along with Treasury Department agents. Nonetheless, Hoover was present to have his photograph taken alongside Colonel Schwarzkopf. The publicity surrounding the case ultimately benefited the Bureau; in June of 1932, Congress passed the Lindbergh Law, which made kidnapping a federal offense.

In March of 1933, Franklin D. Roosevelt was inaugurated for the first of his unprecedented four terms as President. J. Edgar Hoover, fearful of losing his job, had little time to contemplate the ramifications of Roosevelt's proposed New Deal. The man nominated to become the next Attorney General was none other than Montana Senator, Thomas Walsh. The 72-year-old Walsh bore a distinct grudge against the Bureau of Investigation and its Director, who had harassed him during the congressional investigation of the Teapot Dome scandal, a decade earlier. Many, including Hoover, believed Walsh's first act as Attorney General would be to fire the current Bureau Director.

Once again, Hoover proved to be a survivor, but this time he was saved by the hand of fate. Two days before Roosevelt's inauguration, Walsh, who was returning by train to Washington D.C after a Miami Beach honeymoon with his much younger wife, collapsed and died from a heart attack.

FDR's second choice for Attorney General, Homer S. Cummings, elected to retain Hoover as Bureau Director. While Hoover had dodged yet another bullet, he had not yet established his reputation as the nation's top cop, and was soon stung by unexpected criticism. In the August 1933 issue of *Collier's* magazine, reporter Ray Tucker wrote a less than flattering piece about the Bureau Director: "Although Mr. Hoover issued strict orders against publicity on the part of his agents, he was never bound by them. In every newspaper and magazine article and radio broadcast recounting his field agents' activities, there appears the name of 'J. Edgar Hoover, Director of the United States Bureau of Investigation'." Not yet done, Tucker added ridicule to his criticism: "In appearance, Mr. Hoover looks utterly unlike the story-book sleuth. He is short, fat, business-like, and walks with a mincing step. His black hair, swarthy skin, and collegiate haircut make him look younger than thirty-eight, but heavy, horn-rimmed spectacles, give him an air of age and authority. He dresses fastidiously, with Eleanor blue as the favorite color for the matched shades of tie, handkerchief, and socks. A little pompous, he rides in an expensive limousine, even if only to a nearby self-service cafeteria."

Hoover was enraged by the article, which he characterized as the "rantings of a liquor-soaked rat." Tucker had not only questioned his character but also made light of his masculinity and appearance. As might have been expected, Hoover sought consolation from his mother, who informed her son that there was "nothing wrong with solid weight on a man."

More than ever, Hoover felt pressure to prove his worth to the country. In the mind of its Director, the Bureau needed greater responsibilities and bigger cases. Eventually a man named John Dillinger would enable Hoover to fulfill his destiny.

CHAPTER FOUR

I'd rather be dead than ever go back there

While J. Edgar Hoover was trying to establish a foothold at the Department of Justice, John Dillinger began his early adulthood as *Inmate Number 14395* at the Pendleton Reformatory, a 31-acre corrections facility, located 25 miles northeast of Indianapolis. The reformatory's tan brick buildings, each one topped with a red roof, would not have been particularly imposing had the complex not been surrounded by 30-feet-tall concrete walls, with gun towers at each corner. After dark, the facility betrayed its purpose, as powerful search slights illuminated the buildings and prison yards, lessening the appeal of night time escapes.

The Pendleton Reformatory housed minors (less than age 21), who were serving short or moderate-length sentences. Designed to accommodate 1,200 inmates, by the early 1920s, the facility was overcrowded, housing more than 2,000 young prisoners.

The only benefit Dillinger derived from incarceration was his formal disassociation from military service. After learning the deserter was in prison, the Navy issued Dillinger a dishonorable discharge, and elected to pursue no further punitive actions.

Shortly after arriving at the reformatory, Dillinger was diagnosed with Gonorrhea, perhaps a lingering and unwelcome gift from his past contact with prostitutes. In the pre-antibiotic era, he was force to endure painful injections of silver nitrate directly into his penis.

As one of the older inmates, Dillinger was afforded a measure of respect from his peers. More importantly, he was spared many of the cruel indignities inflicted by the more powerful inmates on their weaker counterparts.

Making good on his threat to the reformatory superintendent, Dillinger unsuccessfully attempted to escape within the first 30 days after his arrival. The failed escape added six months to his original concurrent sentences. In December of 1924, Dillinger and two other inmates were caught trying to saw through their cell bars with a hacksaw blade. The second infraction added yet another six months to his sentences; within three months of arriving at the reformatory, Dillinger had already managed to lengthen his incarceration by a full year.

Throughout his stay at Pendleton, Dillinger would behave as a model prisoner for short stretches of time, followed by a series of rules infractions. The inconsistency proved self-defeating, and jeopardized his chances of earning an early parole for good behavior.

Dillinger's wife, Beryl, eventually grew weary of being married to a prison inmate, and after mid-1928, stopped visiting her husband. In April of 1929, Beryl filed for divorce. Two months later, the same judge who had sentenced Dillinger to prison granted her petition.

Other family members visited Dillinger when they could. His favorite niece, Mary, came most often, and also remained a faithful pen pal, which cemented their already close relationship. "I wrote him every week—ten, twelve, fifteen pages," Mary later recalled.

Inside the walls of the Pendleton Reformatory, four companies operated factories that manufactured clothing, furniture, tableware, and manhole covers. By collaborating with the penal system, business owners profited from low-cost, forced labor. Dillinger was initially assigned to the foundry, helping produce manhole covers. Unhappy with the 100- plus-degree-temperatures, Dillinger sought reassignment by pouring hot steel into one of his shoes. When his initial self-inflicted injury failed to achieve the desired effect, Dillinger poured acid on his burned foot, which finally led to his being transferred out of the foundry.

Dillinger's first parole hearing arrived in July of 1929, after he had completed nearly five years of his concurrent sentences. On the day of the hearing, Dillinger played shortstop for the reformatory's baseball team in a game against a semi-professional team. Indiana Governor, Harry Leslie, a member of the three-man parole board, was among the spectators observing the ball game. Impressed by Dillinger's athleticism, the Governor informed an *Indianapolis News* reporter: "That kid ought to be playing major league baseball."

As a result of multiple rules infractions, Dillinger was denied parole. The chairman explained the parole board's reasoning: "Young man, you've served only a small part of your term and apparently you aren't amenable to prison life. Perhaps you better go back for a few years."

A disappointed Dillinger immediately asked to be transferred to the Indiana State Penitentiary in Michigan City: "I want to go up there and play baseball. They have a real good team."

"I don't see any merit in that," the board chairman replied.

At this point, Governor Leslie intervened: "It might be an occupation for him later. I'd be in favor of the transfer."

On July 15, 1929, Dillinger was sent to Michigan City. After arriving at the Indiana State Penitentiary, however, he never played on any of the prison's baseball teams. The most likely reason for Dillinger's transfer request was his desire to associate with older, more experienced criminals, who would serve as seasoned tutors. Incarceration had only reinforced Dillinger's determination to learn as much he could from other criminals. Dillinger biographer, John Toland, summed up the failed attempt at rehabilitation: "Dillinger had seen little reformation at the reformatory, and would see even less penitence at the penitentiary. There was no regret for having committed a crime, only for being caught..."

The 23-acre Indiana State Penitentiary, surrounded by drab gray walls, housed 2,500 inmates. Located 150 miles further distant from Mooresville, Dillinger's new home was not easily accessible by his family members. In the four years that he was incarcerated in Michigan City, Dillinger's beloved sister, Audrey, was only able to visit her brother on one occasion.

Accommodations behind the penitentiary's stone walls were primitive. Dillinger resided in a six by nine feet cell, illuminated by a single 25-watt bulb. A card, taped to his cell wall, enumerated the 27 rules governing every inmate's life. Prisoners were not allowed to possess books, magazines, or newspapers, and were issued a bar of soap, one towel, and tobacco. Three times each evening, the inmates were allowed to smoke their corncob pipes or cigarettes, which they lit from a torch carried by a trusty.

Michigan City was Dillinger's first exposed to an older, more experienced class of criminals—bank and train robbers, burglars, and safecrackers. From this assemblage of felons, he learned more about the finer points of crime, eagerly absorbing the lessons and establishing relationships that would prove beneficial in the future.

As had been the case at Pendleton Reformatory, the private sector worked in conjunction with the Indiana State Penitentiary, operating factories behind the prison walls. Dillinger was assigned to work at the Golden East Coast Shirt Company, where he sewed collars on Blue Yank work shirts. Dillinger was so efficient operating the Tomcat sewing machine that he not only met his daily production quotas, but also kept fellow inmates from falling behind.

While working in the shirt factory, Dillinger made his first contact with a select group of convicted bank robbers, who would later become criminal partners—Harry "Pete" Pierpont, Charles Makley, John "Red" or "Three-fingered" Hamilton, and Russell "Boobie" Clark. Among those felons, Pierpont likely exerted the most influence.

The 26-year-old Pierpont, whose home was Muncie, Indiana, was only one year Dillinger's senior, but possessed a far more impressive criminal resume. Six-feet-tall, with brown hair, blue eyes, and striking facial features, Pierpont was sometimes called "Handsome Harry." He was, however, afflicted with an embarrassing physical defect—his second and third toes were connected in a web. Interestingly, Dillinger's relationship with Pierpont marked his second close association with a fused-extremity criminal mentor. Pierpont's extensive rap sheet included car theft, assault and battery with intent to murder, and several bank robberies. In addition to their mutual interest in thievery, Dillinger and Pierpont were fascinated by guns.

Pierpont, who tried to escape the penitentiary on four separate occasions, endured four separate solitary confinements and multiple beatings from guards. His fearlessness and hatred of lawmen quickly earned him the respect of fellow inmates. Consequently, Pierpont became the established leader of a cadre of imprisoned bank robbers, including Hamilton, Makley, and Clark.

Dillinger also developed a close relationship with 24-year-old Homer Van Meter, a native of Fort Wayne, Indiana. Van Meter's early years had been chaotic and traumatic; his father was declared insane and his uncle ultimately died in an asylum. After running away from home at age 12, Van Meter embarked on a life of crime. After he was convicted of train robbery, Van Meter was sentenced to 10 to 21 years at the Indiana State Penitentiary.

Standing less than six feet tall and weighing only 125 pounds, Van Meter was physically unimposing and possessed a disarming sense of humor. His diminutive build and jovial personality, however, thinly masked a capacity for violence. In no uncertain terms, a Gary, Indiana police officer summarized his experiences with Van Meter: "This fellow is a hardened criminal and would not hesitate to shoot and kill in order to accomplish his purpose."

While incarcerated in Michigan City, Van Meter struck a guard in the head with a lead pipe, which led to a two-month stint in solitary confinement, during which time he was regularly beaten by other prison staffers. At least one prison guard came to understand Van Meter quite well: "...He is a murderer at heart, and if society is to be safeguarded, his type must be confined throughout their natural lives."

Harry Pierpont detested Van Meter, calling him a "clown," but a charismatic Dillinger managed to forge lasting relationships with both men. Even though he was prone to violence, Van Meter's prospects for an early parole appeared promising; perhaps a byproduct of discreet bribes paid on his behalf by outsiders. Van Meter promised Dillinger that once they were both released from prison, he would teach him how to abscond with "the big money."

Unlike Homer Van Meter, Dillinger was never a violent inmate. On the contrary, most of the guards and his fellow inmates considered Dillinger to be likeable and easy going. At the same time, Dillinger was never a model prisoner, and continued to commit his share of petty offenses. During his nearly four-year incarceration at the Indiana State Penitentiary, Dillinger was punished with two stretches of solitary confinement—once for stealing a watermelon and the other time for concealing a straight razor in his cell. In spite of these infractions, Dillinger bragged to his niece about his ongoing rehabilitation, in a letter written on Christmas Day, 1929: "...I'll be out sometime, and believe me, I am going to stay out. I know right from wrong, and I intend to do right when I get out..."

As his next parole hearing drew near, Dillinger's conduct improved, with fewer rules infractions. In April of 1933, Dillinger's family organized a petition supporting his parole; the petition truthfully asserted that his stepmother was in ill health, but laughingly suggested that Dillinger would provide much needed labor at the farm. A total of 188 individuals signed the petition, including the Morgan County sheriff and the clerk of the court, as well as the county's auditor, treasurer, recorder, and assessor. Two rather unlikely signatures were added to the request for parole—Judge Joe Williams, who had sentenced the defendant to prison, and Frank Morgan, the grocer Dillinger had robbed and assaulted. Judge Williams went so far as to include a brief letter of support: "...I believe if this prisoner is paroled, that he has learned his lesson and that he will go straight in the future and will make a useful and honorable citizen..."

While his family labored to secure him an early release from prison, the unrepentant Dillinger was actively plotting future crimes. Ignoring the risk of being captured or killed, Harry Pierpont seduced Dillinger with the lifestyle a successful bank robber might enjoy—pocketsful of cash, fine suits, new cars, luxurious hotel accommodations, and the ability to solicit high-class prostitutes. Pierpont also provided Dillinger with the names and locations of banks to rob, advice on how to stage heists, a list of potential accomplices, and the "how-to" on fencing stolen goods and laundering stolen money. In exchange for this valuable information, Dillinger promised to use a portion of the money he stole during his initial post-parole robberies to purchase weapons and smuggle them into the penitentiary, which would enable Pierpont and his select few to stage a prison break.

Dillinger's much-anticipated parole hearing was held on May 10, 1933. Because he had not yet served his minimum 10-year sentence, Dillinger's parole would be considered by the three-man Governor's Clemency Petition Committee, rather than the Indiana State Penitentiary's Board of Trustees. In Dillinger's case, this was a lucky break, since the prison board was far more familiar with his poor attitude and multiple rules infractions.

Two of the three clemency commissioners, Delus Dean and Tom Arbuckle, voted to grant Dillinger's parole. The third commissioner, Wayne Coy, who also happened to be Governor Paul V. McNutt's personal secretary, voted no, for reasons that he never made known. A two-thirds vote, however, was all that was needed to grant Dillinger his freedom.

On the morning of May 20th, Dillinger's step-mother suffered a catastrophic stoke. Later that same day, Indiana State Penitentiary Warden, Walter H. Daly, received an unexpected telegram from John Dillinger, Sr.: JOHN DILLINGER NO. 13225. MOTHER NOT EXPECTED TO LIVE. CAN YOU SEND HIM AT ONCE? ANSWER.

The warden's assistant informed the elder Dillinger that his son would be available for release in two days. On the morning of May 22nd, Dillinger's half-brother, Hubert, and his nephew, Fred Hancock, arrived at the penitentiary. After prison officials provided him with an inexpensive suit of clothes and $40 in cash, Dillinger exited prison a free man, for the first time in nine and one-half years. As he walked outside the penitentiary's main gate, Dillinger offered an ominous benediction: "I'd rather be dead than ever go back in there."

By the time the trio arrived in Mooresville later that same day, Dillinger's stepmother had already died. What might have been a joyous family reunion was supplanted by grief.

On the day of his stepmother's funeral, Dillinger bragged to the undertaker that he had indeed been rehabilitated: "I'm sick of it. I'm going straight." Dillinger also promised his father that he would walk the straight and narrow. At first, the ex-convict's avowals appeared sincere. Frank Morgan, the grocer who Dillinger had attacked and robbed, was surprised when his former assailant paid him a visit: "He shook my hand and said, 'I want to apologize for socking you that time. I've turned over a new leaf. I've reformed. I want to thank you for helping get my parole.' He seemed to realize that he had been bad."

For a time, Dillinger attended church, perhaps hoping to convince others that he was truly reformed. Just prior to Dillinger's release from prison, the warden at the Indiana State Penitentiary sent a letter to Reverend Gertrude Rainer, pastor of Mooresville's Quaker Friend's Church, asking her to tend to the parolee's "spiritual needs." When Rainer reached out to Dillinger, he gave every indication of reciprocating. On Father's Day, at the conclusion of church services, Dillinger thanked Reverend Rainer for her reflections on the Prodigal Son: "You will never know how much good that sermon has done me."

Not everyone was convinced that Dillinger had changed. When Dillinger paid an unannounced call on his ex-wife, Beryl, she was dubious about his motives: "He just wanted to know how I was getting along. I asked him to leave, and he did."

Many of those who attended church with Dillinger were also skeptical about his self-proclaimed rehabilitation. During an altar call, when church members were asked to kneel at the altar and offer their support to fellow parishioners, no one came forward to join Dillinger. Unable to convince, or perhaps con others into believing that he was a changed man, Dillinger angrily informed his sister, Audrey: "I will never go to church again, as long as I live."

While their attitudes and actions were decidedly un-Christian, the parishioners who professed disbelief in John Dillinger's redemption proved prescient.

CHAPTER FIVE

The Jackrabbit

Within a month of his parole from the Indiana State Penitentiary, John Dillinger reentered the world of crime. His newfound accomplices, Nobel Claycomb, William "The Kid" Shaw, and Paul "Lefty" Parker, were members of the so-called *White Cap Gang*. Mostly in their late teens, the White Cappers had established a reputation for engaging in small-time robberies in the Indianapolis area.

In early June of 1933, just six days after Dillinger promised Frank Morgan that he was a "reformed" man, Dillinger and two White Cappers accomplices robbed an all-night grocery store in Indianapolis. With Nobel Claycomb manning the get-away car, Dillinger and William Shaw entered the supermarket. While Shaw emptied the cash register, Dillinger held the customers and employees at gun point, ordering them to move to the rear of the store. When an elderly gentleman, perhaps paralyzed by fear, failed to move, Dillinger struck him in the mouth with his revolver, shattering the old man's dentures. Dillinger's first post-prison robbery was hardly noteworthy; his share of the stolen money amounted to only $30.

A few nights later, Dillinger teamed up with Shaw and Lefty Parker to rob one of Indianapolis' Haag Drug Stores, located at 5648 E. Washington Street. Earlier in the day, Dillinger and Shaw had stolen a Dodge sedan and replaced its out of state license plates with Indiana tags swiped from another vehicle. Later that day, Dillinger purchased a long-barreled .32 caliber revolver from a weapons broker at a local saloon.

Armed with pistols, Dillinger and Shaw entered the Haag Drug Store, while Parker sat behind the wheel of the get-away car. Dillinger emptied the cash register at the soda fountain, while Shaw targeted the main register in the back of the store. When both robbers repeatedly told the customers and employees to "turn around" and not stare at them while they cleaned out their respective cash drawers, the confused group continually spun around in a comedic dance routine.

After Dillinger and Shaw exited the drug store, flush with cash, they discovered that Parker, who was supposed to keep the get-away vehicle double parked near the entrance, had driven to a different location. On the spur of the moment, the inexperienced wheel man had decided to practice his parallel parking skills! As he anxiously attempted to maneuver out of the cramped space, Parker managed to ram into the cars parked in front and behind. Once the trio was a safe distance from scene of the crime, Dillinger castigated Parker for his stupidity.

A few days after the Haag Drug Store heist, the same trio targeted a Kroger grocery store, located on 3512 North College Street. When Dillinger asked if he had previously robbed this particular store, Shaw lied; in fact, he and Claycomb had held up the same grocery, less than a month earlier. While Parker manned the get-away car, Dillinger and Shaw entered the grocery.

"Oh-oh, here they are again," the Kroger manager said, immediately recognizing Shaw's face, "You guys have started the company collecting, and the collector just left."

Consequently, the bandits discovered very little cash inside the registers. Before leaving the store, Shaw gathered up several tins of cigarettes as a consolation prize.

This time, Parker was careful to double park near the front entrance, rather than wedge the get-away car into a parallel space. After Dillinger hopped in the front seat, an anxious Parker accelerated, leaving Shaw standing in the street with a conspicuous armful of cigarette tins.

"Hold it!" Dillinger shouted, "We left the kid behind!"

Parker slammed on the brakes, shifted into reverse, raced backwards, and nearly ran over Shaw. After tossing the cigarette tins inside the car, Shaw hopped into the backseat, and the bandits sped away.

On the morning of June 21, 1933, just one day shy of his 30th birthday, Dillinger, Parker, and Shaw entered the New Carlisle National Bank in New Carlisle, Ohio. The bandits, wearing handkerchiefs over their faces, confronted the bank's bookkeeper, Horace Grisso, who was the first employee to arrive for work.

"All right, buddy, open the safe," a pistol-wielding Dillinger ordered.

Shaw grew impatient as a nervous Grisso struggled to dial the combination lock: "Let me drill him—he's stalling."

Displaying his uncanny ability to remain calm, Dillinger simultaneously hushed Shaw and reassured Grisso: "Take your time."

When a female clerk entered the bank, Dillinger ordered her to lie down on the floor, and bound her hands and feet with wire. In a chivalric effort to make the woman more comfortable, Dillinger placed a chair slip cover on the hard floor.

"I don't want to hurt you," Dillinger explained.

After Grisso managed to open the vault, Shaw and Parker stuffed their sacks with cash, while Dillinger watched the front door. When two more employees arrived for work, a smiling Dillinger greeted them at gunpoint: "You hadn't ought to come in the bank so early."

Unmolested, the three bandits exited the bank and hopped into their get-away car driven by an unknown accomplice, possibly Claycomb. The four men raced back to Indianapolis. In their inaugural bank robbery, Dillinger and his partners made away with $10,600.

That same night, Dillinger and his cohorts busily robbed a grocery store, as well as another Haag Drug Store. As they drove away from the grocery, Dillinger bragged to Shaw: "I'll never go back to the pen. They're not going to catch me—not (even) if I have to kill someone."

Using a portion of his share of the stolen money, Dillinger paid a bribe to former Howard County Sheriff, Omar Brown—a man he thought might exert influence over the parole board. Dillinger hoped the bribe would secure freedom for his prison mentor, Harry Pierpont, whose parole hearing was scheduled for August 24th.

Unaccustomed to having so much cash in his pocket, Dillinger purchased a new suit, a pair of shoes, and a straw boater hat. He also visited a barber, who transformed his prison "bowl cut" into a more fashionable hair style.

On the night of June 22nd, Dillinger and Shaw robbed an open-air fruit market, making off with a meager $175. A week later, Shaw hot-wired a 1931 DeSoto sedan, which he and Dillinger used as a get-away vehicle later that same day, after robbing Eaton's Sandwich Shop on East Maple Road, absconding with $340.

Dillinger was growing concerned that his continued partnership with the small-time and often bumbling White Cappers might result in his being apprehended and sent back to prison. He was now eager to organize a more experienced gang and target banks, where a robber could steal the big bucks.

On June 30th, the day after the sandwich shop robbery, Shaw married his sweetheart. While Shaw was enjoying his honeymoon, Dillinger drove the recently-purloined DeSoto to Bradsfordsville, Kentucky, where he visited with ex-con, Frank Whitehouse, a fellow alumnus of the Indiana State Penitentiary. Whitehouse put Dillinger in contact with a discreet auto repair specialist, who agreed to repaint the DeSoto and alter the engine's serial numbers, readying the vehicle for further use as a get-away car.

While the DeSoto was in the shop, Dillinger treated Whiteside and his wife with an excursion to the 1933 World's Fair in Chicago. En route to the Windy City, the trio stopped in Fort Wayne, Indiana, where Dillinger met with Whitey Mohler, yet another former Michigan City inmate. A convicted cop killer, Mohler had staged a unique, if not foolhardy, escape from the Indiana State Penitentiary. After drinking shellac from the prison's furniture shop, Mohler developed a high fever and his skin turned yellow. The prison doctors, unaware of the inmate's self-poisoning, misdiagnosed Mohler with tuberculosis, and transferred him to a TB asylum. Once he stopped consuming the shellac, Mohler's health returned to normal, and he easily escaped from the poorly-guarded asylum, finding refuge in a Fort Wayne hide-away.

Dillinger discussed with Mohler his plans to assemble a gang of robbers. Mohler, in turn, suggested that Dillinger contact another former prison inmate, Sam Goldstein, who was living in Hammond, Indiana. Dillinger immediately made another stop in Hammond to visit Goldstein, who had previously teamed up with Mohler and Homer Van Meter to rob more than 10 banks across the Midwest. By the time he reached Chicago, Dillinger had secured tentative commitments from Mohler, Goldstein, and another ex-Indiana State Penitentiary inmate, Fred Brennan, to form a new, more experienced gang.

When Dillinger returned to Indianapolis from the World's Fair, he was flush with cash; some have speculated that Dillinger, perhaps in conjunction with Mohler, Goldstein, and Brennan, robbed a bank or other profitable business. A generous Dillinger gave William Shaw several hundred dollars and the repainted DeSoto as wedding presents. Afterwards, Dillinger purchased a used, maroon-colored V-6 Chevrolet coupe, equipped with red wire wheels.

Dillinger and Shaw soon recruited a new gang member, Harry Copeland. An ex-con, Copeland would remain one of Dillinger's longest standing accomplices.

Shaw soon stole another vehicle—a brand new Chrysler Imperial 80 Roadster that was parked outside Indianapolis' Apollo Theater. Shaw's new bride, Ufah, became party to criminal activity when she drove her husband to the scene of the crime and then followed him to a rented garage, where they stashed the stolen Chrysler.

Joined by yet another newly-recruited gang member, Hilton "Pizzy Wizzy" Crouch, Dillinger, Shaw, and Claycomb plotted to rob a female money collector who worked for the Haag Drug Store chain. Shaw had been trailing the attractive red-headed for several weeks, monitoring her routine of cash pick-ups.

On July 10th, Dillinger and Crouch used the recently-stolen Chrysler to stake out the collector's last stop of the day, a store located at the corner of 16th and Illinois Streets. Even though he had been warned by Shaw not to turn off the car engine, which would burn out the jumper wire the car thief had rigged to steal the vehicle, Crouch apparently did not pay attention, or simply forgot. The bill collector arrived at the anticipated time, but Crouch was unable to start the get-away vehicle, forcing the pair to abort the robbery.

Four days later, Dillinger and Shaw, wearing handkerchiefs over their faces and armed with pistols, robbed the Bide-A-Wee Tavern in Muncie, Indiana, making off with $70. During their exit, the bandits encountered a couple entering the tavern. A smiling Dillinger could not resist the urge to pinch the woman on her rear. When her male companion protested, Dillinger punched him in the face.

The next day, as Dillinger and Copeland were driving back to the Muncie boarding house where gang was temporarily residing, they spotted two police detectives, who were preparing to raid the residence. While Dillinger and Copeland safely sped away, their counterparts were not so lucky. Shaw, Claycomb, and Parker were arrested and taken to the Delaware County Jail. After Shaw's wife, Ufah, managed to convince the authorities that she was an innocent and unsuspecting spouse, the police released her.

The arrestees informed police officials that the name of their accomplice was *John Dellinger*—a name that meant nothing to the authorities. All three men were sentenced to prison, ending their association with Dillinger.

Now just a two-man gang, Dillinger and Copeland staged a daring robbery of the Commercial Bank in Daleville, Indiana on July 17th. At 12:45 p.m., Copeland pulled Dillinger's Chevrolet to the curb outside the bank. Even though the get-away vehicle had been repainted green, the Chevy's red wire rim wheels appeared all the more garish, rendering it quite conspicuous.

While Copeland manned the get-away car, Dillinger, dressed in a dark gray coat, light gray pants, and a straw boater hat, entered the bank, where he found there were no customers and only one employee inside the building (the remainder of the employees were out to lunch). After removing a pistol from his shoulder holster, Dillinger greeted the 22-year-old teller, Margaret Good: "Honey, this is a stick-up. Get me the money."

When Good started to raise her arms, Dillinger stopped her, fearing such movements would attract unwanted attention from those passing by on the sidewalk. In athletic fashion, Dillinger vaulted over the six-feet-high railing separating the lobby from the cash drawers and vault. His agility earned him a new and lasting moniker—*Jackrabbit*. From the tellers' drawers and vault, Dillinger stole $3,000 in cash, along with three diamond rings; the rings belonged to the daughter of cashier, J. N. Barnard, who had left them at the bank for safe keeping, while she was playing tennis.

When three bystanders approached the front door of the bank, Copeland exited the get-away car and marched them inside at gunpoint. After locking Good and the three local citizens inside the vault, the bandits strolled out of the bank, unmolested.

Now a veteran of two bank robberies, John Dillinger was determined to bolster his gang with more experienced talent. There were more and bigger banks waiting to be robbed.

CHAPTER SIX

This is a stick-up

While John Dillinger was establishing himself as a bank robber, criminal activity was rampant across the country, particularly in the Midwest. In 1933, there were 29 bank robberies in Dillinger's home state of Indiana.

The Indiana State Police eventually interviewed enough witnesses to ascertain Dillinger's true identity, thus making him the prime suspect in the Bide-A-Wee Tavern and Daleville bank robberies. At this point in time, the man who would become one of Dillinger's arch nemeses emerged to join the chase—Captain Matt Leach, Director of the Indiana State Police.

Born in Croatia, while his mother was visiting relatives in her homeland, Leach's birth name was Matija Licanin, which he later Anglicized. Leach served as a Sargent in the 151st Infantry's 38th *Cyclone* Division during World War I; he was also under the command of the legendary General, John J. "Black Jack" Pershing, during the Army's pursuit of Mexican revolutionary, Pancho Villa. After completing his military service, Leach returned to his hometown of Gary and joined the Indiana State Police. Diligent in self-study, including the psychology of criminals, Leach worked his way up the ladder, and was eventually appointed to the directorship of the state police.

The rail-thin, 39-year-old Leach was high strung and prone to stuttering when under stress. His work ethic, however, was unquestionable. By the latter half of 1933, Leach was obsessed with capturing John Dillinger, whose wanted posters were affixed to walls throughout the state of Indiana.

On July 19, 1933, just two days after the robbery in Daleville, Dillinger and Harry Copeland struck again. After parking their black Plymouth sedan near the front entrance of the Rockville National Bank in Rockville, Indiana, the pair entered the building. Nattily dressed in a brown suit, Dillinger pointed his newly-acquired .45 caliber automatic pistol at bank President, A. C. Crays: "Do as we say, if you don't want to get killed. Get down on floor!"

Aware of the commotion in the lobby, Roland Crays, the bank President's son, peered through the crack of his partially shut office door. Determined to halt the robbery in progress, the younger Crays retrieved a Colt .38 caliber revolver and took dead aim at one of the bandits. After the bullet whizzed past Copeland's ear and broke a window, an enraged Dillinger stormed into the shooter's office, jammed his pistol into Crays' stomach, and pulled the trigger. To Cray's eternal good fortune, the .45 misfired. Dillinger then punched Crays, knocking him to the floor and disarming him.

Shaken by having been shot at for the first time, Dillinger and Copeland exited the bank after stealing only $120, piled into the get-away car, and raced out of town. While Copeland drove, Dillinger dumped roofing nails in their wake, to slow down potential pursuers. Roland Crays, undaunted by his near-death experience, commandeered a vehicle and briefly gave chase, but was unable to catch up with the bandits' fleet Plymouth.

Twelve miles outside of Rockville, the robbers abandoned the get-away car and boarded a yellow Chrysler Imperial Roadster they had left in waiting. After abandoning the $900 Plymouth, the robbery of the Rockville National Bank ended up costing Dillinger and Copeland $780!

The next day, Dillinger drove to Dayton, Ohio to visit his new love interest, Mary Jenkins Longnacker. Twenty-three-years-old, dark haired, and willowy, Longnacker was no stranger to the world of crime; her brother, James Jenkins, was serving a life sentence for murder at the Indiana State Penitentiary. The attractive Longnacker was still married, but had been abandoned by her husband, who ran off with their two daughters.

Dillinger took Longnacker and her friend, Mary Ann Buchholz, to the World's Fair in Chicago. Among the venues that caught Dillinger's attention was the Hudson Motor Car Company's display of its new sleek and powerful Essex Terraplane Eight. Ever in need of fast get-away vehicles, Dillinger decided that he would one day purchase his own Terraplane.

On their way back from Chicago, Dillinger drove Longnacker to the Indiana State Penitentiary for a visit with her brother. Unwilling to enter the prison grounds where he had previously languished, Dillinger purchased fruit for Mary to give to her brother. Inside one of the bananas, Dillinger concealed an additional treat—a 50-dollar bill.

Having grown infatuated with Longnacker, Dillinger accompanied her to see a Dayton attorney, Farrell Johnson. Dillinger offered to pay Johnson the necessary fee to represent Mary in her forthcoming divorce and child custody cases.

On July 26th, Dillinger made a brief visit to the family farm in Mooresville, presenting his father with a 69th birthday present—a shirt and tie. Dillinger immediately high-tailed it out of Mooresville, after learning that his parole officer planned to arrest him for violating his parole by leaving town without permission.

At 2:40 p.m. on August 4th, a blue Dodge sedan eased to a stop in front of the First National Bank on Main Street in Montpelier, Indiana. A third accomplice, possibly Whitey Mohler or Sam Goldstein, joined Dillinger and Copeland on the heist, manning the get-away car.

Copeland and a gum-chewing Dillinger strolled into the bank lobby, brandishing pistols. In a calm, but authoritative voice, Dillinger announced: "This is a stick-up. All we want is your money. Stand still, and you won't get hurt."

While Copeland forced three bank employees to lie down on the floor, Dillinger vaulted over the railing separating the lobby from the tellers' cash drawers. As he was scooping up cash, Dillinger eyed one of the female tellers reaching for a button: "What are you trying to do, set off that alarm?"

"I would, if I could," she defiantly replied.

In short order, the bandits exited the building with $10,110 worth of cash and coins, as well as a .45 caliber revolver found in one of the tellers' drawers. One of the bank's employees later remembered Dillinger's parting comments: "This was a pretty good haul."

"Looks like the banks being held up again," a bystander on the sidewalk remarked, as the robbers boarded their get-away car.

"I'm not surprised," Dillinger grinned.

As the residents of Montpelier watched the robbers' Dodge race away, the town's police officers were far too slow to offer chase. A farmer outside of town later saw the bandits stop briefly to change the get-away car's license plates. In the early evening, authorities discovered the abandoned Dodge car on a rural road, 100 miles distant from Montpelier. Inside the vehicle, the cops discovered a sack of roofing nails and a map detailing the bank robbers' escape route.

On August 10th, the Indiana State Police issued the first *all-points* bulletin for Dillinger, Copeland, and three other potential accomplices. The legend of the Dillinger Gang was underway.

On Monday, August 14, 1933, Dillinger and five unidentified accomplices robbed the Citizen's National Bank in Bluffton, Ohio. Just before noon, a green sedan parked on Church Street, adjacent to the bank. While one man remained inside the get-away car with the engine running, five others exited the vehicle. Two of the bandits stationed themselves on the sidewalk near the front entrance, while the others entered the bank. One of the men stood just inside the door, while the other two approached the tellers' cages. Assistant cashier, Roscoe Klingler, greeted one of the strangers, who asked to change a five dollar bill, specifically requesting three ones, 10 dimes, and 20 nickels. After pocketing the bills and change, the customer, who the cashier would later describe as "the quiet man," drew a pistol: "Stand back, this is a stick-up."

When an unlucky customer entered the bank, the quiet man ordered him to join Klingler and the bank's bookkeeper, Oliver Locher, behind the counter. At this point, a man, who witnesses would later identify as Dillinger, vaulted over the rail and proceeded to empty bills from the cash drawers into a cloth sack.

"You've got more than this. Where the hell is it?" Dillinger confronted Locher.

The terrified bookkeeper pointed at the vault, just as the outside bank alarm began to ring.

"They're after us, let's go," the quiet man announced.

"Take it easy. We've got plenty of time," Dillinger calmly replied.

As Dillinger finished cleaning out the tellers' drawers, a second alarm, located at the town's water works, began wailing. When he encountered a locked drawer, Dillinger grew impatient: "Where the hell's the key?"

Almost immediately, gunfire erupted outside. The robbers stationed on the sidewalk, having grown antsy by the twin alarms, began firing their handguns at the windows of neighboring businesses, sending proprietors and customers scurrying. *Bluffton News* reporter, Red Biery, was among those seeking immediate cover: "Good men are scarce. I decided to preserve one."

In short order, Dillinger and his accomplices exited the bank and piled into the get-away car. In spite of the uproar they created, the robbers sped out of town without incident, having stolen $6,000.

On September 6th, Dillinger, Copeland, and a third man, possibly a new recruit named John Vinson, entered the State Bank of Massachusetts in downtown Indianapolis. The Jackrabbit scaled the seven-feet-high tellers' counter and confronted assistant manager, Lloyd Rinehart: "This is a stick-up! We mean business." Rinehart, who was on the phone and initially disregarded the order, soon found a pistol pointed in his face.

"Get away from that damned phone!" Dillinger ordered.

While his accomplices forced the bank employees to lie on the floor and the customers to stand in the corner with their hands kept visible, Dillinger filled his sacks with $24,000 in cash and $1,000 in silver half-dollar coins. After exiting the bank, the bandits quickly boarded their get-away car, a blue DeSoto, driven by Hilton Crouch. A portion of the robbers' stolen money included the recently deposited payroll for the Real Silk Hosiery Plant; this particular heist was the second costliest bank robbery in state history.

After robbing the State Bank of Massachusetts, Dillinger had enough money to purchase weapons needed to facilitate the Indiana State Penitentiary break-out that he and Harry Pierpont had previously planned. While Homer Van Meter had been paroled on May 19th, Pierpont had no such luck during his parole hearing, in spite of bribes that were paid on his behalf.

Desperate to get out of prison by any means possible, Pierpont had previously asked his mother to write a letter to Indiana State Police Chief, Matt Leach. In the proxy missive, Pierpont promised that if he was temporarily released from prison with one guard, he would lead Leach directly to Dillinger and Copeland. Interpreting Pierpont's request as little more than a clever ruse designed to allow the inmate to escape, Leach ignored the proposal.

Unaware of Pierpont's offer to betray him, Dillinger continued to work on an escape plan by establishing relationships with Pearl Elliott, the owner of a night club and brothel in Kokomo, Indiana, and 22-year-old Mary Kinder. Kinder, a petite, four-feet, 11-inches-tall red-head, was no stranger to the world of crime—her brother, ex-husband, and an old friend, Harry Pierpont, were prisoners at the Indiana State Penitentiary. Kinder's brother, Earl, had once partnered with Pierpont to rob a bank in Kokomo. Kinder agreed to help Dillinger if Pierpont would include her brother in his escape plan. Dillinger readily agreed, and instructed Kinder to locate a safe house for the escapees.

Dillinger paid a Chicago weapons broker $144 for three .38 caliber automatic pistols and additional ammunition clips. Assisted by Copeland, Dillinger separately wrapped each handgun inside sheets of newspaper and cloth, and then covered the packages with roofing tar.

On the night of September 12th, Dillinger and Copeland drove to Michigan City, parking several blocks from the Indiana State Penitentiary. Travelling the rest of the way on foot, the pair located a portion of the concrete wall surrounding the prison's athletic field. After several tries, they were able to toss the heavy packages over the 25-feet-high enclosure.

After an inmate discovered the strange, tar-covered packages at 5:40 a.m. the following day, he immediately summoned Deputy Warden, H. D. Clardy. When the blocks were cracked open and discovered to contain pistols, an angry Clardy mistakenly targeted three inmates, all of whom were convicted bank robbers, and placed them in solitary confinement. The deputy warden's miscalculation allowed Pierpont and his cohorts to keep their escape plans alive.

After Pierpont sent word that the first shipment of weapons had been intercepted, Dillinger purchased three additional .38 caliber automatic pistols and delivered them to an unidentified middleman. The mysterious middleman then bribed an employee of the Henry Myer Manufacturing Company to conceal the weapons inside a container of sewing thread that was scheduled to be shipped to the shirt factory at the Indiana State Penitentiary. Once the pistols were hidden away, the Henry Myer employee used a crayon to inconspicuously mark the carton with the letter X.

Before Pierpont and the others could stage their prison break, Dillinger was arrested. Based on a tip from Mary Longnacker's landlady, local authorities began staking out the Dayton, Ohio boarding house where Dillinger's girlfriend was living. Shortly after 1:00 a.m. on September 22, 1933, three Dayton police officers, Sargent W. J. Aldredge and Detectives Russell Pfauhl and Charlie Gross, armed with shotguns and a single submachine gun, raided the home. The lawmen discovered an unsuspecting Dillinger in the living room, looking at photographs he and Longnacker had taken during their recent excursion to the World's Fair.

"Stick 'em up, John," Detective Gross ordered the fugitive.

When Dillinger made a move to resist, Detective Pfauhl aimed his shotgun at the suspect: "Don't, John. I'll kill you."

After a thorough search, the arresting officers discovered two .38 caliber automatic pistols on Dillinger's person, a third one wedged between sofa cushions, and five others stored inside a suitcase. They also recovered $2,604 in cash, an ammunition store, and a sack of roofing nails inside Dillinger's car. The handcuffed arrestee managed to appear nonchalant: "When you fellows came in, I thought maybe you were part of another gang. I know uniformed cops, but not you plain clothes guys. I thought you were somebody else."

Even after he was incarcerated in Dayton, Dillinger remained remarkably calm. During a conversation with Detective Gross, the arrestee asked if the police department's bulletproof vests were "any good."

"We don't know, but we feel a little safer with them on. What do you think?" Gross replied.

"I put three steel-jacketed slugs through one, not so long ago—only in practice, of course," Dillinger grinned.

From his Dayton jail cell, Dillinger wrote to his father: "...Maybe I'll learn some day, Dad that you can't win in this game. I know I have been a big disappointment to you, but I guess I did too much time, for where I went in a care free boy, I came out bitter toward everything in general..."

Dillinger's missive was short on remorse and filled with defensive rationalizations: "...Dad, don't believe all that the newspapers say about me, for I am not guilty of half the things I'm charged with and I've never hurt anyone..."

John Dillinger, Sr., however, was encouraged that his oldest son had apparently seen the error of his ways: "I smiled for the first time in years, because, maybe, he'd won after all...Johnnie wasn't a goner, and all he needed was another chance."

While incarcerated, Dillinger was subjected to several witness identification line-ups; a number of eyewitnesses pinpointed him as an active participant in the bank robberies in New Carlisle, Bluffton, Daleville, and Indianapolis. Acting on the advice of his attorneys, Dillinger refused to make any incriminating statements. Matt Leach, who travelled to Dayton from the Indiana State Police headquarters, was among those who tried to wring a confession from the fugitive.

"What are you talking about?" Dillinger slyly smiled.

While Leach was at the Dayton Jail, Detective Pfauhl showed him a hand-drawn map discovered in Dillinger's pocket. Pfauhl was convinced the map was part of a proposed escape plan from the Indiana State Penitentiary. Leach, however, was unimpressed: "You've been reading too many books. This guy ain't that big. They couldn't get out of there, if they tried."

Leach's misjudgment ultimately proved disastrous. On the night of September 26th, utilizing the pistols Dillinger had smuggled into the penitentiary, Pierpont and nine other inmates (including Dillinger cronies, Charles Makley, John Hamilton, Edward Shouse, and Russell Clark) staged their much-anticipated prison break. Mary Kinder's brother, Earl, who was terminally ill with tuberculosis, was unable to accompany the other escapees.

Having disregarded evidence that might have prevented the prison escape, a red-faced Captain Leach was highly concerned that the escaped convicts would try to bust Dillinger out of jail. Under heavy guard, Dillinger was quietly transferred from Dayton to the small and seemingly obscure town of Lima, Ohio, where he would remain incarcerated until he stood trial for the bank robbery in nearby Bluffton.

Pierpont and five of his fellow escapees fled to the safe house Mary Kinder had arranged for them; a residence occupied by Ralph Saffell, a man Kinder had been recently dating. After the escaped convicts hid their stolen vehicle in Saffell's garage, they took refuge behind the house's locked doors and closed blinds. A willing abettor, Kinder purchased new clothes to replace the fugitives' prison dungarees. Kinder's accomplice, Pearl Elliott, who had visited Dillinger in jail, informed the group of their benefactor's recent arrest.

Because Dillinger had fulfilled his end of the agreement by helping them escape from prison, Pierpont vowed that he and the others would spring Dillinger from captivity, once they had obtained the necessary weapons and vehicles. In preparation for the forthcoming jail break, the fugitives traveled to Pierpont's parent's farm, located just outside Leipsic, Ohio, only 28 miles from Lima.

On October 2nd, just a week after breaking out of the Indiana State Penitentiary, Pierpont and four of his fellow escapees robbed the First National Bank in St. Mary's, Ohio. St Mary's, located only a few miles from Lima, also happened to be Charles Makley's home town, which provided the bandits with added familiarity about the surrounding area. At 2:40 p.m., Pierpont, Clark, and Makley entered the bank, while Hamilton and Shouse manned two recently stolen get-away cars.

The heist went smoothly without any shots being fired, and the bandits absconded with two bags of cash, believed to contain nearly $15,000; the small town bank, already on the verge of collapsing, failed soon after the robbery. Outside of town, Pierpont and Makley separated from the others, and boarded another get-away car, driven by Mary Kinder. While the others headed north, Pierpont, Makley, and Kinder spend south to Hamilton, located 125 miles from Lima. By now, Pierpont and Kinder had rekindled their past romance, and the feisty redhead was a willing criminal accomplice. Inside their safe house in Hamilton, Kinder baked the crisply stolen cash in an oven and scorched the individual bills with an iron, making them appear worn and less likely to be traced.

On October 10th, Pierpont traveled to Chicago to retrieved another of Dillinger's love interests—Evelyn "Billie" Frechette. Frechette, the offspring of a French father and a half-French, half-American Indian mother, had been born on an Indian reservation in Wisconsin. No stranger to the underworld, her husband, George "Sparks" Frechette, was serving a 15-year prison sentence at Fort Leavenworth for bank robbery. Dillinger was believed to have met Billie while she was working as a dancer and hat check girl at a Chicago nightclub; he was quickly smitten by Frechette, and Mary Longnacker soon became a distant memory.

Five-feet, two-inches-tall and weighing 120 pounds, the black-haired, brown-eyed Frechette was striking; her only physical flaw was a smallpox-marked face, which she successfully masked with heavy coats of make-up. Billie was equally infatuated with Dillinger: "From the very first night I met him, there was nobody else in my life, and I didn't want anybody else. He treated me like a lady."

In anticipation of springing Dillinger from jail, Pierpont rented an apartment in Cincinnati for Mary Kinder and Billie Frechette. Kinder was concerned about the proposed jail break, but Pierpont assured her there would be no "killing or rough stuff"—a promise he would be unable to keep.

The jail in Lima was a concrete-block structure attached to the home of Allen County's 47-year-old sheriff, Jess Sarber. Affable, heavy-set, and balding, Sarber was a former used car salesman who was forced to make a career change after his business fell victim to the economic woes of the Great Depression. The Allen County Jail was literally a mom and pop operation—Sarber supervised the incarceration of the prisoners and his wife prepared and served the inmates' meals. Unbeknownst to Sheriff Sarber, Harry Pierpont and his associates had arrived in Lima in early October, and immediately began staking out the jail and its immediate surroundings.

On the night of October 12th, Sheriff Sarber and his wife were enjoying a quiet evening at home. While he read the newspaper at his desk, Mrs. Sarber sat nearby, working a crossword puzzle. Wilbur Sharp, a 32-year-old deputy sheriff, off-duty and dressed in civilian clothes, was sitting on the Sarber's couch playing with the couple's dog. Not expecting trouble, Sharp left his holstered pistol on the sheriff's desk, while Sarber's service revolver was inside his desk drawer. Just down the hall, Dillinger was playing pinochle with three other inmates in the cell block.

At 6:25 p.m., Pierpont, Makley, and Clark entered the jail office, while Shouse, Copeland, and Hamilton kept watch outside, adjacent to their two get-away cars. Sheriff Sarber was surprised by the arrival of three unexpected visitors, all of whom were dressed in nice suits. A suspicious Sarber immediately asked about the nature of their business.

"We're from Michigan City. We want to see John Dillinger," Pierpont explained, falsely claiming that he and his two companions were Indiana State Police detectives.

"Let me see your credentials," Sarber replied.

"Here's our credentials," Pierpont angrily announced, before drawing his pistol and shooting Sarber.

The bullet fired by Pierpont struck the sheriff in his left side, traveled downward through his abdomen, lodged in his thigh, and severed his femoral artery. Profusely bleeding, Sarber somehow managed to stay on his feet.

"Give us the keys to the cells!" Pierpont shouted.

When the sheriff failed to respond, Pierpont fired two warning shots into the wall near the sheriff's head. Makley then struck Sarber in the head with the butt of his pistol, splitting the sheriff's scalp open to bone, and knocking him to the floor. The impact of the blow caused Makley's pistol to discharge and fire a bullet into the floor. Fearing the sound of the gunshots might alert outsiders to call the sheriff's office, Pierpont ripped the telephone line out of the wall.

Mistakenly believing that Deputy Sharp was a jail trusty, the intruders had made no efforts to subdue him. However, when the alarmed deputy made a move to assist the wounded sheriff, Makley pointed his pistol at him: "Take it easy boy."

"Give us the keys!" Pierpont repeated.

"Don't hurt him no more!" Mrs. Sarber wailed, and quickly retrieved the keys from the desk drawer.

When the jailhouse prisoners heard gunshots from the sheriff's house, one of Dillinger's card-playing companions remarked: "John, your gang is after you." Dillinger calmly got up from the table and retrieved his coat from his cell, while Pierpont was unlocking the series of doors at the end of the corridor leading to the cell block. Armed with three pistols, his own and the two belonging to the sheriff and his deputy, Pierpont announced his arrival by firing a warning shot.

"Get back, you son of a bitch! We want John. The rest of you can get out when I'm gone," Pierpont shouted to an inmate who was eyeing him closely.

Now armed with one of the pistols supplied by Pierpont, Dillinger hustled down the hall into the Sarber's house. Having grown fond of the kindly sheriff and his wife, Dillinger was shocked to see Sarber lying on the floor in a growing pool of blood.

"Men, why did you do this to me?" the sheriff moaned, as Dillinger silently knelt beside Mrs. Sarber.

"Mother, I believe I'm going to have to leave you," a gravely wounded Sarber informed his wife.

Pierpont shared none of Dillinger's compassion. Ignoring Mrs. Sarber's pleas to remain beside her dying husband, Pierpont locked her and Deputy Sharp inside the cell block, before the gang fled the scene of the crime.

As they sped away from Lima, Dillinger confronted Pierpont and Makley about their unnecessary display of violence: "Did you have to do that?" When neither man offered a satisfactory answer, Dillinger let the matter drop, perhaps realizing that it was both unwise and ungracious to criticize the orchestrators of his jail break. Heading south, the fugitives took refuge in their safe house in Hamilton, Ohio.

Less than two hours after being shot, Sheriff Sarber died at Lima Memorial Hospital. Both Dillinger's escape and Sarber's murder were widely covered by the newspapers. The members of what was now being referred to as the *Dillinger Gang* were characterized by the press as "cold-blooded cop killers." One reporter wrote that Dillinger was "more deadly than Machine Gun Kelly ever dreamed of being." Another eager newsman tracked down John Dillinger, Sr., who was at a loss for words: "Well, I don't know what to think, but it's pretty bad."

Two days after the murderous jail break, the Indiana State Police raided the Dillinger farm house in Mooresville. John Sr. had little to offer the authorities: "If John was here, I didn't see him."

Nearly 2,500 Lima-area residents attended Jess Sarber's funeral. His son, Don, only 21 years old, was sworn into office as the new sheriff, which made him the youngest person in American history to hold such a title. The Allen County Commissioners expressed their outrage by posting a $5,000 reward for the capture of Sheriff Sarber's killers.

Two days after the jail break, the Dillinger Gang broke into separate groups, with the understanding that they would rendezvous later in Chicago. Dillinger and Pierpont drove to Cincinnati, 140 miles to the south of Lima, reuniting with their girlfriends. Mary Kinder recalled the happy gathering: "It's real nice with Johnnie home and all of us sitting here."

Pierpont provided his girlfriend with sketchy details about what had transpired during the jail break, explaining that they "had to beat up the sheriff to get Johnnie out." At the same time, Pierpont offered Kinder an opportunity to leave, before the situation grew more tenuous. Convinced that she was in love with Pierpont, Kinder declined: "No, it wouldn't be right me leaving you boys just because you're in trouble."

In the wake of the violent jail break, there was considerable finger pointing. Matt Leach immediately blamed law enforcement officials in Ohio: "We would have taken adequate precautions against any attempt to liberate Dillinger." The Ohioans soon fired back, accusing Leach of arrogantly disregarding the map found in Dillinger's pocket on the night of his arrest; a clue that might have enabled prison officials to block the escape of Pierpont and the others from the Indiana State Penitentiary.

On Saturday night October 14th, just two days after escaping from jail, Dillinger, accompanied by Pierpont, entered the police station in Auburn, Indiana, located just across the Ohio state line. While Dillinger and Pierpont were inside police headquarters, Makley kept watch outside the door. The two duty officers were caught off guard by the pistol-wielding intruders.

"You might as well sit still. We don't want to kill anyone, unless we have to. Have you got any guns?" Dillinger inquired.

After relinquishing the key to the gun cabinet, the police officers were locked inside a jail cell. The bandits quickly seized two .38 caliber revolvers, a Thompson submachine gun, a .30 caliber Springfield rifle, a Winchester semi-automatic 16-shot rifle, a .45 caliber Colt automatic pistol, a .25 caliber Spanish-made automatic pistol, a 9 mm German Luger, three bulletproof vests, and several hundred rounds of ammunition.

After raiding the Auburn police department, the Dillinger Gang rendezvoused in Chicago, where they hid out in various rented apartments. The newspapers immediately spotlighted the gang's brazen theft of weapons from the Auburn Police Department. Reporters soon christened Dillinger as "Public Enemy Number One," the "Hoosier Hellcat," and the leader of a "Terror Gang." Captain Leach also added to the shrill chorus: "When all of the facts about Dillinger are dragged into publicity, it will be found that no desperado in America can approach this bad man's record."

On Friday October 20th, just six days after the daring raid in Auburn, Dillinger and Pierpont entered the police station in Peru, Indiana, once again catching the locals by surprise.

"I haven't plugged anyone for a week, and I would just as soon punc-ture one of you cops, as not," a gun-wielding Pierpont announced to police officers.

From a glass-encased gun cabinet, Dillinger and Pierpont stole two Thompson submachine guns, a tear gas gun, nine bulletproof vests, two sawed-off shotguns, three rifles, a 12 gauge automatic shotgun, a .32 caliber au-tomatic pistol, five .38 caliber revolvers, 10 magazines loaded with machine gun bullets, two boxes of shotgun shells, three uniform badges, and a pair of handcuffs. After spying a locked door, Dillinger asked Officer Eldon Chittum what was stored in the room. When told that it contained confiscated liquor, Dillinger smiled: "Well forget it then—I don't drink." Mary Kinder was amazed when the gun thieves returned to their hide-away: "My God, what are you going to start—a young army?"

On Monday October 23rd, the freshly-armed Dillinger Gang robbed the Central National Bank in Greencastle, Indiana; a small town of 4,600 resi-dents, located 30 miles northeast of Terre Haute. Pierpont, who had once worked at a sand gravel plant in nearby Ferndale, targeted the Greencastle bank as an easy mark.

At 2:45 p.m., five men (Dillinger, Pierpont, Makley, Hamilton, and either Copeland or Clark) parked their black Studebaker just outside the bank's front entrance. Forgoing the established practice of leaving someone behind the wheel of the get-away car, all five bandits, dressed in overcoats to con-ceal their weapons, entered the bank. While Dillinger hurdled the railing to access the tellers' cages, Pierpont, armed with a submachine gun, ushered bank employees inside the open vault. The robbers quickly filled their muslin sacks with $75,000 in stolen cash and bonds. As Dillinger exited the bank, witnesses later recalled his bold declaration: "Boys, take a good look at me, so you will be sure to know me the next time you see me!"

When departing the bank building, the bandits encountered a local gro-cer, Rex Thornton, who was oblivious to the robbery. When Thornton reached into his pocket to retrieve the cash he was about to deposit, Pierpont sus-pected the grocer was drawing a pistol, and walloped him on the head with the barrel of his submachine gun.

Without a shot being fired, the Dillinger Gang sped out of town, bound for Chicago. When a black Studebaker stopped at a service station in nearby

Ferndale, the attendant was astonished to see several men clad in nice suits, holding submachine guns in their laps. When the attendant kept staring at one the robbers, who was surveying the surrounding area through binoculars, Pierpont grew impatient: "What the hell are you waiting for? Fill it up!" After purchasing $1.70 worth of gas, the bandits left the filling station employee a 30 cent tip—a handsome reward during the Great Depression.

Within seven days, the Dillinger Gang had raided two police stations and robbed a bank, leaving Indiana lawmen and politicians in a state of panic. Legislation was quickly enacted, which empowered sheriffs to deputize anyone willing to take up arms against bank robbers. The Governor dispatched 765 National Guardsmen, all of whom were qualified as marksmen, to armories throughout the state, placing the soldiers under the supervision of the state police. The National Guard further offered to make aircraft and tanks available to law enforcement. Indiana State Police officials were nearly hysterical, cautioning Halloween trick or treaters not to wear costumes mimicking the attire of gangsters.

The editor of the *Indianapolis News* telegraphed the newspaper's out of state owners: *CONVICT GANG RUNNING LOOSE*, and urged them to petition Attorney General Homer Cummings to send federal agents to the state. At this point, however, J. Edgar Hoover considered the so-called Dillinger Gang a minor annoyance, and not yet worthy of Bureau manpower and resources.

For the immediate future, the Indiana State Police assumed the lead role in tracking down and apprehending the Dillinger Gang. Led by Captain Leach, the state law enforcement agency, which employed only 90 officers to police 92 counties, faced a formidable task. The Governor tried to bolster the state police's resources, appropriating $10,000 for the purchase of bulletproof vests and 10 additional squad cars.

Captain Leach, mistakenly believing that Pierpont was the true ringleader of the gang, adopted the role of amateur psychologist. Characterizing the murderous robber as a "super egoist," Leach instructed officers to never mention Pierpont by name. By focusing exclusively on the name Dillinger, Leach hoped to foment insurrection amongst the band of criminals. Pierpont, far more interested in stealing money than garnishing headlines, was decidedly unperturbed by Leach's strategy.

The press had their own doubts about the quirky, stutter-prone Leach, and featured articles detailing the state police's failed efforts to capture the bank robbers. Reporters began forwarding letters to Leach, supposedly written by Dillinger and directed to the state law enforcement agency. One newspaperman anonymously sent Leach a copy of the book, *How to be a Detective*; an enraged Leach immediately concluded that Dillinger was the source of the prank. As might have been expected, Dillinger could not resist adding fuel to the fire—a week after the bank heist in Greencastle, he telephoned Leach: "This is John Dillinger. How are you, you stuttering bastard?" From that point forward, Dillinger periodically telephoned Leach, who repeatedly and unsuccessfully attempted to trick the fugitive into revealing his location and future plans.

Believing they could remain more inconspicuous in a large metropolitan area, the Dillinger Gang members dispersed throughout Chicago. At first, Dillinger and Billie Frechette rented unit #311 at the Parkside Avenue apartments; next door, Pierpont and Mary Kinder took up residence in apartment #312. Russell Long reunited with his ex-wife, Opal Long, who happened to be the sister of Harry Copeland's girlfriend, Pat Cherrington. Homer Van Meter soon joined his penitentiary alums, moving into an apartment with his attractive brunette girlfriend, Marie Marion Conforti

The bank robbers stayed in touch on a regular basis, often meeting to play poker. A pool hall and bookie joint, both of which were located on North Sheridan Road, served as message centers for the Dillinger Gang. Arthur "Fish" Johnson and Jack Perkins, both of whom were associates of an up and coming gangster named Baby Face Nelson, facilitated communication between the various gang members.

Dillinger, Frechette, Pierpont, and Kinder eventually moved into a shared, fully-furnished, two-bedroom apartment at 4310 Clarendon Avenue. The exclusive apartment complex, located a half-mile from Lake Michigan, offered the services of bellboys and housed a delicatessen, the Mary Ann Food Shop, on the first floor. The delicatessen offered two of Dillinger's favorite indulgences—Schlitz beer and frog legs.

Wary of prying eyes, Dillinger and Pierpont warned Frechette and Kinder not to wear "flashy dresses" or engage in "movie star behavior." They also instructed their girlfriends to refrain from drinking heavily, which might lead to careless chatter in front of the wrong people. While the women often drank hard liquor, Dillinger and Pierpont, who were on alert around-the-clock, limited themselves to beer.

Enjoying his share of the stolen money, Pierpont gave Mary $1,000 to open a bank account under the alias of *Fred Ross*, and purchased her an expensive watch for $190. Dillinger was also generous, treating Billie to a fur coat that cost $150.

Disagreements occasionally flared between the women, largely related to Billie's unwillingness to perform her share of the cooking. Mary convinced a reluctant Pierpont to broach the subject with Dillinger, who confronted Billie.

"I'm not much of a cook," she explained.

"Do your share," Dillinger admonished her.

Fearful of being caught and sent back to prison so soon after escaping, Pierpont remained inside the apartment much of the time. In contrast, Dillinger wanted to enjoy his freedom and spend his money; whenever possible, he attended sporting events, went out to dinner, shopped for clothes, and patronized night clubs. In early November, Dillinger took Frechette and Kinder for a day-long excursion to the World's Fair, which exasperated Pierpont: "Our pictures are in every newspaper, and you're out gallivanting around the Fair! You're gonna get us all sent back to prison."

"Well, you gotta take chances now and then," Dillinger nonchalantly replied.

A cautious Pierpont continued to be reclusive. When delivery boys brought groceries to the apartment, Pierpont sometimes hid in the bathroom. Dillinger often occupied his idle time by reading, including his favorite magazine, *Popular Mechanics*, and the flurry of newspaper articles about the gang.

On November 3, 1933, Pierpont, Copeland, Hamilton, Shouse, and Burns (the latter of whom had actually not been present in Lima on the night of Dillinger's jail break), were indicted by the Allen County Ohio prosecutor for the murder of Sheriff Jess Sarber. The formal charges induced little remorse among the gang members, only intensifying their resolve to never be captured alive.

For the most part, the gang members got along well, with the exception of Ed Shouse, who Dillinger accused of making romantic advances toward Billie Frechette. When Shouse tried to recruit Hamilton to join him in a two-man bank heist, it was the last straw for Dillinger. After the other gang members voted to pay Shouse his full share of their stolen reserve funds, Dillinger bid him a hasty and testy farewell: "There's your money. Now get your ass out!"

Dillinger managed to survive a close call when insurance investigator, Forrest Huntington, learned that the fugitive bank robber was discreetly cashing out stolen bonds. Huntington persuaded one of Dillinger's less than savory bond exchangers, Art McGinnis, to function as an undercover informant. On the night of November 13th, McGinnis met with Dillinger to make arrangements to cash eight $1,000 World War I Liberty Loan bonds. During the course of their meeting, McGinnis learned that Dillinger had an appointment scheduled the following night with a dermatologist, who was treating his inflamed hair follicles; McGinnis had been the one who originally referred Dillinger to this particular physician.

That next night, three squads of Chicago policemen, two Indiana State Police detectives, and Investigator Huntington staked out the office of Dr. Charles Eye. At 7:23 p.m., the lawmen watched as an Essex Terraplane sedan parked outside the physician's office. While Billie Frechette waited in the car, Dillinger entered the building for his appointment. Twenty minutes later, when he exited the office, Dillinger immediately grew suspicious at the number of vehicles congregated in the area, some of which were parked at odd angles. Once he was behind the wheel, Dillinger jammed the car in reverse and rapidly backed onto Irving Boulevard and then sped away, catching the authorities by surprise.

Chicago Police Department detective, John Artery, joined by Indiana State Police officer, Art Keller, immediately gave chase, and eventually pulled even with Dillinger's car. Frechette, who had been instructed to lie down on the floorboard, was nowhere in sight when Officer Keller leaned out the open window of the pursuing vehicle and opened fired on Dillinger's car. After emptying his handgun, Keller fired five shotgun blasts at Dillinger, none of which struck the fugitive. Consumed by the need to escape, Dillinger never fired back.

The lawmen chased the elusive Dillinger for several miles, until he managed to slip through a narrow gap between two trolley cars that were approaching from opposite directions. One of the pursuing police officers was impressed by Dillinger's daredevil stunt: "That bird sure can drive!"

After abandoning the bullet-riddled Essex on the north side of Chicago, Dillinger and Frechette made their way safely to Russell Clark's apartment in a taxi. The local press had a field day with Dillinger's most recent escape. The *Chicago Tribune* characterized him as the "desperate leader of a band of outlaws which has been terrorizing northern and central Indiana for weeks." As usual, the newspaper stories were filled with embellishments; one article falsely reported that Dillinger had driven with one hand and fired with the other during the wild chase. Another proclaimed that the fugitive's car was not only bulletproof, but also equipped with a "concealed porthole" for a hidden gunman to fire "a rat-a-tat of bullets."

The Chicago police, embarrassed by their failure to capture Dillinger, soon posted a $10,000 bounty. Now also referring to the Dillinger Gang as the "savage seven," the police department authorized officers to shoot Dillinger and his minions, on sight.

Dillinger and Pierpont correctly assumed that McGinnis had betrayed them, and both couples abandoned the Clarendon Avenue apartment, to temporarily reside at Clark's apartment. Avoiding further contact with McGinnis, Dillinger began using a fence in Milwaukee to cash out his stolen bonds.

After McGinnis' betrayal, Dillinger was warier than ever about who could be trusted. Ed Shouse had already been dismissed from the gang, and the hard-drinking Harry Copeland, who was considered a loud-mouthed liability, was soon sent packing. The latter decision proved fortuitous; on November 19th, Copeland was arrested during a drunken argument with a prostitute, who apparently had not fulfilled a previous obligation. Copeland was sent back to the Indiana State Penitentiary to complete his prison sentence. Once sober, the captured fugitive refused to share any information with the authorities about his association with Dillinger Gang.

The Bureau of Investigation remained reluctant to join in the hunt for any of the country's fugitive bank robbers. The unwillingness stretched to the highest level of the federal government; President Franklin Roosevelt, backed by civil libertarians, was wary of establishing a national police force, reminiscent of totalitarian regimes. Roosevelt and his supporters argued that Treasury Department agents, who had done an admirable job of bringing down the famed gangster, Al Capone, were sufficient resources to assist state and local authorities. The Bureau was also limited in its manpower, employing only 266 agents and 60 accountants, none of whom were authorized to carry guns or make arrests.

The entire dynamic changed on June 17, 1933—the date of what would become known as the infamous *Kansas City Massacre*. One day earlier, Bureau agents Joe Lackey and Frank Smith had arrested a well-known fugitive, Frank Nash, in the Arkansas resort town of Hot Springs. Nash, sentenced to 25 years in Fort Leavenworth for robbing a mail train, had escaped prison in October of 1930. Otto Reed, the police chief of McAlester, Oklahoma, who could identify Nash by sight and was authorized to make arrests, joined the agents on their manhunt.

That same night, the three lawmen drove the arrestee to Fort Smith, Arkansas and boarded a train bound for Kansas City. An *Associated Press* reporter in Fort Smith soon made it public knowledge that Nash was en route to Kansas City and would arrive the next morning, where he would be transported by car, to the federal penitentiary in Fort Leavenworth.

At 7:00 a.m. on June 17th, the Special Agent in Charge (SAC) of the Bureau's Kansas City office, Reed Vetterli, accompanied by fellow agent, Ray Caffrey, and police officers, Bill "Red" Grooms and Frank Hermanson, were waiting at the Union Station train depot to greet the fugitive and his captors. His manacled hands covered by a handkerchief, Nash was led off the train onto to the platform, and then escorted down a flight of stairs to the depot's main lobby. Even though Bureau agents were not authorized to carry firearms, Agent Caffrey nonetheless had a .38 caliber revolver pressed against Nash's midsection.

After exiting the train station, Agent Lackey and Chief Reed climbed in the back of Caffrey's Chevrolet coupe. Lackey directed Nash where to sit: "Get up front. We'll ride like we did out of Hot Springs." After Nash settled in the passenger's front seat, Agent Smith joined Lackey and Reed in the back.

Agents Vetterli and Caffrey were still outside the car, along with Officers Grooms and Hermanson, when all hell broke loose. A voice soon emanated from somewhere in front of the car: "Up! Up! Get your hands up!"

Before any of the lawmen could react, a burst of machine gun fire raked the vehicle. Grooms and Hermanson were struck multiple times in the chest, instantly killing them both. Even though the attack was ostensibly staged to free the fugitive, Nash was fatally wounded in the head during the barrage of bullets. In the Chevrolet's back seat, Chief Reed was also killed by a shot to the head. Agent Caffrey, who was pinned against the hood of the car, was severely wounded and dropped to the pavement. Agent Vetterli, superficially wounded in the right arm, sprinted toward the depot, dodging the bullets that were kicking up shards of concrete near his feet. Agent Lackey, armed with a shotgun in the backseat, raised his weapon, but after being shot three times, dropped it. Both Lackey and Agent Smith, who was not wounded, played dead, falling forward and tucking their heads between their knees. While assuming the postures of dead men, Lackey and Smith heard footsteps approaching the bullet-riddled automobile.

"Everyone's dead in here," a voice announced, before the mysterious attackers disappeared.

Police officer, Mike Fanning, who had been on foot patrol inside the depot, was the first person to reach the car. He found Agent Caffrey lying on the pavement near the front fender. Caffrey silently mouthed indecipherable words—he would be dead within a few minutes—only the third Bureau agent to be killed in the line of duty.

Drawing his pistol, Fanning yanked open the car door. A stunned Agent Smith stammered: "Don't shoot, I'm a federal officer."

Agent Vetterli, his right arm grazed by a bullet, soon returned to help lift a moaning Lackey from the car and place him on the pavement. Lackey was rushed to the Research Hospital; he would eventually recover from his wounds and return to duty.

After returning to the Kansas City field office, located in the Federal Reserve Bank building, Agent Vetterli telephoned Bureau headquarters in Washington D.C.: "It was a massacre, Mr. Hoover! Ray Caffrey is dead. Joe Lackey may not pull through. Two Kansas City detectives and the Chief of Police from McAlester, Oklahoma were killed. So was Frank Nash."

The aftermath of the blood bath was confusing. Witnesses gave conflicting stories concerning the number of shooters and escape vehicles, as well as divergent descriptions of the gunmen. An enraged J. Edgar Hoover decided that he needed an experienced hand to coordinate the investigation, and immediately summoned Gus Jones, the SAC of the Bureau's San Antonio office.

Unlike the stereotypical "college-boy" lawyer image of most agents, 51-year-old Gus Jones wore a cowboy hat and hailed from a family filled with generations of lawman. Jones had earlier established his reputation by tracking down and arresting Martin Durkin, the car thief who shot and killed Bureau agent, Ed Shanahan, in 1925.

Jones, who was under pressure from Hoover to bring the Kansas City killers to justice, had little in the way of hard evidence, even after sifting through the statements of his surviving fellow agents. Agent Lackey, who had been wounded three times, was unable to identify any of the shooters. Agent Smith, who had played dead to avoid being shot, never caught sight of the gunmen. Agent Vetterli, who had fled inside the depot after being wounded in the arm, was the only one who claimed to recognize any of the attackers. According to Vetterli, one of the gunmen was prison escapee, Robert "Big Boy" Brady; with the passage of time, however, the agent grew less sure that the shooter was really Brady. Lottie West, who was manager of the train station's Travelers Aid, identified Charles "Pretty Boy" Floyd as one of the attackers, but her description was shaky, at best.

The case was further complicated by evidence discovered during the autopsies of Frank Nash and the deceased lawmen; based on the bullets recovered from their bodies, as well as wound locations and trajectories, it appeared likely that another Bureau agent, perhaps Lackey, had accidently shot Caffrey, Nash, and Hermanson. As might have been expected, J. Edgar Hoover immediately squelched any notion that *friendly fire* might have been responsible for the wounding or deaths.

Agent Jones developed a tentative and broad list of potential suspects, including Pretty Boy Floyd, Alvin "Creepy" Carpis, Harvey Bailey, Wilbur Underhill, and even the infamous Bonnie (Parker) and Clyde (Barrow). It would be months before any arrests would be made, and many of the questions surrounding the Kansas City Massacre would remain forever unanswered.

Hoover attempted to mobilize public opinion via the press, declaring war on "America's gangsters" and "hoodlums." In an interview with a reporter from the *Kansas City Star*, Hoover emphasized the Bureau's mission to capture the perpetrators of the massacre: "We will never stop until we get our men, if it takes ages to accomplish it. There will be no let-up in this case." Attorney General Cummings echoed the Bureau Director's resolve: "We are now engaged in a war that threatens the safety of our country—a war with the organized forces of crime." In another interview, Hoover expressed continued outrage: "The problems of organized gang warfare and the defiance of the forces of society and civilization can no longer be ignored. Sooner or later, the penalty which is their due will be paid."

Hoover argued that Bureau agents should be authorized to carry weapons. At the same time, he neglected to mention that Agents Caffrey, Smith, and Lackey had actually been armed on the day of the Kansas City Massacre.

Cummings appointed a special prosecutor, Joseph Keenan, and established *special squads* within the Bureau, to focus on specific, high-profile cases. The Attorney General lobbied Congress to pass his proposed *Twelve Point Anticrime Program*. Cummings informed lawmakers that gangsters had "more men under arms than the Army and Navy of the United States." In addition to new statutes broadening the powers of the Bureau, Cummings asked for additional funding to hire 200 new agents, increasing the total force to 600, as well as purchasing armored cars and aircraft.

Fully aware that the newly-christened *War on Crime* was a hot political issue, President Roosevelt gave Cummings his full support. The President pressured Congressman Halton Sumners, Chairman of the House Judiciary Committee, to submit a favorable recommendation on the Attorney General's proposed anticrime bills.

Over the course of a year, Congress passed nine of Cummings' major bills. One of the new laws made it a federal crime to kill or assault a federal officer. The *Fugitive Felon Act* gave Bureaus agents full powers to arrest federal lawbreakers. Robbery of any Federal Reserve System bank was designated as a federal crime, as well as the transportation of stolen property across state lines. Those who fled across state lines to avoid prosecution or to avoid giving testimony in federal crimes were also subject to arrest by Bureau agents. Racketeering in interstate commerce was also designated as a federal offense. The Lindbergh Law was amended, adding the death penalty as a potential penalty for kidnapping.

Even though the Bureau struggled to identify and arrest the perpetrators of the Kansas City Massacre, the agency was able to solve one high profile case. On July 23, 1933, Oklahoma oilman, Charles F. Urschel, was kidnapped from his home; his captors demanded a $200,000 ransom. By virtue of the Lindbergh Law, the Bureau took charge of the case.

In less than a week, before the ransom was paid, Urschel was released by his kidnappers. After being questioned by Bureau agents, Urschel provided enough information for the feds to locate the remote farm house where he had been held. On September 26th of that year, Bureau agents raided the house, which was owned by the step-parents of Kathryn Kelly, wife of outlaw, George "Machine Gun" Kelly. According to the story proudly circulated by Hoover, a surprised Kelly shouted: "Don't shoot, G-Men! Don't shoot!"

Kelly disputed Hoover's rendition of the arrest, indicating that his actual response had been: "I've been waiting for you." Irrespective of the accuracy of Hoover's boast, Bureau agents earned what would become a legendary moniker—*G-Men*. Kelly was ultimately convicted for kidnapping and sentenced to life imprisonment.

While the famed G-Men were not yet on John Dillinger's tail, the Chicago Police Department remained on high alert. Seeking a lower profile, the Dillinger Gang moved to a hide-out in Racine, Wisconsin. When Dillinger learned about Harry Copeland's arrest, he was delighted to have disassociated from the drunken, former gang member.

The gang, now running short of funds, surveyed area banks as potential targets for their next heist. Homer Van Meter suggested teaming up with an up and coming felon named "Baby Face" Nelson to stage a train robbery. Dillinger and Pierpont rejected the proposal, wary of associating with unproven and potentially untrustworthy partners. It would not be long, however, before Nelson would play a major role in the John Dillinger story.

CHAPTER SEVEN

Baby Face

The outlaw whose felonious path would soon intersect with John Dillinger's had a rather innocuous birth name—Lester Joseph Gillis. From the Depression-era onward, however, history would remember him as the enigmatic *Baby Face Nelson*. Clean cut, with a youthful, chubby, face, Nelson neither drank nor smoked, and unlike the womanizing Dillinger, was devoted to his wife and children, who frequently accompanied him throughout the country on his law-breaking escapades.

Standing only five-feet, four-inches-tall, the 133-pound Nelson often wore an extra set of clothing to bulk up his physique. With the added clothes, augmented by a bulletproof vest, the diminutive Nelson was often described by witnesses as appearing *stocky*.

Irrespective of his short stature, Nelson was one of the most violent gangsters of the 20th century. J. Edgar Hoover labeled him as a "crazy killer" and a "vicious half-pint rat, who shoots without provocation."

Born on December 6, 1908 to a middle class family in Chicago's Near West Side, Gillis was the youngest of seven children. Undersized, Gillis compensated by picking fights with much bigger boys. Childhood friend, John Alfred Perkins, remembered those days quite clearly: "He was the toughest kid I ever met—tougher than rat shit. He never backed down from a fight, no matter how big, old, or ugly the other kid was." Gillis' parents found it difficult to control their youngest son's behavior; like John Dillinger, Lester refused to cry when spanked. Julie Gillis later recalled that her mother and father possessed little leverage when dealing with her younger brother: "Whippings, making him work—punishments of all kinds—made no difference."

Before reaching their teen years, Gillis and John Perkins were already stealing from the cash registers of Chicago-area merchants. Gillis' fascination with firearms resulted in the first major disruption of his young life. At age 12, he fired a pistol over the heads of a group of children playing in an alleyway—a dangerous practical joke that resulted in one of the bullets ricocheting off a brick wall and striking another boy in the jaw. A juvenile court judge, rejecting Gillis' claim that the shooting was an accident, sentenced him to 12 to 15 months at an area juvenile detention facility—the Cook County School for Boys.

After serving 12 months of his sentence, Gillis was released, but soon began indulging another obsession, stealing automobiles for joy rides. In October of 1922, when he was 14 years old, Gillis was arrested for car theft and sent to the Illinois State School for Boys, where he remained until his parole, 18 months later. Less than six months later, the wayward youth was arrested for stealing yet another automobile, which lead to a nine-month sentence at the same reformatory.

When he returned home in July of 1925, Gillis' family was in disarray; the previous Christmas Eve, Lester's father had committed suicide. Now forced to help support his mother, Gillis was employed as a mechanic at Parkview Motor Company, a local Chrysler dealership. Before three months had passed, the 16-year-old was arrested a third time for car theft, leading to yet another stent (nine months) in juvenile detention.

When he was 18 years old, Gillis and two cronies were arrested for stealing tires from a local car dealership. For reasons that are not clear, he managed to avoid serious punishment, and was sentenced to one-year probation.

While pursuing honest work as a mechanic, Gillis fell in love with Helen Wawrzyniak, a petite, black-haired, blue-eyed daughter of Polish-German immigrants. Less than six months later, when 15-year-old Helen became pregnant, the young couple were married. On their marriage certificate, the groom inflated his age to 21, while his bride lied that she was 20 years old. In April of 1930, Helen gave birth to a son the couple named Ronald. A year later a daughter, Darlene, was born.

Gillis continued to supplement his mechanic's income by stealing tires and driving shipments of bootleg whiskey throughout Illinois and neighboring states. In spite of his blatant disregard for the law, Gillis, by all appearances, was a loyal husband and loving father. His sister, Julie, remembered her brother's dual lives: "He loved to stay around the house, cuddling his little boy and helping Helen in the kitchen."

Gillis' lifelong fascination with automobiles was not solely limited to theft. He and a friend, Clarence Lieder, built their own race car, which they entered in a number of dirt track races. Lieder boasted that Gillis was "one of the best drivers I've ever seen;" a useful skill for a thief and whiskey-runner.

Gillis eventually graduated to more lucrative felonies, adopting an alias, *George Nelson.* He assembled a small gang that raided affluent Chicago-area homes, sometimes binding and gagging the residents, before stealing their jewelry.

On October 3, 1930, Nelson and a second, unidentified man robbed the State Bank of Itasca in Du Page County, 15 miles northwest of Chicago. The pair stole $4,678—four times the average yearly income of an American of that era. Teller, Emma Droegemuller, vividly remembered the youthful bandit: "He had blond hair and the bluest eyes I've ever seen. I always wondered how someone so innocent-looking could be robbing us."

Three days later, Nelson and two accomplices robbed Mary Walker Thompson, wife of Chicago Mayor, William Thompson, as she was walking down the sidewalk toward her apartment. After slugging and holding Ms. Thompson's male bodyguard at gunpoint, the trio stole a diamond ring, a diamond-laced bracelet, and a brooch—$17,000-worth of jewelry. That night, an infamous nickname was born. During an interview with a reporter from the *Chicago Herald* newspaper, the mayor's wife offered a fitting description of one of the thieves: "He had a *baby face.* He was good looking, hardly more than a boy, had dark hair and was wearing a gray topcoat and brown felt hat, with a turned-down brim."

On November 7th of that year, Nelson and a new accomplice, Stanton John Randall, robbed a bank in Plainfield, Illinois, 30 miles southwest of Chicago. When he entered the building, Nelson drew a pistol, dramatically ordering the bank customers and employees to: "Stick 'em up!"

The bandits soon encountered difficulty, discovering the tellers' cages were separated from the lobby by a glass partition. When the bank president refused to open the door to the area where the money was kept, Nelson and Stanton angrily fired shots at the partition, which was made of bulletproof glass. Amidst the cacophony of gunfire, one of the ricocheting bullets struck a female customer above the right eye. After the president activated the alarm, the frustrated robbers exited the building, piled into their get-away car, and sped out of town.

Less than two weeks later, on November 22nd, Nelson and three unidentified partners, one of whom manned the get-away car, robbed the Hillside State Bank in the Chicago suburb of Cicero. After firing several warning shots into the lobby ceiling, one of the bandits, most likely Nelson, ordered the bank employees to line up and face the wall: "Anyone (who) twitches, gets drilled."

The robbers quickly cleaned out the tellers' drawers, stealing $4,155. When a cashier made a move to activate the alarm, one of the bandits issued a stern warning: "Do it, and you're dead!" Nelson and his accomplices exited the bank and fled town, unmolested.

Before the end of the month, Nelson and his gang robbed a roadhouse bar on the outskirts of Chicago. Three nights later, the robbers struck another tavern in the Chicago suburbs. When one customer, a stockbroker named Edwin R. Thompson, made the mistake of smiling after being ordered to raise his hands, Nelson fired a fatal shotgun blast into the man's chest; as a result, the youthful bandit added murder to his growing list of crimes.

In February of 1931, law enforcement agents finally caught up with Nelson and two of his partners, Stanton John Randall and Harry Lewis Powell, at their apartment hide-away in Cicero. An article in the *Chicago Tribune* provided the gang leader with his first widespread recognition, referring to him as George "Baby Face" Nelson.

On the 20th of that month, Nelson, Randall, and Powell were indicted for the Hillside State Bank robbery, as well as one of their earlier jewelry heists. Each man's bail was set at $25,000, forcing them to remain in jail, pending trial. Powell soon pled guilty and was sentenced to one-year probation. After initially condemning Powell for cowardice and betrayal, Randall eventually pled guilty to bank robbery, and was sentenced to one to ten years at the Illinois State Prison.

Even after being subjected to harsh interrogation, Nelson stubbornly professed his innocence. Assistant State's Attorney, John Swanson, characterized him as a "tough little shit." When Mary Gillis visited her son in jail, he stubbornly maintained his innocence: "Mother, I didn't do this."

When Nelson's trial began on June 22, 1931, Powell testified that the defendant was the leader of gang. Three days later, after deliberating for two hours, the jury convicted Nelson for the Hillside bank robbery. On July 9th, Judge John Prystalski sentenced Nelson to one year to life at the Illinois State Prison, located in Joliet, Illinois. On the day he was transported from the Cook County Jail to the state penitentiary, Nelson embraced his wife, children, mother, and sisters. His mother distinctly remembered her son's lack of remorse: "Les told me it was all up now—there was no use trying to live right. His only thought from that time on was escaping from prison, I believe."

Nelson, *Inmate Number 5437*, arrived at the Illinois State Prison on July 17, 1931, where he cohabitated with nearly 1,000 other convicted felons. For the first five months of his incarceration, Nelson was a model prisoner. After learning that his request for a new trial had been rejected and the Du Page County Prosecutor was seeking to try him for the Itasca bank robbery, Nelson grew uncooperative. On December 23rd, Nelson's visitation privileges were suspended, and he was transferred to a more secure area of the prison; stern punishment for calling the guards "obscene names."

On January 6, 1932, Nelson was transported to Wheaton, where he was formally charged with the bank robbery in Itasca. After pleading not guilty, he was sent back to Joliet, pending the start of his trial on January 26th. Shortly before the start of the trial, Raymond Frantzen, the assistant cashier of the State Bank of Itasca, was visited at his home by Nelson's mother, Mary, and his wife, Helen. Mary pleaded with Frantzen not to testify against her son. When an uncomfortable Frantzen asked the women to leave, Helen angrily accosted him: "You'd better not testify, if you know what's good for you."

During his trial testimony, Frantzen identified Nelson as the ringleader of the bank robbers. At day's end, as he was being led out of the courtroom, Nelson glared at the bank cashier: "I'm gonna get you for this."

On February 17th, Nelson was convicted for his second bank robbery and sentenced to an additional one year to life. Later that same day, prison guard, R. N. Martin, escorted Nelson back to the state penitentiary. The pair traveled by rail, changing trains in Chicago. Once they reached Joliet, Martin and his prisoner boarded a taxi for the short drive to the prison. As the cab neared the penitentiary, Nelson drew a .45 caliber pistol, which apparently had been smuggled to him aboard the train.

"If you move, I will kill you," Nelson warned Martin, "Now, unlock the cuffs."

Once Martin removed the handcuffs, Nelson asked cab driver, Joseph Candic, his name.

"Well, Joe, just keep driving. Head for Chicago and stay under the speed limit. No stops, unless I say," Nelson instructed him.

"I've got a family," Candic protested.

"Small world, so do I; don't sweat it, Joe. No one gets hurt, if we all behave," Nelson replied.

When the taxi driver reached the Chicago suburb of Summit, located four miles southwest of Cicero, Nelson ordered Candic to stop: "This looks good." Once the cab came to a stop, Nelson took $10 from Martin's wallet.

"Take it all—you'll need it," the prison guard advised him.

"This is enough," Nelson replied, before ordering Martin and Candic to exit the cab, hopping behind the wheel, and speeding toward Chicago.

The authorities were interested in how Nelson obtained a pistol. Nelson later reported that "an angel" delivered the pistol to him. It is likely the angel was either his wife or mother, who had planted the weapon in one of the rail car's restrooms.

Aware that it was far too risky to remain in Chicago, Nelson, along with his wife and children, headed west, first stopping in Reno, where he began employing the alias Jimmie Burnett. From Reno, Nelson traveled to San Francisco, where he spent six months working for a bootlegger, guarding whiskey shipments. During this time, Nelson recruited two future gang members—John Paul Chase and Joseph "Fatso" Negri.

When Nelson's mug shot appeared in the magazine, True Detective Lineup, California local law enforcement officials learned the fugitive had been sighted in the Bay Area, forcing him to relocate. Nelson and his family returned to Reno, where he was introduced to Alvin "Creepy" Karpis, who was one of the principals in the infamous Barker/Karpis Gang. Nelson and Karpis, both of whom hailed from Chicago, soon developed an easy rapport. Nelson informed his fellow outlaw that he wanted to resume robbing banks, and hoped to join an experienced group of thieves, in order to pursue more exclusive targets. Karpis informed Nelson that his own gang was fully staffed, but provided the names of experienced contacts in the Midwest, particularly in St. Paul. Nelson later remembered Karpis' enthusiasm about the Minnesota city: "St. Paul was a good spot for both pleasure and business. You could relax in its joints and speakeasies without any fear of arrest, and when you were planning a score, you could have your pick of all the top men at all the top crimes."

In the spring of 1933, after spending a month in Reno, Nelson departed for St. Paul. As Karpis had advised, the Minnesota capital was a safe haven for felons. Two major underworld figures, Harry "Dutch" Sawyer and John "Jack" Peifer, bribed enough local law enforcement officials and politicians to keep the authorities from nosing into the affairs of those afforded their protection. St. Paul was governed by the so-called *O'Connor System*, whereby local and out of town criminals were safe from arrest and prosecution, as long as they did not commit illegal activities within the city limits. At the Green Lantern Saloon, Alvin Karpis, who had since returned to St. Paul, introduced Nelson to Dutch Sawyer. As a favor to Karpis, Sawyer extended protection to the newcomer.

Nelson soon established relationships with Thomas Gannon and Pat Reilly, the Green Lantern's manager and bartender. Gannon expressed interest in joining Nelson's proposed bank robbing gang, but an anxious Reilly was only willing to serve as an errand runner and abettor. Reilly did, however, put Nelson in touch with another prospective gang member, Tommy Carroll, who happened to be dating the bartender's sister.

A muscular 36-year-old, Carroll had already served four prison sentences related to armed robbery, burglary, possession of stolen property, and automobile theft. In addition to his experience, Carroll was also well-acquainted with the geography of the Midwest, having committed crimes in Iowa, Kanas, Minnesota, Nebraska, Missouri, and Illinois. Carroll, though older and more experienced than Nelson, was eager to team up with his newfound acquaintance, who promised to equip the gang with bulletproof vests and powerful weapons.

Nelson also paid a visit to Jack Peifer, who was St. Paul's other underworld boss. Peifer recommended that Nelson consult with his "good friend" Eddie Bentz, who was a "real gentleman."

Six-foot tall and solidly built, Edward Wilhem Bentz sharply contrasted with most early 20th century bank robbers—intelligent, cultured, well-mannered, and opposed to violence. Aside from his criminal activities, Bentz was an accomplished photographer, architecture buff, and aficionado of classic literature.

After serving a series of prison sentences between 1916 and 1926, Bentz resolved to never return to jail. When he first met Baby Face Nelson, Bentz was considered one of the country's most skilled planners of bank heists. Carefully selecting his accomplices and partners, Bentz seldom partnered with the same men more than once. Bentz was a detailed planner, often working weeks in advance to carefully scrutinize a targeted bank's floor plan, security system, and the personalities of its employees. In addition, Bentz precisely calculated his circuitous get-away route, which was never more than 300-miles-long. To avoid undue publicity and assume unnecessary risks, Bentz never robbed more than three banks per year.

In May of 1933, after trading his Ford for a more powerful Essex Terraplane, capable of reaching a speed of 83 miles per hour, Nelson drove to Chicago to meet with Eddie Bentz. When Nelson first encountered the famed bank robber, Bentz was living in a cottage on the shores of Lake Michigan.

"I don't mean to interrupt your siesta, Ed. I was hoping we could talk," Nelson said, when he discovered Bentz napping in a hammock behind his cottage.

"Sure. What's on your mind?" Bentz replied.

"Some friends and I are thinking of doing a job in Gary," Nelson explained.

"You're talking about knocking off a bank?" Bentz clarified.

"Absolutely," Nelson answered.

As the pair strolled leisurely along the lake shore, Bentz inquired more about Nelson's ambitions: "You want me to share some of my expertise? So here it is. It includes a lot of dos and don'ts—you might not care to hear."

"No, that's fine. We want your help. Hell, we need it!" Nelson reassured him.

"Okay, then. An area like Gary is too congested. That's a major don't. You want to stay away from big cities. They're nice to hole up in, but hell to get out of. You run into a traffic back-up, and you're done for. You might get away with more money, but chances are you won't be going far," Bentz lectured.

"You see, Jimmie, any idiot or bunch of idiots can walk into a bank, pull out guns, and grab the cash. It's the ones who are smart and careful enough to make a clean escape and do it again a month, a year later, whatever; they are the real pros. Small towns are your best bet. They're the only kind of scores I'll even consider—fewer cops, less traffic, lots of countryside to lose the heat in. If you do your homework right, you can find some pretty ripe banks in hick towns—you just have to know what to look for," Bentz continued.

"That's our problem," Nelson explained, "None of us know shit about casing a job—which bank to pick—which ones to stay away from. We figured you could help us out."

"You mean recommend a mark?" Bentz asked.

"I'm talking about setting us up all around—you pick the jug, you do the casing, you work out the get-away chart—the whole thing. You don't have to be along when we take it, and we'll cut you in for an even share," Nelson proposed.

Bentz paused, before continuing: "Tell me about your gang."

"I've got the people lined up in St. Paul. I'll head over there next week and get them over here," Nelson answered.

"How many?" Bentz asked.

"At least three, for sure," Nelson replied, "They're all good hold-up men—kind of raw, but very reliable."

"Any experience with bank jobs?" Bentz questioned.

"Not a one, unless you count me," Nelson answered, "I was in a couple of small capers a few years back—nothing to brag about. How many men will we need?"

"You can take a bank with three, if they're all pros and you want to live dangerously. Four or five is ideal. Since you boys are just starting out, I'd suggest no fewer than six—three inside, three covering the outside," Bentz recommended.

"I should be able to come up with a couple more men. What else do we need?" Nelson inquired.

"Money—at least a thousand, probably more," Bentz explained, "There's certain essentials you need. A clean get-away car is the top priority, because you're just going to abandon it later, unless you're a fool. You can use a hot car, if you want, but it only increases the risk; better to buy one like any businessman, as long as you make sure it can't be traced back to you."

When Nelson asked if Bentz had a target in mind, the veteran robber suggested a small bank in Grand Haven, Michigan. Bentz estimated that they could steal upwards of $50,000.

On June 7th, after his first lesson in the ABC's of bank robbery, Nelson returned to St. Paul to recruit gang members. Neither Tommy Carroll, who was working with his attorney to get suspicion of burglary charges dropped, or Tom Gannon, who was tied to his management duties at the Green Lantern, were available to participate in the Green Haven heist.

Frustrated by his inability to quickly assemble a gang, Nelson returned to meet with Bentz on June 22nd. Bentz told him not to fret about recruiting accomplices—the longer they had to plan the forthcoming heist, the better.

"How are you boys set for firearms?" Bentz inquired.

When Nelson explained that he had several pistols and a single shotgun, Bentz cut him short: "You'll need some heavier hardware—at least one machine gun, probably two. I'll talk to a fellow I know in Chicago, and see what he can do."

Bentz also provided Nelson with a list of other items needed before undertaking the heist—several stolen Michigan license plates, a keg of roofing nails, extra ammunition, a shovel, an axe, and several gas cans. Bentz and Nelson soon met with the discreet owner of an Army-Navy store in Chicago, purchasing a sawed-off 12 gauge riot shotgun with a pistol grip, two Remington rifles, and several .38 caliber pistols mounted on .45 caliber frames—a weapon specifically designed for the Pennsylvania State Police.

On June 27th, when he again met with Bentz, Nelson learned that his mentor's Chicago gun broker would be unable to obtain Thompson submachine guns for three months. Bentz soon telephoned a weapons dealer in San Antonio, Texas, who agreed to sell Nelson the necessary weapons.

Nelson and newly recruited gang member, Chuck Fisher, agreed to travel to Texas to purchase the weapons. In the meantime, Bentz and another new gang member, Earl Doyle, would travel to Grand Haven, where would they would case the bank and plan a get-away route. Just prior to Nelson's departure, Bentz instructed him to visit Lebman Sporting Goods in San Antonio: "Ask for Hymie."

On the morning of June 28th, Nelson, along with his wife and son (their daughter was left behind with another family member), mother, and Chuck Fisher drove from Chicago to San Antonio. Two days later, Nelson and Fisher entered Hyman Saul Lebman's sporting goods store.

Lebman, a 30-year-old Russian Jew, was born in Odessa, Texas and became a naturalized American citizen at age nine. A master gunsmith, Lebman not only ran a legitimate gun shop, but he also smuggled weapons into the country from Mexico, including the submachine guns favored by gangsters, which he sold for handsome profits. Lebman informed his newfound customers that he had not yet received all of the parts necessary to assemble the requested Tommy guns, telling them it might take several days to fulfill their order.

Nelson and his travel companions spent a week in San Antonio. Nearly every day, Nelson dropped by Lebman's store, where he was particularly fascinated by one of the gunsmith's ongoing projects—the conversion of an automatic pistol into a miniature machine gun. By July 6th, Lebman had assembled two submachine guns and four automatic pistols for Nelson; the total sales price was $300. Before returning to Chicago, Nelson informed Lebman that he would return at a later date to purchase one or more of his machine gun pistols.

On July 10th, Nelson, Fisher, and Doyle met with Bentz in Chicago, to learn more about his surveillance of the People's Savings Bank in Grand Haven. By now, Thomas Gannon had freed up his schedule and was able to join the gang, all of whom rented cottages along Lake Michigan, adjacent to Bentz's.

For the next five weeks, Bentz conducted a bank robbery school for his eager students. On a secluded section of Lake Michigan beachfront, Bentz taught Nelson and the others to aim, fire, and rapidly reload the newly purchased submachine guns. At the same time, he cautioned them to be careful with Tommy guns: "Make sure you never actually shoot anyone. It's not worth it. It'll only make the cops come after you with everything they've got. Plus, if you grab any securities in the hold-up, they'll be worthless—too hot to handle, if there's a killing attached to them."

Bentz continued with his lessons: "Remember, the object is to scare the hell out of people. Blast the glass in store windows or shoot the shit out of some parked cars. The noise will drive people off the street and out of your way, which is really all you want. I've been knocking off banks for the last 10 years and I've never shot a single soul."

Bentz also outlined the specific roles of the participants in a bank heist. The *wheelman* would remain in the driver's seat of the get-away car at all times, keeping the engine running, with a submachine gun at hand, in case the bank alarm sounded before the robbers had finished their job. The *tiger* would be stationed just outside the bank's front entrance, to serve as a look-out and to prevent anyone from entering or exiting the building while the robbery was underway. Three men would enter the bank; the *center fielder*, armed with a submachine gun, would keep the customers and employees at bay, while the *skimmer* emptied the tellers' cash drawers, and the fifth bandit (absent a specific name) would clean out the vault. In light of the gang's in-experience, Bentz recommend a six-man crew, adding an extra *tiger* to guard the bank's rear door.

Aware that he was still short of gang members, Nelson eventually approached Bentz about a revision in their plans: "The boys and I were thinking we almost have to have you along on this job."

"That wasn't our deal, Jimmie," Bentz protested.

"I know. But, we'll botch it for sure, if you're not there to make sure things go right," Nelson pleaded.

"I've got other things to do. Besides, I already earned my share of the take. Our agreement was I set you boys up with a score and teach you how to pull it off like professionals. My work is done. The rest is up to you," Bentz explained.

"Think it over, please. Along with your share of the cash, we'll let you have all the securities we snatch, if you go with us," Nelson bargained.

Doyle, Fisher, and Gannon also lobbied Bentz to join in the bank heist. After several days, Bentz relented, but only if he could serve as the wheelman. Bentz also demanded that the tentative date for the Grand Haven heist, set for mid-July, be rescheduled for mid-August, if he became involved in "another venture."

On the morning of July 18, 1933, Nelson greeted Bentz and Doyle: "Looks like great weather for a bank robbery." Three miles outside of Grand Haven, the gang pulled off to a side road and donned their bulletproof vests. Nelson managed to convince Bentz that newly-recruited gang member, Freddie Monahan, was "too green" and should be assigned to man the get-away car. Bentz reluctantly agreed, assigning each gang member a specific role— Monahan would be the wheelman, Doyle would serve as the rear entrance tiger, Gannon would function as the front entrance tiger, Nelson would be the centerfielder, Fisher would serve as the skimmer, and Bentz would clean out the vault. Bentz gave the group last minute instructions; speak very little, try not to leave fingerprints, order the customers to lie on the floor rather than raise their hands (which might attract the attention of passersby), and do not treat women employees or customers abusively (they might start screaming and draw the attention of outsiders).

At 2:40 p.m., the robbers drove into the town of 10,000, parking in front of the bank. Once inside the building, Bentz went directly to the office of the head cashier, Ted Bolt, and after patiently waiting for the man to finish a phone call, ordered him to open the vault. At the same time, Nelson approached teller, Art Welling, asking to change two one-dollar bills into nickels. Up until this point, the operation was flowing smoothly. Then, for unknown reasons, Fisher broke into laughter which quickly spread to Nelson.

As Bentz led the head cashier out of his office at gunpoint, Nelson's smile instantly transformed into a scowl, and he lashed out at Welling: "Step back and lie down on the floor, damn you!" The teller complied, but not before pushing the foot pedal that activated the bank's silent alarm.

While Fisher emptied the cash drawers in the tellers' cages, Bentz escorted the assistant cashier to the vault. When Bolt was unable to open the combination lock, Bentz told Nelson to bring over Art Welling. Nelson complied, and tried to speed the teller along: "Hurry it up, or we'll shoot you. Come on, come on!" Once an anxious Welling finally opened the vault, Bentz went to work collecting cash, checks, and bonds.

By this time, the alarm had attracted a small crowd outside the bank, including, Edward Kinkema, who owned the furniture store next door, and Charles Bugielski, the manager of a nearby dime store. Kinkema exited his business armed with a Remington shotgun, while Bugielski carried a .38 caliber pistol.

As Kinkema neared the bank's front entrance, he spied a sedan idling at the curbside. Surmising that it was likely the robbers' get-away car, Kinkema aimed his shotgun at the driver. A panicked Freddie Monahan ducked down, jammed the accelerator, and sped away, abandoning his fellow gang members. The sight of the shotgun-wielding Kinkema and the sound of screeching tires immediately drew the attention of more Grand Haven citizens, who began clustering in front and back of the bank.

Aware of the growing commotion outside the building, the five robbers inside the bank led eight hostages out the rear door. Kinkema and Bugielski had already made their way to the back of the building and soon opened fire with their shotgun and pistol, purposely aiming high, hoping to frighten the bandits, but not wound the hostages. Nelson immediately fired back with his more powerful submachine gun, shattering store front windows on the opposite side of the street where Kinkema and Bugielski were standing, forcing both men to hit the deck.

When a sheriff's patrol car approached, Nelson opened fire on the vehicle, shattering a side window, flattening a tire, and puncturing the fuel tank, which caused gas to leak onto the street. Undersheriff Edward Rycenga and Deputy Maurice Rosema immediately abandoned their patrol car, took cover, and started shooting at the bank robbers. When Doyle joined Nelson in returning fire, the panicked hostages scattered, seeking refuge from the gun battle.

"Car! Car! Where the hell is our car?" Bentz yelled.

As the confused bandits rushed down Third Street in search of another vehicle, one of the hostages, Ted Bolt, grabbed for Doyle's pistol. During the ensuing struggle, the pistol discharged, blowing a hole through Doyle's hand. Though his shot gun was now empty, Kinkema had moved close enough to club Doyle over the head with the weapon's wooden stock. As he fell to the pavement, Doyle badly wrenched his leg, fracturing his femur in two places. Though disarmed and lame, Doyle tried to crawl away and join his fellow gang members.

"Shoot him! Kill him!" a crowd member shouted.

Unbeknownst to Doyle, Bugielski had already emptied his pistol. Nonetheless, the dime store manager cocked the hammer and pointed the weapon at the crippled bandit's head, which resulted in his immediate surrender: "Don't kill me. My leg is broke. I'm not going anywhere."

As the bank robbers continued to make their escape on foot, Nelson fired repeated machine gun bursts, shattering plate glass windows of businesses along the way. A frustrated Bentz, who had inadvertently dropped a bag containing several hundred dollars in cash and more than $100,000 in securities near the rear door of the bank, cautioned Nelson: "Go easy on the soup. All our extra ammo is in the car." Chuck Fisher, who tried to hold onto his sack of loot and shoot at the same time, left a trail of cash in his wake.

Bentz eventually spotted an approaching Chevrolet occupied by two women in the front seat and four small children in the back. Waving his arms, Bentz ordered the driver to stop, and threatened to "plug" both women, if they did not immediately exit the vehicle. When the driver hesitated, Bentz abandoned his chivalric, non-violent code of behavior, jerking her out of the car and tearing her dress.

As Bentz climbed behind the wheel, the displaced driver wailed: "Wait! Don't take our babies!"

Fisher and Cannon allowed the frightened children to exit the rear seat, before taking their places. After hopping in the passenger's side front seat, Nelson informed Bentz: "We gotta go back for Doyle."

"Not a chance. We don't have the ammo. Hell, we don't even have our *get*, thanks to your pal Freddie. I'm afraid Doyle is on his own," Bentz replied, referring to their escape map, which had been left behind inside the get-away car.

"He's right. We can't go back," Gannon agreed.

The frustrated bank robbers raced out of town. Four miles outside of Grand Haven, after discovering the Chevrolet was nearly out of gas, the bandits stole a farmer's Chrysler. After traveling 160 miles, the stolen vehicle blew a tire, causing Bentz to crash into a tree. The gang then hijacked yet another vehicle—a Ford driven by a teenage boy, who was accompanied by three other adolescents.

At 4:00 a.m. the following day, the exhausted bandits arrived at their lakeside cottages in Chicago. While Gannon and Fisher ditched the stolen Ford, Nelson and Bentz drove to Michigan City, intent upon confronting Monahan, but soon learned the wheelman and his wife had suddenly left town. Later in the day, the four remaining gang members divided the loot, which consisted of $2,568 in cash, $6,410 in bank checks, and seven Pacific Railway bonds. Bentz was more disappointed and angry—he had counted on stealing at least $50,000.

The robbers split the cash six ways, setting aside one share for the captured Doyle's wife. Bentz asserted that Nelson deserved Monahan's share, in exchange for having purchased the weapons and other equipment used to stage the heist. Bentz and his wife soon departed, settling into another lakeside cottage in Union Pier, Michigan.

After his arrest, Earl Doyle refused to give the authorities his real name, instead using the alias, *Harry Harris*. The arrestee was charged with *bank robbery, possession of firearms*, and *felonious assault*. Doyle initially pled not-guilty, but later changed his mind. On September 9th, a judge sentenced him to life imprisonment at the Michigan State Penitentiary.

Freddie Monahan, assuming that was his real name and not an alias, was never heard from again. The run-away wheelman's disappearance proved fortuitous, as Nelson vowed to kill him for his cowardice and betrayal.

On August 29th, Nelson and Bentz met briefly for the final time. During their post-mortem evaluation of the poorly-executed Grand Haven bank robbery, Bentz tried to reassure his disgruntled young accomplice: "Don't let it discourage you. Bank robbing is a business, and in every business, there's an element of risk. Just consider this a learning experience. Next time, you avoid the mistakes we made." In spite of Bentz's encouraging message to Nelson, the veteran bank robber had no further interest in associating with the fledgling gang.

Nelson emerged from his association with Bentz convinced that he had learned the finer points of bank robbery, and was eager to stage further heists. Nelson believed that he was clearly capable of leading his own gang, which was soon augmented by the arrival of veteran bank robber, Homer Van Meter.

Nelson also welcomed another newcomer—Eugene "Eddie" Green. Wiry-built with an acne-scarred face, the short-tempered, 31-year-old Green had served three prison terms related to robbery and grand larceny. Defiant of authority and handy with his fists, he spent considerable time in solitary confinement while imprisoned. Green was renowned for his skill as a *jug marker*; adept at identifying and sizing-up the easiest banks to rob. Green, who was eager to make money, provided Nelson with a list of potential bank targets in Iowa, South Dakota, Wisconsin, Minnesota, and Nebraska.

Thirty-six-year old James Murray also joined the Nelson Gang. Heavy-set, with a scarred face and pencil-thin mustache, Murray was a bootlegger, who had served five years in Leavenworth for masterminding a train robbery. After his parole, Murray operated the Rainbo Barbeque joint on Chicago's North Avenue, a frequent meeting place for outlaws.

When Freddie Monahan fled with their get-away car, Nelson lost most of his weapons and ammunition. Down to only one submachine gun, Nelson and his wife drove to San Antonio in early September of 1933. At Hymie Lebman's gun shop, Nelson purchased six Tommy guns, four automatic pistols, and two rifles, as well as two of Hyman's newly-designed machine gun pistols—one was a .45 caliber and the other was a .38 caliber.

In late October, the so-called *Nelson Gang* travelled to Brainerd, Minnesota, which was located 135 miles north of St. Paul. For several days, Nelson, Homer Van Meter, Tommy Carroll, Eddie Green, Chuck Fisher, and Thomas Gannon rented cottages at Louge Lake, some 15 miles north of Brainerd, affording them the opportunity to case the First National Bank.

On October 23rd, the heavily-armed gang entered the bank building. When the bank's frightened vice-president expressed uncertainty about his ability to open the vault, Nelson issued a harsh warning: "You'll open it or get killed." A cashier managed to open the combination lock, allowing the robbers to clear out the vault. After herding all 14 bank employees into the men's room, Nelson offered a parting threat: "I'll blow off the first head I see come through this door."

As the gang sped out of town, $32,000 richer, the impulsive and trig-ger-happy Nelson and Van Meter could not resist the urge to fire their submachine guns from the windows of the get-away car, shattering the plate glass windows of area businesses and sending bystanders scurrying for cover. A Brainerd policeman vividly recalled the bandits' brazenness: "They wanted to let folks know they were here."

In the late fall of 1933, Baby Face Nelson and John Dillinger met face-to-face; a meeting brokered by their mutual acquaintance, Homer Van Meter. It is possible the two bank robbers had crossed paths before; if not, they were certainly aware of one another's reputation. It proved to be a cordial meeting between the two men who aspired to become the most infamous outlaws of their generation.

"You know, they've already hung that Grand Haven job on me, along with every other damn thing over the last couple of months," Dillinger joked with Nelson.

"You're welcome to take credit for that one," Nelson lightheartedly responded.

Dillinger was eager to learn about Nelson's contacts for purchasing weapons, automobiles, and licenses plates, as well as discreet locations for automobile body shop repairs, and potential locales for cashing out stolen securities and bonds. When the pair met again in mid-November, Nelson offered to purchase weapons on Dillinger's behalf from Hymie Lebman in San Antonio. Like Nelson, Dillinger was intrigued by the Texan's machine gun pistol, and authorized his fellow outlaw to purchase one, "as long as the price is right."

With winter approaching, both outlaws were preparing to seek warmer climates. Inside a year, Dillinger and Nelson would meet again and establish a tenuous alliance.

CHAPTER EIGHT

The Number One Criminal at Large

With the departure of Ed Shouse and the arrest of Harry Copeland, the Dillinger Gang, previously known as the "Savage Seven," was renamed the "Furious Five." On November 20, 1933, the felonious quintet struck again. At 2:30 p.m., a resident of Racine, Wisconsin watched a vehicle pass in front of the American Bank and Trust Company twice, dropping off two men, dressed in topcoats, each time. The wheelman, Russell Clark, piloting a rather conspicuous get-away car, a Black Buick with jump seats and yellow wire wheel rims, parked behind the bank and left the engine idling.

Harry Pierpont was the first to enter the building, where he taped a Red Cross poster over the front window, covering nearly 80 percent of the plate glass. Dillinger, Charles Makley, and John Hamilton followed Pierpont into the lobby. Makley approached the head teller, Harold Graham, who was busy counting money in front of a sign that read "next window, please."

"Stick 'em up!" Makley ordered.

"Stick 'em up!" Makley repeated, when Graham failed to look from his work.

"Next window, please," Graham replied, preoccupied with the task at hand.

His patience exhausted, Makley squeezed the trigger on his Tommy gun sending a bullet through the teller's right arm and into his hip; fortunately for Graham, Makley's submachine gun was set in single-fire mode. As he was falling backwards to the floor, the wounded teller somehow managed to activate the alarm, which rang loudly outside the bank, and also triggered two separate alarms at the police station.

Dillinger and Pierpont immediately ordered bank employees to lie down on the floor. An unnerved teller, George Ryan complained to Pierpont: "For God's sake, Mister, point that (machine) gun the other way!"

"As long as you're a good boy, you don't have to worry," Pierpont chuckled.

After forcing the bank's president, Grover Weyland, to open the vault, Dillinger began filling sacks with cash. Accustomed to false alarms, the local police responded in an unhurried fashion. Three officers did manage to arrive while the robbery was in progress; a first for the Dillinger Gang. The first policeman to enter the bank, Chester Boyard, immediately encountered a machine gun-wielding Clark.

"Stick 'em up!" Clark ordered, before relieving Boyard of his service revolver.

"Come right in and join us," Dillinger cheerfully added.

A second officer, Sargent Wilbur Hansen, armed with a submachine gun, soon entered the building. Pierpont reacted instantly: "Get that cop with the machine gun!"

Makley fired his Tommy gun, disabling Hansen with wounds to his right hand and torso. A third officer, who was poised to enter the bank, instead ran in the opposite direction to summon help. Makley stepped outside to the sidewalk and discovered the manager of nearby Goldberg's Shoe Store standing on the window ledge, trying to peer around the poster and catch a glimpse of what was happening inside the bank. After Makley fired a burst from his submachine gun, shattering the window, the curious shoe store manager ran for his life.

By now, a crowd was gathering in front of the bank. After concluding that the drop from the bank's rear windows to the parking lot was too great, Dillinger announced: "We'll have to shoot our way out the front."

At gunpoint, Pierpont ordered Weyland and three female employees to accompany the robbers as they exited the front door. When Weyland was slow to respond, Pierpont slapped him in the face.

"If you didn't have that gun in your hand, you wouldn't have that much guts," Weyland brazenly responded, before another bandit bloodied his nose with the barrel of his submachine gun.

The bank robbers and hostages literally had to force their way through the crowd gathered on the sidewalk. Just then, two police detectives rounded the sidewalk on foot, a half-block away. After Makley unleashed a burst from his submachine gun, the detectives were forced to seek cover in the doorway of a nearby business. When the lawmen briefly reemerged from the protective alcove, Makley again sprayed the doorway with bullets, forcing them to dive for safety.

As the group rounded the corner and neared the get-away car parked in the rear of the building, Dillinger addressed the bloodied Weyland: "Come on, Mr. President, you're coming with us."

"And you in the red dress," Dillinger motioned to teller, Anna Patzke.

"You mean me?" a startled Patzke asked.

"Yes, and be quick about it," Dillinger replied.

After the bandits piled inside the black Buick, Weyland and Patzke were forced to mount the driver's side running boards. Officer Boyard was ordered to assume the same position on the opposite side of the vehicle.

After running two red lights and driving west out of town, the car halted briefly; Boyard was let go, while Weyland and Patzke were pulled inside the vehicle. A few miles outside the city limits, the bandits halted on a dirt side road to change the car's license plates and fill the tank from previously-hidden gas cans (the fuel gauges on 1930's-era automobiles were notoriously unreliable, forcing bank robbers to carry surplus gasoline).

After the brief pause, the fugitives and their hostages hit the road again. When Patzke complained of feeling cold, Pierpont draped his suit jacket over her shoulders. Weyland soon reported that his balding head was getting chilled, prompting Pierpont to hand the bank president his hat.

Keeping to the back roads, the bandits, who had made away with $32,000, departed the Racine area. As they passed an old man driving a tractor, Dillinger extended a jovial greeting: "Hi, Joe."

Sufficiently distant from Racine, the bandits stopped again and ordered their hostages to exit the vehicle. When Patzke paused briefly to tie her silk shoelaces, an impatient Makley cursed.

"Cut it out, man. There's a lady in the car," Dillinger reminded him.

In the woods adjacent to the road, Pierpont told Weyland and Patzke to hug a tree trunk, facing one another: "Time for ring-around-the-rosy; you'll be a little late for supper." Using shoelaces, Pierpont bound the two hostages together.

Realizing that he could easily free himself from the thin restraints, Weyland asked for clarification: "How long do you want us to wait? Ten minutes?"

"Better make it twenty," Pierpont replied, before removing his coat from Patzke's shoulders, and plucking his fedora from Weyland's bald head: "Sorry, Mister, I'll have to have my hat back." When later questioned by reporters, Weyland described the robbers as "genial," remembering how Dillinger had reprimanded another gang member for cursing in front of a woman.

Dillinger's good manners and acts of courtesy humanized him, unlike most of the other outlaws. For many downtrodden, Depression-era Americans, Dillinger was no more evil than the banks, which were steadily foreclosing on home and farm mortgages. A man in Indiana wrote a letter to his local newspaper editor: "Why should the law have wanted John Dillinger for bank robbery? He wasn't any worse than bankers and politicians who took the poor people's money. Dillinger did not rob poor people. He robbed those who became rich by robbing the poor. I am for Johnnie."

State and local law enforcement agencies, however, considered Dillinger to be nothing more than a flamboyant criminal, and totally dismissed any notion that he was a modern-day Robin Hood. Among pictures posted in the December 1933 issue of the *Chicago Police Department Bulletin*, eight of the *ten most wanted criminals* were members of the Dillinger Gang.

Those who had any association with the Dillinger Gang were subjected to harassment. When Captain Matt Leach received a tip that Harry Pierpont's mother and brother were passing through Terre Haute, Indiana, he advised the chief of police and sheriff to trail the pair, but not arrest them, believing they might lead authorities directly to the gang members. Disregarding Leach's advice, local lawmen arrested both of them.

Enraged that his mother had been temporarily incarcerated, Pierpont drove to Indianapolis and parked outside state police headquarters. When Leach eventually exited the building, he unknowingly found himself in Pierpont's gun sight. Only after Detective Harvey Hire, who was walking alongside Leach, blocked the line of fire, did Pierpont decide not to shoot.

The Dillinger Gang laid low for nearly three weeks after the Racine bank robbery. During the lull, Dillinger purchased a new Hudson Terraplane sedan for $813.96. In early December, Dillinger and Billie Frechette took a short vacation to Hot Springs, Arkansas. At the same time, Pierpont and Mary Kinder made a brief get-away to Houston, Texas.

Unexpected trouble arrived on December 14th, when Chicago Police Department Detective William Shanley received a tip that one of the Dillinger gang members was having his car repaired at Tower Auto Rebuilders on Broadway Street. The 43-year-old Shanley lay in wait at the body shop until John Hamilton and his girlfriend, Elaine Dent, arrived to pick up his vehicle, which had undergone a five-dollar bumper repair.

When the detective attempted to question the fugitive, Hamilton shot him in the chest; Shanley was rushed to a nearby hospital, where he died 15 minutes later. Hamilton and his girlfriend immediately ran from the scene of the crime. Less fleet-footed, Dent was captured by police officers, but her boyfriend managed to escape.

The authorities mistakenly identified Harry Pierpont as Shanley's killer, until Dent clarified the situation. Even though the young waitress did not know Hamilton's name, she told police detectives that her boyfriend had only three fingers on one of his hands. Dent naively believed that her male suitor was a man of influence: "Once, he showed me $70,000 in thousand-dollar notes...My folks thought he was a great catch and encouraged me to marry him. He was awfully nice. He used to take two baths a day and never used curse words."

After Dent was arraigned on charges of *accessory to murder*, she revised her opinion of Hamilton: "If I ever get out and he tries to get in touch with me, I'll put a bullet in him." After the prosecutor concluded that Dent was far too unsophisticated to be a criminal accomplice, the charges against her were dropped.

After the loss of one of its own, the Chicago Police Department declared war on the Dillinger Gang. Captain John Stege, who was selected to head the newly-formed *Get Dillinger Squad*, summarized the task force's ultimate goal: "We hope, although their trails are cold, to be able to drive them out of town, or bury them. We'd prefer the latter." Stege handpicked marksmen to work the squad's night shift; after dark was considered the most likely time that lawmen might encounter the Dillinger Gang.

After returning from his vacation in Hot Springs, Dillinger learned that Detective Shanley's murder had intensified the authorities' determination to capture him—*dead or alive.* Consequently, Dillinger and Frechette frequently changed hide-away locations; the decision proved fortuitous, when the Chicago Police Department raided one of Dillinger's apartments, just days after the fugitive had vacated the premises.

After murdering Shanley, the red-headed Hamilton sought greater anonymity by dyeing his hair brunette. Pierpont also changed his hair color to a darker shade. Not to be outdone, Dillinger dyed his hair red and grew a mustache, the latter of which helped disguise an easily recognizable scar on his upper lip.

In spite of the intensified manhunt, Dillinger could not resist the urge to taunt his pursuers. In mid-December, Dillinger telephoned Matt Leach to inquire about the progress of the Indiana State Police's manhunt. Dillinger also called Chicago Police Department Sargent, Frank Reynolds, who was the night shift commander of the 40-man Get Dillinger Squad: "You'd better watch your ass. We'll take you." When Reynolds offered to meet Dillinger one-on-one, any time of the day or night, the fugitive laughed and hung up the phone.

The murder of Detective Shanley had nationwide ramifications. J. Edgar Hoover was still reluctant to commit federal resources to the case, but in mid-December of 1933, the Bureau did designate Dillinger as *the Number One Criminal at Large,* a precursor to the FBI's later and widely-acclaimed, *Ten Most Wanted List.* While Dillinger had not yet killed anyone, his gang members had committed murder, implicating him by association.

On December 18th, local law enforcement agents cornered former Dillinger gang member, Ed Shouse, and two female companions in front of the France Hotel in Paris, Illinois. Once the police hemmed in his car, Shouse unsuccessfully tried to escape on foot. While firing at the fleeing suspect with his shotgun, police lieutenant Chester Butler inadvertently shot and killed 24-year-old State Trooper, Eugene Teague. A distraught Butler, while exonerated of wrong-doing, resigned from the police force.

While Dillinger was nowhere near Paris, the accidental shooting was indirectly blamed on him. Matt Leach was among those who vented their anger and frustration at the Dillinger Gang: "It will cost the lives of more officers before we get them. I may be the next one to pay." Twenty-eight-year-old, Frances Colin, one of the women who had been inside the car with Shouse on the night of his arrest, directed her animus at the authorities: "They ought to hang that copper for killing another policeman. But, he's a copper—that makes a difference."

After he was arrested, Shouse informed authorities that he was no longer associated with the Dillinger Gang, and provided them with little new information about his former partners. The arrestee was soon sent back to the Indiana State Penitentiary to complete his original 25-year sentence for automobile theft. Once incarcerated, Shouse did offer a few tidbits of information, explaining how the armed gang members would take prearranged positions, whenever someone knocked on the door of their hide-away. He also reported that the Dillinger Gang often talked about killing lawmen, and were so vigilant that they sometimes slept in their bulletproof vests.

"They're all kill crazy. That's why I left them," Shouse disingenuously and self-servingly claimed.

With their names plastered on wanted posters throughout the Midwest, the Dillinger Gang decided to take a lengthy holiday vacation. A week or so before Christmas, the group departed Chicago, travelling in three separate automobiles. Billie Frechette and "Three-Fingered" John Hamilton joined Dillinger in his new Terraplane sedan. Charles Makley and Mary Kinder rode with Harry Pierpont in his Studebaker, while Russell Clark drove his newly purchased Ford V-8, accompanied by his wife Bernice and her sister, Pat Cherrington.

To appear less conspicuous, the caravan separated as it headed south. Dillinger visited his half-brother Hubert in Indianapolis, his sister Audrey in Maywood, and other relatives, dropping off Christmas presents along the way.

Two days after Dillinger left Chicago, acting on an anonymous tip, Sargent Reynolds and other members of the Get Dillinger Squad raided an apartment on Farwell Avenue, where the fugitive was thought to be staying. The lawmen entered the residence with blazing guns, fatally wounding the three men who were living there. The dead men, named Katzewitz, Tattlebaum, and Gingsberg, were Jewish criminals, none of whom had any association with John Dillinger.

Near the Indiana and Kentucky border, Russell Clark skidded on a rain-slicked road and collided with a truck. Neither Clark nor Cherrington were hurt, but Bernice gashed her head and briefly lost consciousness. Before attendants could load her aboard an ambulance, Bernice cleverly stuffed $4,000 in her shoes. After stashing the bulk of his money inside suitcases, already heavily-laden with firearms, Clark took a taxi to the police station. Accepting full responsibility for the accident, he paid the truck driver for the damages to his vehicle.

At the hospital, Bernice was fearful of becoming loose-lipped, and insisted that the doctors suture her head laceration without using pain killers. She also resisted all efforts by the nurses to remove her shoes. The next morning, absent a vehicle, the trio chartered a plane to Nashville—the gang's predetermined meeting place.

In Nashville, the gang members and their significant others stayed at the Hermitage Hotel, where Dillinger registered under the alias of *Frank Sullivan*. The fugitives freely spent their money in Tennessee; Hamilton purchased a new V-8 Ford, while Pierpont bought Mary Kinder a $500 diamond ring and an $85 gold wedding band.

From Nashville, the group departed for Florida, arriving in Daytona Beach two days before Christmas. At a cost of $100 per month, Dillinger rented a three-story, 17-room beach house at 901 South Atlantic Avenue.

For many in the vacation party, it was the first time they had ever seen the ocean. The group enjoyed fishing, sunbathing, swimming, walking and riding horses on the beach, playing cards, and going to the movies. Dillinger, as usual, read newspapers and listened to radio news broadcasts, amused by the national hysteria that he had created. The press attributed nearly every new bank robbery in the Midwest to the Dillinger Gang. After hearing radio news reports accusing the gang of robbing a roadhouse tavern outside of Chicago, which resulted in two policemen being shot, Dillinger complained to Pierpont and Hamilton: "Now they'll blame everything on me."

Unlike so many of the news reporters, Matt Leach no longer believed the Dillinger Gang was in Chicago, but instead had travelled to a warmer climate—either Texas or Florida. Accordingly, Leach sent photographs and fingerprint samples to Miami, Miami Beach, and Dade County law enforcement officials, warning them that the gang members were heavily armed and "will not be taken alive." While Leach correctly surmised that the Dillinger Gang might be in Florida, he was unaware that they had settled 300 miles north of the Miami area. On December 26th, the *Daytona News Journal* headlined: *POLICE WARN AGAINST KILL CRAZY GANGSTERS.* Unbeknownst to the coastal community residents and lawmen, the outlaws were enjoying a holiday vacation right under their noses.

On Christmas Day, Russell Clark's wife, Bernice, alias *Opal Long,* who was also nicknamed "Mack Truck," prepared dinner for the vacationers. Continuing his pattern of lavishing affection through jewelry, Harry Pierpont presented Mary Kinder with a diamond watch. Dillinger was also generous to Billie Frechette, giving her a Boston Bulldog puppy, silk undergarments, and $ 1,000 in cash.

Pierpont purchased a new Buick for $1,600, employing the alias, *J. C. Evans,* which happened to be the name of a much-despised guard at the Indiana State Penitentiary. Ever fearful of being discovered by the authorities, Pierpont sent Mary Kinder to a Jacksonville dealership to pick up his new car. The *Jacksonville Times Union* sent a photographer to commemorate the car dealership's first sale of a 1934 Buick. The story accompanying the newspaper picture detailed the purchase of the new car by *Mrs. J. C. Evans,* who was vacationing in Florida.

Dillinger and Pierpont drove across the Florida peninsula to examine an estate in Tampa that was listed for sale. When the seller began asking questions about their background and asked for references, Dillinger and Pierpont decided against making an offer on the $15,000 property.

On Christmas Eve, Dillinger and Billie reportedly engaged in a violent argument that left her with a black eye; while this story has been reported as fact by some Dillinger biographers, the other women who accompanied the gang to Florida later claimed to have no memories of the altercation. Irrespective of the alleged fight, Dillinger lavished Billie with Christmas gifts, and also signed over to her the title of his newly-purchased Hudson Terraplane. Shortly after Christmas, employing the alias *Frank Kirtley,* Dillinger visited a notary public, D. R. Beach, and signed over the automobile, "free of all encumbrances," to *Evelyn Frechette,* reported to be his sister, and a resident of Neopit, Wisconsin. The week after Christmas, Billie and Pat Cherrington departed Florida in the Terraplane; Frechette planned to make a holiday visit to her family in Wisconsin.

On New Year's Eve, Dillinger and his gang members held a raucous party. The celebration marked the first and only time that many of them would see Dillinger intoxicated. Nearing midnight, as he stood on the beach house balcony, armed with a submachine gun, a drunken Dillinger pointed to the moon. "Think I can hit it?" he asked Mary Kinder.

At the stroke of midnight, as church bells tolled and fireworks exploded, heralding the arrival of what would be the final year of his life, Dillinger unleashed a burst of machine gun fire over the Atlantic Ocean. The next day, perhaps still hung over, Dillinger wrote his niece, Mary, a letter tinged with self-pity: "...I see in the papers where I'm robbing cabarets and most anything that comes along, but you know that's a lie don't you, honey? When I steal anything, it isn't going to be a few hundred dollars. They blame me for most everything now a days..."

On Sunday January 14th, Dillinger and Hamilton left Daytona Beach bound for Chicago, in the latter's newly-purchased car. Makley, Clark, Pierpont, and the two women departed for Tucson, Arizona, hoping to extend their warm-weather vacation. After rendezvousing with Billie, Dillinger planned to join the others in Arizona. Driving through the night, Dillinger and Hamilton reached Chicago the next day.

Monday, the 15th, was a busy day for Dillinger. Continuing his pattern of taunting the authorities, Dillinger telephoned Sargent Frank Reynolds, commander of the Get Dillinger Squad's night shift, threatening to visit his house and kill him. A defiant Reynolds encouraged the fugitive to come ahead, vowing that he could "take down two Dillinger's, single-handedly."

That same day, Dillinger and Hamilton staged a daring robbery of the First National Bank in East Chicago, Indiana, located 25 miles from its namesake city. At 3:45 p.m., the pair entered the bank, while an unidentified accomplice remained behind the wheel of the get-away car. Once inside the lobby, Dillinger opened a black leather case, which some witnesses later described as a trombone case, and removed a submachine gun. After inserting a 50-round drum in the Tommy gun, Dillinger announced: "This is a stick-up! Everybody put your hands up!"

Hamilton ordered the women and children, among the nearly 20 customers and employees in the bank, to stand in a corner, and instructed the men to face the wall. After spying a woman pushing a baby carriage, Dillinger told her to move to a safer location behind the tellers' cages. While the bandits were repositioning the customers, the bank's vice-president, Walter Spencer, pushed a button in the keyhole of his desk, activating a silent alarm that was received at the police station, a block away.

Hamilton quickly filled a leather satchel with cash from the tellers' drawers. When a customer tried to leave his cash on the counter, Dillinger stopped him: "You go ahead and take your money. We don't want your money—just the bank's"

Police officer, Hobart Wilgus, entered the front door of the building, unaware that a robbery was in progress, and was immediately disarmed by Dillinger. When an anxious Wilgus kept staring at the fugitive's submachine gun, Dillinger smiled: "Oh, don't worry about this. I'm not even sure it'll shoot."

As a group of lawmen, answering the alarm, approached the front of the bank, Dillinger reassured Hamilton: "Don't let those coppers worry you. Take your time, and be sure you get all the dough. We'll take care of them birds on the outside, when we get there."

After Hamilton had collected a bit over $20,000 in cash, the robbers made their way toward the front door. Dillinger ordered Walter Spencer to join them: "Come on out here with me, Mr. President." When Spencer asked if he could put on his coat as protection against the cold, Dillinger shook his head: "You're not going far."

Heading out the front door, Dillinger positioned Officer Wilgus in front of him, while Hamilton had his arm around Spencer, employing him as a human shield. Dillinger instructed Wilgus to remain cool: "You go first. They might as well shoot you, as me. We love you guys anyway."

Making their way across the sidewalk toward the get-away car, the bandits and their two hostages encountered seven East Chicago police officers. Sargent Patrick O'Malley, who was standing 10 feet to Dillinger's left, suddenly shouted: "Wilgus!"

On cue, Wilgus turned to one side, giving O'Malley and unobstructed shot at Dillinger. The Sargent fired four times, with at least one of the shots striking Dillinger's bulletproof vest. Though not seriously wounded, Dillinger was in pain, and his calm demeanor instantly transformed into rage.

"Get over! I'll get that son of a bitch!" Dillinger shouted, as he shoved Wilgus to one side, and fired a machine gun burst at O'Malley. Struck eight times in the chest, the 43-year-old policeman was instantly killed.

As Dillinger and Hamilton sprinted to the get-away car, the remaining six officers opened fire. While Dillinger managed to dodge the lawmen's bullets, Hamilton was hit several times in areas not protected by his bulletproof vest. With amazing luck and agility, Dillinger not only pulled Hamilton, who had fallen to the pavement, inside the car, but also managed to grab the cash-filled satchel his wounded partner had dropped.

Amidst a barrage of bullets, the bank robbers sped away. Two Indiana State Game Wardens gave brief chase, firing at the escaping Ford, but were unable to keep pace for very long.

For the first time, Dillinger was a murderer, joining ranks with gang members, Pierpont, Makley, and Hamilton. For the remainder of his life, Dillinger would repeatedly and disingenuously deny killing Sargent O'Malley, to the point of telling family members that he was not even present in East Chicago on the day of the bank robbery. At the same time, Dillinger was clearly troubled by his actions, and later complained to an attorney that the policeman had shot him first: "What else could I do?"

After arriving back in Chicago, Dillinger drove his wounded accomplice to the hotel where Pat Cherrington was staying. Cherrington climbed in the backseat and comforted the bleeding Hamilton, who was lying down and covered with a blanket. Dillinger then sped to Dr. Joseph P. Moran's office, located on Irving Park Boulevard. Moran, a 39-year-old alcoholic, had made acquaintances with numerous inmates while serving a two-year prison term, after one of his patients died following an illegal abortion. After being released from the penitentiary, Moran continued to perform abortions and was also available to discreetly treat gunshot wounds and other injuries sustained by criminals.

Moran's examination revealed six bullet holes scattered in Hamilton's shoulders, left arm, and hip. Even after the physician concluded that the wounded man had lost so much blood that his survival was doubtful, Dillinger instructed Moran to remove the slugs and dress the wounds. The physician earned a handsome fee for this discreet services; Dillinger paid him $5,000 (equivalent to $67,000 by today's standards).

Once Dr. Moran had done all that he could to treat Hamilton, Dillinger drove his wounded partner to an apartment occupied by Hazel Doyle. A nightclub hostess, Doyle was married to an associate of Baby Face Nelson, who had been imprisoned for bank robbery. At the rate of $100 per day, Doyle agreed to take care of Hamilton. In spite of serious blood loss, Hamilton slowly improved, and was eventually relocated to the home of his half-sister and brother-in-law in Fort Wayne, Indiana. After equally dividing the money stolen in the bank robbery, Dillinger left Hamilton in Fort Wayne to complete his lengthy recovery.

With the death of another policeman, both the police and the press began using the phrase, *wanted dead or alive*, in association with the Dillinger Gang. When Dillinger's blood-stained Ford was found abandoned in Chicago, the authorities assumed that he was still in the area. In reality, after rendezvousing with Billie Frechette and visiting a divorce attorney to speed up the dissolution of her marriage, Dillinger and his girlfriend left Chicago to meet up with fellow gang members in Arizona. En route to Tucson, the couple made a brief stop in Mooresville to visit Dillinger's father. Afterwards, they travelled to Saint Louis, where Dillinger attended an automobile show and purchased a new Hudson sedan with a more powerful V-8 engine. While the couple was completing the necessary paperwork for the new car, Billie's puppy got loose from its collar. A gracious police officer helped Dillinger capture the runaway dog, totally unaware that he was assisting America's most wanted fugitive.

After spending one night in St. Louis, Dillinger and Billie headed to Arizona, arriving on January 24th. Later that same day, Harry Pierpont and Mary Kinder drove into Tucson, settling in the same tourist court where Dillinger and Billie had earlier registered as *Mr. and Mrs. Frank Sullivan*, from Green Bay, Wisconsin. Charles Makley, along with Russell Clark and his wife, Bernice, had arrived several days earlier, first living in a hotel, before renting a house.

Around noon on the following day, Dillinger met with fellow gang members two miles outside of town, near the Veterans Hospital. During their initial reunion, the bank robbers discussed future targets.

In a more relaxed environment, distant from the scenes of their past crimes, the gang members grew remarkably careless. For unknown reasons, Pierpont stopped to talk with two police officers, reporting that he was visiting from Florida and was being trailed by a mysterious vehicle. While one of the cops followed the suspicious automobile, Pierpont showed off his newly-purchased Buick to the other officer, and foolishly gave him the address of the tourist court where he was staying.

On Tuesday, January 23rd, an oil furnace in the basement of the Congress Hotel caught fire and spread up the elevator shaft, forcing Clark and Makley to abandon their rooms. After the blaze was brought under control, William Benedict, a Tucson fireman, discovered the two fugitives situating a ladder against the outer wall of the hotel, in hopes of gaining access to luggage in Makley's third-floor room. Benedict stopped them, but agreed to retrieve the luggage from Room 329; one item, a fabric box containing submachine guns, appeared suspiciously heavy to the fireman, who was also shocked when Makley gave him a generous tip for his assistance.

Three days later, Benedict was reading a recent issue of *True Detective* magazine, when he came across Charles Makley's photograph, and immediately recognized him as the *Mr. Davies*, whose luggage he had rescued from the fire-damaged hotel. Benedict immediately reported his discovery to local police officers. After hearing Benedict's story, one of the policemen, Harry Lesly, remembered that earlier in the week two tourists had shared information about a strange encounter at a local night club. A man, identifying himself as *L. L. Long* (Russell Clark's alias) had bragged how easy it was to endure the economic hardships of the Great Depression, if one was proficient with a submachine gun. The tourists also recalled that *Long* and his male companion appeared to be wearing shoulder holsters.

After police detectives studied their collection of wanted posters and determined that Makley and *Davies* were one in the same, they phoned the fire-damaged Congress Hotel and learned that the fugitives' luggage had been sent to a bungalow at 927 North Second Street. By early afternoon of that same day, three Tucson police officers were stationed in a squad car outside Makley and Clark's rental house. Before long, Makley and his newly-acquired girlfriend, Madge Ritze, exited the house and boarded his Studebaker. The lawmen followed closely behind as the couple drove to Grabbe Electric and Radio, where Makley had left a radio to be repaired.

When the officers arrested the fugitive inside the appliance store, Makley immediately identified himself as *J. C. Davies*, a businessman visiting from

Florida. After the arrestee refused to be fingerprinted at the police station, he was locked inside a jail cell.

Tucson Police Chief, C. A. Wollard, suspected that at least one other member of the Dillinger Gang was in the area, and soon dispatched two police officers, Frank Eyman and Dallas Ford, along with Detective Chet Sherman, to stake out Makley's bungalow. After waiting for over an hour, an impatient Sherman exited the squad car and rang the front doorbell, posing as a letter-carrying, special delivery clerk.

When Russell Clark's wife, Bernice, answered the door, Sherman forced his way inside, where he immediately came face-to-face with the fugitive. When the detective drew his pistol, Clark grabbed the barrel, and the two men struggled for control of the weapon, in a mad dance that carried them from the living room into one of the bedrooms. Alerted by the commotion, Officers Eyman and Ford stormed the house, bursting through the door before Bernice could lock it. Ford clubbed Clark over the head with his service revolver just as the outlaw was reaching for a .38 caliber pistol hidden beneath a pillow on the bed.

Clark and his wife were hustled to jail. Had the lawmen hung around longer, they would have soon encountered another one of the gang members. Later in the afternoon, when Pierpont dropped by Makley and Clark's house, he discovered the open front door, overturned furniture, and bloodstains on the floor. Aware that his partners had likely been arrested, Pierpont rushed back to his cabin, where he and Mary Kinder began furiously packing.

Chief Wollard now believed that John Dillinger and Harry Pierpont were also in Tucson. The two patrol officers, who had interacted with an amiable businessman driving a new Buick a few days earlier, informed Wollard that the stranger's face matched the photographs on Harry Pierpont's wanted poster. One of the officers also remembered the name of the tourist camp where the man said he was staying.

Wollard immediately dispatched Sargent Eyman and the two patrolmen to Pierpont's cabin. Just as the lawmen were arriving, Pierpont and a female companion were driving away in his new Buick. After following Pierpont and Mary Kinder for a short distance, Eyman honked the patrol car's horn and motioned Pierpont to pull over to the side of the road.

"How do you do? May I please see your driver's license?" Eyman addressed Pierpont, through the open driver's side window.

After examining the license issued in the name of Pierpont's alias, Eyman informed him that his vehicle lacked a proper visitor's inspection sticker, which could be readily obtained at the police station. Eyman hopped in the back seat of the Buick, sitting atop the couple's luggage, and told them he would direct them to police headquarters. When he spotted Pierpont eyeing him through the rearview mirror, Eyman discreetly drew his pistol. Unbeknownst to Eyman, Pierpont had already concealed his .45 caliber handgun between his legs.

At the police station, Pierpont and Kinder were escorted to Chief Wollard's office, where the weapons and luggage confiscated from Makley and Clark were in plain view. When he realized what was happening, Pierpont tried to draw his pistol from his shoulder holster.

Eyman was quicker on the draw: "Drop it!"

After relinquishing his weapon, Pierpont suddenly stuck a piece of paper in his mouth. To keep the arrestee from swallowing evidence, police officers squeezed a device, known as the iron claw, on Pierpont's arm, until the pain forced him to spit out the paper, which contained the address where Dillinger was staying.

"You're treating me pretty rough, aren't you?" Pierpont complained.

"What do you want us to do—kiss you?" Eyman replied.

Pierpont immediately grew enraged: "I'll get you...I can get out of any jail, and I'll not forget."

The police confiscated $10,000 in cash from Pierpont, Makley, and Clark. They also discovered Pierpont was carrying the .38 caliber pistol that had belonged to the murdered Ohio sheriff, Jess Sarber. When asked how he came into possession of Sarber's handgun, Pierpont muttered: "I can't remember."

The only member of the infamous Dillinger Gang not in custody was the leader, himself. Certain that Dillinger was nearby, the authorities placed the arrested fugitives' residences under constant surveillance. At Makley's bungalow, two patrol officers, Kenneth Mullaney and Milo Walker, snuck inside the back door and lay in wait. Across the street, Detective James Herron was stationed inside a car.

The lawmen's patience was rewarded, when later in the afternoon, a Hudson sedan parked in front of the bungalow. Dillinger, dressed in a brown suit, approached the front door, while Billie Frechette waited inside the car with her puppy. Detective Herron immediately followed Dillinger to the front door.

"Who are you looking for?" Herron inquired.

"I'm at the wrong house," Dillinger replied.

"Oh no, you're not," Herron asserted, "Stick 'em up!"

Officers Mullaney and Walker quickly exited the front door of the bungalow, guns drawn. When Dillinger slowly began to lower his raised arms, Walker cocked the hammer on his shotgun: "Reach for the moon, or I'll cut you in two."

Dillinger was arrested and taken to the police station, where he identified himself as a Wisconsin businessman named *Frank Sullivan*. Sargent Mark Robbins reviewed a stack of photographs of wanted men while Dillinger stood in front of him: "Look what we have here!" Robbins then examined the arrestee's left wrist and beneath his mustache, discovering the identifying scars referenced in the wanted posters.

"This man is John Dillinger," Robbins announced.

A .45 caliber pistol and $6,875 in cash were discovered in a body search of the arrestee. After closely examining Dillinger's clothing, an additional $200 was found hidden inside the lining of his suit coat. After Dillinger's possessions were inventoried, the rabbit's foot found in one of his pockets was returned to him.

"That's one time your rabbit's foot didn't work, boy," the booking officer commented.

"That rabbit was a lot luckier than I was," Dillinger grinned.

Inside Dillinger's Hudson, police officers discovered two submachine guns, 500 rounds of ammunition, and two shortwave radios. At the fugitives rented cabin, the search uncovered two Winchester .351 rifles with Maxim silencers, as well as $6,500 packed in a suitcase and $1,000 locked inside a closet.

Dillinger did not abandon the use of his alias until the fingerprint technician verified his true identity. The authorities realized they had hit pay dirt, when serial numbers on 200 of the five-dollar bills found in Dillinger's possessions were traced back to the First National Bank in East Chicago, Indiana.

A more thorough search of Makley and Clark's rented bungalow uncovered three submachine guns, handcuffs, brass knuckles, two Colt .45 caliber automatic pistols, two bulletproof vests, and abundant stores of ammunition.

In just one day, the Tucson Police Department had captured John Dillinger, three of his gang members, a small arsenal, and $27,000 in stolen money, without firing a single shot. From that day forward, on or around January 26th, the city of Tucson has celebrated an annual *Dillinger Days Festival*, which includes reenactments of the arrests.

Reporters from all over the country rushed to the Pima County Jail in Tucson, to cover the story of the Dillinger Gang's arrest. Motion picture cameramen from *Movietone News*, *Universal Newsreels*, and *Pathe* soon joined the mass of reporters and still photographers in Tucson. Proud of their accomplishment, the local authorities were cooperative with the press. When Harry Pierpont tried to hide his face from photographers, two police officers forced him to pose for the camera.

The day after their arrests, amidst the popping sound of camera flashbulbs, the four gang members and three women were taken to the courtroom in shackles. Security was tight, with 30 deputies stationed along the walls of the courtroom. When Dillinger slumped down in his chair, Justice of the Peace, C. V. Budlong, was not amused: "Stand up!"

"I ain't Dillinger," the gang leader replied, before a bailiff forced him to stand.

Attorney John L. VanBuskirk represented the entire group, entering pleas of *not guilty*. VanBuskirk argued that Arizona statues prohibited his clients from being held without bail, since they had not committed any crimes within the state. Justice Budlong responded by fixing each gang members' individual bail at $100,000; an amount large enough to ensure that they would remain behind bars. The individual bails for Billie Frechette, Mary Kinder, and Bernice Clark were set at $5,000.

Pierpont erupted when Kinder was remanded into custody: "I don't care what you do to me, but that little woman had nothing to do with it!" Pierpont was also unhappy when the gang's arsenal of weapons was openly displayed in the courtroom: "Just because a fellow has money, does that make him a fugitive from justice?"

Hoping to prevent the banks and insurance companies from immediately seizing their *assets*, the gang members signed over their money and automobiles to their attorney. A Hudson car dealership managed to obtain temporary use of Dillinger's automobile, displaying it with an accompanying banner: *DILLINGER CHOOSES THE 1934 HUDSON FOR HIS PERSONAL USE.*

After their arraignments, the three female prisoners were incarcerated separate from the men, on the top floor of the county jail—a cell block referred to as the *penthouse.* Sheriff John Belton added extra men and firepower to secure the entire jailhouse. The sheriff also segregated Dillinger from his three fellow gang members. Belton sternly informed all four men about the consequences of an attempted escape: "You're worth just as much to me dead as alive, and I don't intend to get a bunch of good men killed, just to see you get away."

Dillinger was an instant media sensation, even when his tone was indignant: "You're framing me for crimes I never even read about! You can't keep me in any two-by-four jail like this...I'll get out and kill you all." At the same time, he could not resist the temptation to brag about his exploits: "I'm an expert in my business. I can play tag with the police any time. They just dodge around on old trails, like fox hounds that don't know what's going on. And, the dumbest ones in the world are the Chicago kind. Right now, none of these smart-alek coppers have got a bit of evidence that I killed anybody or robbed any bank. And, they can't keep me penned up anywhere, here, Atlanta, Leavenworth, or Alcatraz Island—any more than they could keep (me and) my men in Ohio or Indiana." At the conclusion of a press appearance, Dillinger lightheartedly advised reporters to encourage their readers to "vote for Sheriff John Belton in the next election."

Even Dillinger's tight-lipped accomplices eventually opened up a bit. Makley informed a reporter that Pierpont was the most dangerous of the gang members: "If anything happens here, you watch out for Pete. He's a wild man." In spite of the charges levied against him, Makley reminded the press that he came from a good family: "They were honest at least, even if never rich. Look at my Dad, he worked like the devil all his life, and what did he get out of it? I've lived as long in 40 minutes, at times, as Dad did in 40 years."

From her jail cell in the so-called penthouse, Billie Frechette captivated the press with stories about her boyfriend. Billie characterized Dillinger as a "dashing Romeo," who was as "gentle as a lamb."

Dillinger managed to charm his captors: "We're exactly like you cops. You have a profession; we have a profession. The only difference is you're on the right side of the law—we're on the wrong." He also gave credit to the Tucson Police Department: "Where you were smart was getting us one at a time."

Even the surly Pierpont credited the local lawmen for not being trigger happy: "...There are two kinds of officers—rats and gentleman. You fellows are gentlemen, and the Indiana and Ohio cops are rats...If all this had happened in Ohio, we'd be laying (sic) on a slab. They'd have murdered us." When Patrolmen, Milo "Swede" Walker, visited with Clark in jail, the outlaw pointed to the bandage on his head and joked about purchasing a football helmet: "Every time we get in trouble, I get hit on the head."

Reporters were not the only ones interested in eyeballing the infamous gang. When Arizona Governor, B. B. Moeur, passed by Pierpont's cell, the prisoner engaged him: "These cops out here ain't like the ones in Indiana. They pull (their weapons) too fast for us." When Clark encountered the Governor, he was cordial, yet exhibited a measure of bravado: "When I get out of here, I'll be hotter than ever. I've gotten out before."

Now that the Dillinger Gang had been captured, the next big question was where they would be tried for their crimes. Law enforcement agencies and politicians throughout the Midwest were itching to get their hands on the infamous bank robbers.

CHAPTER NINE

The wooden gun

Within days of their arrest, prosecutors and lawmen from Indiana, Ohio, and Wisconsin rushed to Tucson to lobby for extradition of the Dillinger Gang to their respective states. A jurisdictional fight ensued over Dillinger in particular, with each state clamoring to bring him to trial first. Wisconsin offered one of the stronger arguments; the Badger State's judicial process, from trial to conviction to sentencing, was among the fastest in the country. Arizona officials, however, were most interested in claiming reward money: "Give them to the state that will pay us the most."

Matt Leach was among the first out of town lawman to arrive in Tucson. The Director of the Indiana State Police was ecstatic: "This stamps out the so-called Dillinger Gang." Harry Pierpont exploded when he first encountered Leach: "I should have killed you when I had the chance, you dirty son of a bitch! You put my mother in jail...If I ever get out of this, the first thing I'm gonna do is kill you, you rat!"

"There's a man who really loves his mother," Leach calmly told a reporter, who witnessed Pierpont's outburst.

When Leach confronted Dillinger, the two of them shook hands: "Well, we meet again, John." When Leach asked if the fugitive was prepared to return to Indiana, Dillinger appeared nonchalant: "I'm in no hurry. I haven't a thing to do when I get there."

A day after the gang's arrest, a grand jury in Lake County, Indiana indicted Dillinger for the murder of Sargent William Patrick O'Malley. If convicted, Dillinger would receive a mandatory death sentence. Allen County Sheriff

Jess Sarber's widow soon added to the gang's legal hurdles, filing a $50,000 wrongful death civil suit against Dillinger, Pierpont, Makley, and Clark.

Robert Estill, Lake County's politically ambitious prosecuting attorney, soon made his way to Tucson. Hoping to run for Governor, Estill was aware of the enormous publicity and political capital he would derive from successfully convicting John Dillinger. Indiana Governor, Paul McNutt, who was contemplating running for President, knew the execution of Dillinger in the Hoosier State's electric chair would appeal to law and order voters, nationwide. Indiana's argument for extradition was bolstered by Patrolmen Hobart Wilgus, who accompanied Estill to Tucson, and positively identified Dillinger as Sargent O'Malley's killer.

Dillinger was ultimately extradited to Indiana, while Pierpont, Clark, and Makley returned to Ohio to stand trial. Before relinquishing custody of the Dillinger Gang, Sheriff Belton allowed the general public to catch a glimpse the infamous outlaws. Over 1,500 locals passed by the jail cells where Dillinger, Pierpont, Makley, and Clark were held captive.

When the sheriff informed Dillinger that he was being sent to Indiana, Pierpont overheard the exchange. Pierpont's spontaneous rant unnerved Dillinger: "They're not taking you to Indiana. They're putting you on the spot, boy!"

"You're shanghaiing me! They can't take me east without a hearing!" Dillinger protested, retreating into the corner of his jail cell and resisting the guards' efforts to handcuff him.

"I won't forget it. I'll come back and get the whole damn bunch of you!" Dillinger loudly threatened, as he was dragged from his cell.

At the airport in Tucson, Dillinger was hustled aboard a Bellanca Skyrocket monoplane; it was the first time the outlaw had ever flown in an airplane. After he was handcuffed to the frame of the pilot's seat, Dillinger quipped: "Hell, I don't jump out of these things."

A chase plane, piloted by World War I ace, Charles Mayse, followed the aircraft that flew Dillinger to Douglas, Arizona, located 100 miles southwest of Tucson, near the Mexican border. At the airport in Douglas, the fugitive was hustled aboard a commercial American Airways flight to El Paso. Multiple stops followed, including Abilene, Fort Worth, Dallas, Little Rock, Memphis, and St Louis. The flight to Chicago was exhausting; the propeller-driven aircraft could only reach a maximum speed of 100 miles per hour. During one leg of the journey, 22-year-old flight attendant, Marguerite Brennan, got a first-hand look at the famed prisoner, and was less than awed: "I felt sorry for him. He looked like a little puppy with his tail between his legs."

During the lay-over in St. Louis, a photographer for the *Chicago Times*, Sol Davis, boarded the airplane. When Davis asked if he could take the fugitive's picture, Dillinger consented: "All right, kid, what the hell—go ahead and shoot."

While taking a series of flash photographs, Davis doubled as a reporter: "How'd this happen, John?"

"Oh, some dumb cluck slipped up," Dillinger replied.

"The breaks aren't coming your way, huh?" Davis probed.

"The bastards won't give me a break. I was supposed to be brought before the Tucson judge, but those Chinamen hustled me out! When those pricks nabbed me, I wish I'd had five seconds," Dillinger lamented.

"Why five seconds?" Davis inquired.

"If I'd had those five seconds, they wouldn't have taken me that way," Dillinger boasted.

The prisoner eventually grew tired of bantering with Davis: "I thought you was (sic) a cameraman. What the hell's the use of me answering all these questions over again? Go away and let me sleep!"

By now, the photographer had captured valuable images for his newspaper. Davis would forever remember his exchange with the captured outlaw: "I served a long stretch in the Army and I met plenty of tough guys, but I don't think I ever met a tougher one than Dillinger."

The remainder of the Dillinger Gang and Mary Kinder were extradited to Ohio to stand trial for the murder of Sheriff Sarber. The group travelled from Tucson aboard a Southern Pacific railroad car, christened *Camp Pike*. Pierpont, Makley, and Clark so detested the prospect of returning to the Indiana State Penitentiary that they were willing to take their chances in Ohio, where conviction for Sarber's murder would likely result in the death penalty. During the train trip from Tucson to Chicago, an Indianapolis newspaper reporter was allowed to interview Pierpont.

"My conscience doesn't hurt me. I stole from the bankers. They stole from the people. All we did was help raise the insurance rates," Pierpont informed the reporter.

"I suppose I'm what you'd call an abnormal mental case—a case for a psychiatrist. Maybe I am. But, once I was normal. Place your own construction on what I've said," Pierpont declared.

After arriving in Ohio, Mary Kinder was released from jail by court order, after the presiding judge concluded there was not enough evidence to suggest she was an active participant in the Dillinger Gang's crime spree. While still in Tucson, the charges against Bernice Clark, alias *Opal Long*, and Billie Frechette were dropped, and they were released from jail and allowed to leave for Chicago by bus. After witnessing Frechette's reunion with her puppy, a Tucson newspaper reporter wrote: "The Dillinger Gang has come and gone—even to the dog."

The *Arizona Daily Star* headlined: *TUCSON SIGHS AS GANGSTERS LEAVE ARIZONA.* In the accompanying story, reporter Fred Finney offered his benediction: "They brought a lifetime of tension and excitement to the Old Pueblo. Tucson was on the map of the country's front pages, but Tucson also had the tiger by the tail, and the tiger was a sinister animal."

At 6:10 p.m. on Tuesday, January 30, 1934, John Dillinger arrived at Chicago's Midway Airport. On hand to greet the fugitive were 150 Chicago police officers, as well as a host of lawmen from Hammond, Gary, and East Chicago, Indiana. One newspaper reporter remembered that there were "enough policemen to scare hell out of Japan."

A caravan consisting of 13 automobiles and 12 motorcycles was assembled to escort Dillinger to Indiana. Sargent Frank Reynolds, night shift director of the Get Dillinger Squad, escorted the prisoner to a waiting automobile: "You yellow son of a bitch, if anyone tries to stop us, you'll be the first dead man."

Dillinger was placed in the backseat of the car and handcuffed to two Indiana State Police officers. Reynolds, seated in the passenger's side front seat, looked over his shoulder at Dillinger and warned him again: "Just (you) start something."

With flashing lights and screaming sirens, the caravan departed Chicago, bound for the small northwestern Indiana town of Crown Point—population

4,000. Shortly after 7:30 p.m., the group arrived at the Lake County Jail, where the 43-year-old sheriff, Lillian Holley, greeted them. Holley, who had succeeded her murdered husband as sheriff, was wearing a dress, rather than a uniform. In spite of her display of femininity, Holley took her job quite seriously and was a skilled marksman, including the submachine gun.

Dillinger was immediately taken to an isolated cell, while Holley treated the crowd of escorting lawmen to a supper of sandwiches, coffee, and beer. Twenty minutes after his arrival, Dillinger was brought to the sheriff's office, which was crowded by nearly 30 reporters. Dillinger, who was dressed in dark pants, a white open-collared dress shirt, and a dark vest, the latter of which had a pencil sticking out of one pocket and a comb crammed in the other, appeared relaxed. No longer in need of a disguise, Dillinger had recently shaved his mustache.

"Are you glad to see Indiana, again?" a reporter asked.

"About as glad as Indiana is to see me," Dillinger quipped.

"You're credited with having smuggled the guns into the Indiana State Penitentiary just before the big outbreak of September 26th," another reporter challenged him.

"I'm not denying it," Dillinger smiled.

"How did you get them in?" a newsman asked.

"You're too inquisitive," a grinning Dillinger replied.

Robert Estill, the Lake County Prosecutor who had traveled to Arizona to arrange for Dillinger's extradition, found the outlaw amiable, if not charming. When a photographer suggested that Estill put his arm around Dillinger, the prosecutor consented. Adding to what was already an inappropriate sense of familiarity, Dillinger propped his elbow on the prosecutor's shoulder.

The nationally-circulated photograph of Dillinger and Estill was poorly received in many parts of the country. J. Edgar Hoover was enraged that the prosecutor, who was charged with sending Dillinger to the electric chair, would adopt such a friendly posture with the outlaw. Attorney General Homer Cummings characterized Estill's chummy pose as "disgraceful." The New York Times ridiculed the photograph as "a modern version of the return of the prodigal son." The controversial photograph proved to be the beginning of the end for Estill's once-promising political ambitions.

Dillinger thrived in the eye of the media, and during his initial press conference, provided reporters with juicy tidbits, irrespective of their truthfulness. He falsely reported that fellow gang member, John Hamilton, was dead, and accused his attorney in Tucson of taking "everything I had." Dillinger did proudly admit to owning five submachine guns. When a reporter mentioned that today was President Roosevelt's birthday, Dillinger quipped: "You can say that I'm for him all the way and the NRA (National Recovery Act)—particularly for banks."

When a reporter asked Dillinger if he was responsible for sending Matt Leach a copy of *How to be a Detective*, the prisoner (who, in fact, was not the one who mailed the book to the Indiana State Police Captain) smiled: "Well, I was there when it was sent." When asked how long it took to rob a bank, Dillinger never hesitated: "One minute and forty seconds flat."

Dillinger provided the newsmen with a brief biography, including his youthful arrest for mugging and ensuing prison sentence. He explained his reasons for helping the "good fellas" escape from the Indiana State Penitentiary: "There's no denying that I helped fix up the break at Michigan City last September, when 10 men got away. Why not? I stick to my friends, and they stick to me."

The prisoner went on to elaborate about his lone vice: "I don't drink much and I smoke very little. When you rob banks, you can't very well do a lot of drinking. I guess my only bad habit is robbing banks." By the end of the interview, Dillinger had charmed a number of the reporters: "I am not a bad fellow, ladies and gentlemen. I was just an unfortunate boy who started wrong."

Many in the press were amazed by Dillinger's charisma and seemingly care-free attitude. A reporter for the *Chicago Daily News* chronicled his observations: "He had none of the look of the conventional killer—none of the advertised earmarks of the crook...There was no hint of hardness about him, save for the set of his mouth—no evidence save in the alert presence of armed policeman that he had spent his formative years in a penitentiary. He had none of the sneer; the blatant toughness of the criminal...The whole business seemed to be a joke to him..." Another newspaper reporter was equally impressed: "Looking at him for the first time (one) can hardly realize that in a very few days, a month or two at the outside, this cheery, affable young man will probably be a corpse—and a very good one. For, though the finger is definitely on Mr. Dillinger, he still rates in the eyes of calloused observers as the most amazing specimen of his kind ever seen outside of wildly imaginative moving pictures."

Now that his son was a national media sensation, reporters could not wait to track down John Dillinger, Sr. The elder Dillinger shared his mixed emotions: "Look at his mother's picture up there on the wall. Thank God, she's beyond knowing of this disgrace. I don't uphold what John has been doing. No, I don't do that. But, I love him and I would do anything I could to get him a lighter sentence..."

On Monday February 5, 1934, John Dillinger was brought in shackles to the Lake County Criminal Courts Building for a pre-trial hearing. Rumors abounded that John Hamilton, the only gang member not currently behind bars, planned to launch a raid to free Dillinger. More than ever, security was tight in the courtroom.

Nattily attired in a blue shirt, with blue suit pants and a matching vest, Dillinger was accompanied by Joseph Ryan, the attorney his father had hired to represent him. When Ryan asked for additional time to prepare his case, Judge William Murray scheduled Dillinger's arraignment for Friday, February 9th.

Two days later, five eyewitnesses positively identified Dillinger as the man who shot to death Sargent O'Malley in East Chicago. Prosecutor Estill was growing more confident: "There is no doubt about these identifications. They will stand up in court."

Sargent Frank Reynolds of the Get Dillinger Squad interrogated the prisoner, inquiring about the whereabouts of gang member, John Hamilton. Not surprisingly, Dillinger lied, reporting that Hamilton had died after being shot four times, and his body had been dumped in the Calumet River. Reynolds doubted Dillinger's story, and remained convinced that Hamilton would eventually try to break his partner out of jail.

A key figure soon emerged in Dillinger's life—Louis Piquett (his last name rhymed with *ticket*). The charismatic and verbose 49-year-old Piquett, who was short, portly, and sported a gray pompadour, was the son of a blacksmith. A Chicago bartender turned lawyer, Piquett never attended law school, and finally earned a law license after passing the bar exam on his fourth attempt.

During his brief tenure as a prosecutor, Piquett had been indicted, but never convicted, of accepting bribes. The attorney's subsequent private practice catered to criminals, including bootleggers, robbers, abortionists, and murderers. When asked why he chose to represent outlaws, Piquett offered a simple explanation: "They're the only ones who have money these days."

Aware of the enormous potential for publicity, Piquett was eager to represent John Dillinger. Prior to the prisoner's preliminary hearing in Crown Point, Piquett sent Dillinger a business card, and was also present in the courtroom gallery. After the defendant's arraignment was delayed, Piquett was delighted when Dillinger sent a message through the head jailer that he wanted to meet him.

In spite of his outwardly cool demeanor, Dillinger was aware of his precarious position. During his first jailhouse conversation with the flamboyant attorney, Dillinger complained about his current legal representation: "Mr. Piquett, I can't have that fellow Ryan. My God, he's going to send me to the hot seat! He all but convicted me, just in asking for a continuance."

"Ryan's all right," Piquett replied, masking his eagerness to take over Dillinger's case.

"I want you to represent me—how about it?" the prisoner proposed.

"I'll be frank with you. It's going to cost you money," Piquett explained.

Dillinger, certain that money would not be a problem, immediately designated Piquett as his counsel. For the remaining months of Dillinger's life, Piquett and his private investigator, Arthur O'Leary, would not only provide Dillinger with legal services, but also serve as aiders and abettors.

On the morning of February 9th, Piquett made his public debut as Dillinger's newly-hired attorney. At the beginning of the arraignment, Piquett asked the judge to rule on behalf of his client: "The clanging of shackles brings to our minds the dungeons of the Czars, not the flag bedeckled liberty of an American courtroom. I request the court to direct the shackles be removed."

Overriding the objections of Prosecutor Estill, Judge Murray ordered the defendant's handcuffs removed. Piquett also successfully petitioned the judge to order the lawmen not to display their submachine guns in the courtroom. When Piquett requested four months to prepare for the forthcoming trial, Estill objected, recommending 10 days, at most.

"To go on trial in 10 days would be a legal lynching of this poor lad! There is a law against lynching in this state!" Piquett proclaimed.

"There is a law against murder, too!" Estill fired back.

Piquett went on the offensive: "Then why don't you observe it? Why don't you (just) stand Dillinger against a wall and shoot him down...Could it be that a political campaign is approaching? That man's life is at stake."

When Judge Murray asked why he needed extra time, Piquett audaciously replied: "I've got $40,000 in bonds from the Greencastle robbery, and I'm willing to fence it to get my fees." Murray agreed to a one-month continuance, scheduling the opening of the trial for March 12th.

"Your honor, why don't you let Mr. Piquett take Dillinger home with him, and bring him back on the day of the trial? You've given him everything else he has asked for!" an aggrieved Estill vainly protested.

"Atta boy, counsel," Dillinger whispered to Piquett, before he was escorted back to his jail cell.

Estill soon leaked to reporters that Piquett had quietly offered to plead Dillinger guilty, in exchange for a life sentence, rather than the death penalty, but the prosecutor had refused. Piquett immediately denied that any such deal had been proffered.

Rumors continued to circulate that John Hamilton was poised to bust Dillinger out of jail. Sheriff Holley grew concerned enough to petition Judge Murray to transfer the defendant to the Indiana State Penitentiary, pending the start of his trial. The prosecutor, who believed Dillinger was being coddled, agreed with the sheriff.

During a discussion in Judge Murray's chambers, Piquett managed to manipulate the system on behalf of his client. When Sheriff Holley explained to the judge that the state prison was the only place secure enough to house Dillinger, Piquett made his move: "I think that's a very nice jail you have here. What makes you think there's anything wrong with it?"

"There isn't anything wrong with it. It's the strongest jail in Indiana," Holley asserted.

"That's what I thought. But, of course, I don't want to embarrass *Mrs. Holley*. I appreciate that she's a *woman*, and if she's afraid of an escape..."

"I'm not afraid of an escape. I can take care of John Dillinger or any other prisoner," Holley fired back, cutting Piquett off in mid-sentence.

Piquett also informed the judge that he would file a change of venue motion if Dillinger was transferred from the jail in Crown Point to the state penitentiary, fully aware the jurist would be reluctant to pass up the opportunity to officiate such a high profile case. The attorney's intuition proved prescient; Judge Murray ordered Dillinger to remain in the local jail until the end of his trial.

Responsible for overseeing Dillinger's continued incarceration, Sheriff Holley armed members of the local Farmer's Protective Association, establishing a voluntary militia. Floodlights were soon installed outside the jail to keep the surrounding area visible at night. The Governor mobilized the Indiana National Guard's 113th Engineers to help protect the jail. The guardsmen were armed with Browning automatic rifles, capable of firing 120 shots per minute, with a muzzle velocity that could penetrate the bulletproof vests customarily worn by gangsters.

Sheriff Holley's frustrations were just beginning. On February 5th, a Chicago newspaper reported that Holley had sent her twin 19-year-old daughters to Mary Baldwin College in Stanton, Virginia, after they had become the subjects of kidnapping threats by presumed Dillinger supporters. Public disclosure of her daughters' whereabouts infuriated Holley who suggested that the offending newspaper "ought to be blown into Lake Michigan."

"I think the story is heartless and whoever wrote it didn't have much consideration for the heart of a mother!" Holley complained.

Adopting a hard line, the sheriff infuriated Louis Piquett by opening and reading Dillinger's incoming and outgoing mail, as well as prohibiting potential witnesses in his forthcoming trial from visiting the prisoner. Piquett publicly challenged Holley's authority: "Mrs. Holley has, it seems, taken on herself the duties of the Supreme Court."

When the sheriff refused to allow Billie Frechette to visit her boyfriend, Piquett once again clamored for a change of venue. Holley ultimately relented, and allowed Frechette to visit Dillinger on February 16th, but not before she was strip-searched and forced to suffer the indignity of a body cavity search. In a written report, the sheriff was critical of Frechette, claiming that Dillinger's girlfriend was intoxicated, spoke "with a great deal of slang," and wore "cheap" clothing. With Piquett's continued threats to seek a change of venue, Holley eventually expanded Dillinger's visitation list, to include family, friends, and potential trial witnesses.

Near the end of a jailhouse visit from Piquett and his investigator, Art O'Leary, Dillinger passed along a note to be delivered to Frechette. When they later read the missive, Piquett and O'Leary discovered that Dillinger had sketched a floor plan of the Lake County Jail and included instructions on how to use dynamite and blow torches to access the cell block where he was being held. Dillinger intended for Frechette to give the note to fellow gang member, John Hamilton. Amazed by Dillinger's audacity, Piquett and O'Leary nonetheless gave Frechette the written message, without reporting it to the authorities.

Hamilton, who was barely a month into recuperating from the gunshot wounds he received during the East Chicago bank robbery, was not physically able to participate in a jail break. Instead, Hamilton passed along the message to Dillinger crony, Homer Van Meter, who was now living in St. Paul. Before Van Meter had time to formulate an escape plan, Dillinger took the matter into his own hands.

On a rainy Saturday morning, March 3, 1934, 60-year-old janitor, Sam Cahoon, was preparing to clean the cells in the Lake County Jail. Cahoon, who had been employed by the jail for six years, made a procedural error—one that he had never committed before that day. Cahoon carelessly opened the main cell block door separating the day room from the outer walkway leading to the jail offices, *after* the inmates were let outside outside of their cells. That morning, Dillinger and 14 other prisoners were already congregated inside the day room.

Dillinger, who had patiently waited for someone to make even the smallest of mistakes, instantly made his move, shoving what appeared to be a pistol into Cahoon's stomach, then spinning him around and jamming the object into the small of his back. The origin of the dummy weapon, carved from wood into the shape a .38 caliber pistol, remains somewhat of a mystery. Dillinger would later take credit for designing the fake gun, but others believe it might have been smuggled into the jail by a visitor—perhaps Piquett or O'Leary.

"I don't want to kill anyone, so you just do what I tell you," Dillinger instructed Cahoon.

"What's the matter, John? Haven't we been good to you?" Cahoon asked.

"Never mind," Dillinger replied, less interested in sentimentality than the task at hand, "Come on, Sam. We're going places. You're gonna be good, aren't you?"

"I'm always good," an anxious Cahoon replied.

Wilred Bryant, the unarmed jail guard assigned to the cell block, had little opportunity to react, before he was threatened by Herbert Youngblood, a menacing black inmate armed with the wooden handle of a toilet plunger. Bryant knew that Youngblood, who was charged with murder, meant business, and kept quiet.

Dillinger immediately locked Bryant and several jail trusties inside a cell. When Cahoon attempted to join the others, Dillinger stopped him: "No, I got use for you. You're gonna help me out of here."

Dillinger escorted Cahoon to the end of the walkway near the jail's front offices: "How many doors between me and the outside?"

"Four," Cahoon replied.

Dillinger peppered the anxious janitor with questions about the number of officers on duty, the types of weapons stored in the main office, and the locations of building exits. With a pencil, Dillinger drew a rough sketch of the jail's floor plan on a nearby shelf, and ordered Cahoon to verify it for accuracy.

"Who's that?" Dillinger asked, after spying a man moving from one room to another at the end of the corridor.

"Ernest Blunk," Cahoon answered, identifying the deputy sheriff by name.

"Call him back here," Dillinger ordered.

"Blunk, come here a minute," Cahoon obediently called out.

Deputy Sheriff Blunk unsuspectingly strolled down the hall, where he was shocked to see what appeared to be a pistol in Dillinger's hand. Before the image could fully register, Dillinger threatened Blunk in a quiet voice: "Get up here, you son of a bitch or I'll kill you."

"I've got it on you. You haven't got a chance," Dillinger warned the deputy sheriff, before escorting him to the locked cell to join the others.

After returning to their previous position, Dillinger instructed Cahoon to call out the name of jailer, Lew Baker. Cahoon resisted: "I'll be God damned, if I'll help you get out of here. I'm not going any further. Shoot me and be God damned!"

When Youngblood raised his toilet plunger handle to strike Cahoon, Dillinger calmly intervened: "None of that—I'll handle this."

"Contrary to what people say, I'm not a killer. But, I want to get out of here," Dillinger informed Cahoon, before marching the janitor back to the cell block and locking him up.

"They'll kill you before you get half-way down the hall," Cahoon warned him.

"Watch me," Dillinger replied.

After shoving Cahoon inside the cell with the others, Dillinger ordered Deputy Sheriff Blunk to accompany him: "I'm gonna make (it out) this day."

"You can't. They'll kill you," Blunk warned Dillinger, as they walked down the corridor.

"I have everything to gain and nothing to lose. You can either be a dead hero or a live coward," Dillinger explained.

When Blunk said he would not help him escape, Dillinger's tone grew harsh: "You have a wife and baby that you love dearly and would like to see again, haven't you?"

"All right," Blunk relented.

"How many guards are in the office?" Dillinger asked.

"I don't know," Blunk answered.

"Don't lie to me, you son of a bitch, or I'll kill you," Dillinger growled, before instructing him to call out the jailer's name.

When Lew Baker responded to Blunk's summons, Dillinger grabbed him by the shirt and hustled the jailer down the hall and shoved him inside the rapidly-crowding cell: "Get in there and you won't get hurt."

One-by-one, Blunk called jail staffers from the warden's office into the day room, where Dillinger locked them up—in the end, the outlaw managed to take 17 lawmen captive. Only one of the officers, Kenneth "Butch" Houch, tried to wrestle away the "pistol," but was soon overpowered by Dillinger and Youngblood.

Once all the duty officers were locked up, Dillinger retrieved two sub-machine guns from the warden's office. Youngblood was puzzled by the unfamiliar weapon Dillinger handed him: "How does this thing work?" An amused Dillinger gave his fellow inmate a quick tutorial on how to operate a Tommy gun.

Dillinger made one final trip to the cell block, tapping his fake weapon on the bars in front of his captives: "This is how tough your little jail is. I did it all with this little wooden pistol." On his way back through the day room, Dillinger addressed the other inmates: "We've got to get going. We're wasting too much time. Any of you want to come along?" In addition to Youngblood, who stayed with Dillinger, inmates Fred Beaver, Leslie Carron, and James Posey also escaped on that Saturday morning.

Dillinger and Youngblood, accompanied by a single hostage, Deputy Sheriff Blunk, made their way outside to the jail garage, where they discovered none of the police cars had keys inside them; Dillinger realized that the warden had lied to him when he asked about the location of the keys—they were actually kept in his office. The trio quickly made their way next door to the Main Street Garage, where Dillinger asked mechanic, Edwin Saager, to point out the fastest vehicle.

"The V-8 Ford," Saager answered, pointing out Sheriff Holley's newly purchased vehicle.

Dillinger forced the mechanic to join in his escape; Blunk drove the sheriff's car, Dillinger sat in the passenger's side front seat with a submachine gun positioned in his lap, and Youngblood and Saager rode in the back seat. Dillinger instructed Blunk to drive west out of town, sticking mainly to dirt roads. When the anxious deputy sheriff nearly collided with another vehicle, Dillinger issued him a stern warning: "If we hit somebody, I'll plug you first."

"Keep it at forty and watch what you're doing. We don't want a speeding ticket," Dillinger instructed his captive lawman-turned-chauffer.

As Blunk drove outside the city limits of Crown Point, Dillinger hummed *The Last Roundup*, breaking into song at the refrain: "Git along little doggie, git along."

Outside of town, on a muddy road, Blunk lost control of the vehicle and slid into a ditch. The driver and three passengers were forced to exit the Ford and wrap chains around the rear tires to maneuver it out of the muck.

Once they were on the road again, Dillinger regaled his small audience with specific details of how he had whittled the dummy gun from a washboard, attached the handle of a safety razor to serve as the barrel, and painted the fake weapon with black shoe polish.

"You wouldn't think a guy could make a break with pea shooter like this, would you?" Dillinger playfully taunted the deputy sheriff.

Blunk eventually grew comfortable enough to inquire about Dillinger's future plans: "I suppose you'll be going to Lima to bust your men out of jail?"

"They'd do as much for me," Dillinger replied.

When the group had traveled far enough from Crown Point, such that he no longer saw telephone poles dotting the roadside, Dillinger ordered Blunk to stop: "I'd probably get a better start if I shot you two up, right here. But, I never killed nobody (sic), especially that cop, O'Malley, and I don't want to start now. You guys do whatever you have to do, but I can tell you that's the last jail I'll ever be in."

Dillinger offered Blunk and Saager each four dollars from the money he had earlier stolen from the warden and jail guards: "This'll get you to town. It's not much, but it's all I can spare." The mechanic readily accepted the money, but Blunk stubbornly refused. After shaking both their hands, a grinning Dillinger hopped behind the wheel: "Maybe I can remember you at Christmas time." Instructing Youngblood to lie down on the back floorboard out of sight, Dillinger drove away, bound for Chicago.

In Crown Point, Sheriff Holley, who had not been inside the building when Dillinger escaped, was enraged. Describing the jail break as "too ridiculous for words," she burst into tears: "If I ever see John Dillinger, I'll shoot him through the head with my own gun!"

By late Saturday afternoon, Dillinger's dramatic escape was being broadcast nationwide over radio air waves. The next day, newspaper readers learned that Dillinger had ingenuously employed a wooden gun to bluff the jail staff, and then stole the sheriff's car. John Dillinger, Sr. learned the news from the editor of the *Mooresville News*: "What? Escape how? Is he all right?" After hearing the details of his son's jail break, the elder Dillinger offered a cautious assessment: "Well, it makes a fellow feel a little better, but of course, they may catch him..."

Prosecutor Estill and Sheriff Holley were widely ridiculed. At Bureau Headquarters in Washington D.C, J. Edgar Hoover was apoplectic: "It's a damnable outrage. Someone is either guilty of nonfeasance or malfeasance. Either negligence or corruption must be at the bottom of this." Chicago Police Department Captain, John Stege, who had already disbanded the Get Dillinger Squad, could not believe what he was hearing: "How in the name of common sense could a prisoner go through six barred doors to freedom?"

"What's the use of arresting Dillinger if we can't keep him in jail? I'm sending squads all over the city to nab him, if he tries to cross the Indiana border. But, even if we do get him, it will probably be the same thing over again. I'm discouraged," Stege lamented.

The press immediately began referring to the town where Dillinger escaped as *Clown Point*. Area Republicans suggested Sheriff Holley's Democratic Party should replace the donkey with the *wooden gun* as its symbol. Sexists blamed the escape on the *female sheriff*. An embarrassed Holley vowed to never speak again about the incident—a lengthy silence that she maintained until her death in 1994, at the age of 103.

Robert Estill's cozy photograph with John Dillinger was the death knell for his political career. Not only were his aspirations of running for Governor thwarted, but it also cost him his re-election bid as Lake County's Prosecutor.

Some Americans were delighted to hear about Dillinger's escape, and applauded the resourcefulness of their modern day Robin Hood. The Governors of Indiana and Illinois were besieged with requests to pardon Dillinger. A Hoosier State farmer summed up the sentiments of many of his fellow citizens: "As tough as times are, John's doing the country a favor by getting the money of the banks and back into circulation."

In Lima, Ohio, where Dillinger gang members, Harry Pierpont, Russell Clark, and Charles Makley, were incarcerated pending trial, security was heightened; local and state law enforcement officials were certain Dillinger would attempt to bust his partners out of jail. The National Guardsmen already assigned to the Lima area were soon augmented with reinforcements.

Dillinger's attorney, Louis Piquett, and his investigator Art O'Leary, both of whom had advance knowledge of their client's intent to break out of jail, were nonetheless amazed by his audacity. From his office in Chicago, Piquett followed the breaking news over the radio. After Billie Frechette arrived,

Piquett telephoned Warden Baker in Crown Point for official confirmation. When Baker acknowledged Dillinger's escape, Billie squealed with joy. Meyer Bogue, the man who had facilitated the initial meeting between Piquett and Dillinger, arrived at the lawyer's office with the ingredients necessary to make Gin Rickey cocktails. The impromptu party ended with Frechette passed out drunk on Piquett's office couch.

Dillinger drove directly to Chicago, arriving in the middle of the afternoon on Saturday, and immediately encountered trouble. An off-duty police officer, Lorimer Hyde, spotted a black Ford with Indiana license plates, matching the description of Sheriff Holley's stolen vehicle. Hyde trailed the vehicle to the corner of Broadway and Belmont Avenue, and watched as the driver parked by the curb and exited the vehicle. The officer climbed out of his car, which was parked 100 feet behind the stolen Ford, with his pistol drawn. When Dillinger spotted the armed man, he jumped back into his stolen automobile and sped away. Sheriff Holley's abandoned vehicle was found two days later in the suburbs of Chicago.

At 3:00 that same afternoon, the telephone rang in Piquett's office. Investigator O'Leary quickly answered.

"Where will I go?" Dillinger asked.

"Go to 434 Wellington Avenue. Piquett will be waiting," O'Leary replied.

While Youngblood, who was now armed with both submachine guns, remained out of sight on the backseat floorboard, Dillinger drove to the address supplied by O'Leary. Outside the apartment building, he found Piquett waiting.

"Hi ya, counsel," Dillinger smiled.

The two men soon stepped inside the building's lobby, where Billie Frechette was waiting. After Dillinger and his girlfriend embraced, the couple departed for her half-sister's apartment on 3512 North Halstead Street. Piquett gave the fugitive the money in his pocket ($300) to help with Dillinger's immediate living expenses. En-route to his new hide-out, Dillinger stopped to allow Youngblood to board a street car, and continue with his own escape plans. After thanking him for his assistance, Dillinger gave his fellow escapee $100; two weeks later, Youngblood was shot and killed by law enforcement officials in Michigan.

A day after settling into Frances "Patsy" Frechette's apartment, Dillinger spoke with John Hamilton. Largely without a gang, Dillinger was receptive to Hamilton's plans to hook-up with Baby Face Nelson in St. Paul. That same night, Nelson gang member, Tommy Carroll, arrived in Chicago. Dillinger and Frechette ducked out through a side entrance to the apartment building, carrying suitcases and concealing Tommy guns beneath their overcoats. Carroll drove them to St. Paul, where Dillinger was set to begin the next and final phase of his infamous career.

Since his last visit with John Dillinger, Baby Face Nelson had made another visit to Hymie Lebman's gun shop to purchase additional weapons. While in San Antonio, Nelson purchased Dillinger one of the gunsmith's modified .38 caliber machine gun pistols.

In early 1934, Nelson had once again travelled to the west coast. While in California, Nelson's wife was hospitalized for nearly two weeks under the alias of *Helen Williams*; the specifics of her illness were unknown, but possibly related to complications from a recent miscarriage. After the doctors recommended that she rest for at least a month after discharge, the couple drove to Reno.

While in Nevada, Nelson learned that Dillinger and his fellow gang members had been arrested in Tucson. Nelson was bemused, questioning how "a bunch of hick cops in a two-horse town" had managed to capture all four men, without firing a shot.

"The idiots must've been wearing name tags," Nelson quipped.

Nelson returned to St. Paul on February 26th, itching to rob more banks. Within a week, Dillinger, fresh from his daring jail break, also arrived in St. Paul. The same night Dillinger hit town, Nelson and his fellow gang member, John Paul Chase, became involved in a traffic altercation that rapidly escalated into violence.

Thirty-five-year-old paint salesman, Theodore Kidder, was driving home from a birthday party with his wife and mother when Nelson suddenly cut in front of him. In retaliation, Kidder impulsively sped up and gave the offending driver a dose of his own medicine. An enraged Nelson pulled back even with Kidder's car and tried to force him against the curb. Kidder managed to pull ahead, but Nelson stayed hot on his tail. To avoid a confrontation at his home, the paint salesman drove to a drug store, where he planned to telephone the police. When he exited his vehicle, three gunshots, likely fired by Nelson, sounded in the still night air. Two of the bullets struck Kidder, mortally wounding him.

"You've killed him!" Kidder's wife screamed.

"Keep your damned mouth shut or I'll let you have it, too!" the shooter angrily replied, before driving away.

Nelson had once again proven that he was impulsive and prone to violence. The 24-year-old bank robber, however, was savvy enough to realize an association with John Dillinger would not only enhance his reputation, but also fatten his wallet.

While the melding of two such strong personalities would prove challenging, the country was about to witness the birth of the *Second Dillinger Gang*.

CHAPTER TEN

The Second Dillinger Gang

Just a day and a half after his daring escape from the Crown Point jail, John Dillinger settled into an apartment with Billie Frechette at 3252 South Girard Avenue in St. Paul's sister city of Minneapolis. The couple rented a $45-per-month flat using the aliases of *Mr. and Mrs. Olson*. John Hamilton and his new girlfriend, Pat Cherrington, shared the residence with them. Hamilton and Cherrington had struck up a romance while she was nursing him after his shooting.

Fellow Indiana State Penitentiary alum, Homer Van Meter, employing the alias *John L. Ober*, was living with his girlfriend, Marie Conforti, in an apartment near Dillinger and Frechette. On March 5th, Van Meter informed Dillinger that Baby Face Nelson and another ex-convict, Eugene "Eddie" Green, were planning to rob a bank in Sioux Falls, South Dakota the following day, and had invited both of them to join in the heist. Thus began the brief but tumultuous association between Dillinger and Nelson

In spite of the differences in their personalities, Dillinger and Nelson shared certain commonalities. Both came from working-class and close knit families. They shared obsessions with fast cars, firearms, and bank robberies. Dillinger, however, was not as short-tempered, impetuous, and trigger-happy as Nelson. Slow to anger, Dillinger kept a mental list of people that he wanted to kill; including certain lawmen and former associates turned informants, but he never put those threats into action. Nelson, on the other hand, was fully capable of suddenly and impulsively taking his rage out on others.

On Tuesday, March 6, 1934, Dillinger, Nelson, Homer Van Meter, John Hamilton, Eddie Green, and Tommy Carroll robbed the Security National Bank & Trust in Sioux Falls, South Dakota. At 10:00 a.m. on a chilly, 35-degree day, the six men, all dressed in overcoats, arrived in Sioux Falls in a green Packard sedan.

Hamilton remained behind the wheel of the get-away car, while Carroll manned the tiger position on the sidewalk, adjacent to the front door. Dillinger, Nelson, Van Meter, Green, and Carroll entered the lobby, where they encountered uniformed police officer, Peter Duffy, who happened to be in the bank conducting personal business. Green and Van Meter immediately disarmed the unsuspecting lawman. An impetuous Nelson made his presence immediately known, withdrawing a submachine gun from his overcoat: "This is a hold-up! Everyone on the floor!" Among the 10 to 15 customers and employees inside the building, an assistant cashier made the mistake of staring at Nelson, who immediately took offense: "Get your head down, or I'll blow you to hell!"

At first, the confusion in the bank's lobby was comedic. Following the lessons taught to him by Eddie Bentz, Nelson ordered the customers and employees to lie down on the floor. Green and Van Meter, however, soon instructed them to face the wall with their arms raised. When Nelson saw a line of people standing near the front entrance, he exploded, instructing them to "get those arms down," and to "get back" from the window. Nelson soon took a more commanding position atop a marble-covered counter, where he walked back and forth, brandishing his Tommy gun: "If any of you wants to get killed, just make some move!"

Amidst the confusion, bank clerk Don Lovejoy managed to push the alarm button, which loudly sounded inside the building. Seemingly unfazed by the ringing bells, Dillinger and Van Meter began bagging up cash from the tellers' cages. Nelson, however, exploded in rage: "I'd like to know who set that alarm off! Who did it? Who?"

"If you want to get killed, just make some move!" Nelson repeated, "If you want to get killed, just make some move!"

Officer Homer Powers was the first lawman to arrive at the bank in response to the alarm, where he was promptly greeted by Carroll's submachine gun, disarmed, and forced to put his hands above his head. Police Chief M.

W. Parsons and a detective arrived next, and were also disarmed by Carroll. Within minutes, a small crowd had gathered on the sidewalk in front of the bank, unnerving Carroll, who fired a burst of machine gun fire into the air: "Get back there or I'll blow the daylights out of you!"

When motorcycle policeman, Hale Keith, arrived on the scene, an agitated Nelson fired his submachine gun at him through the bank's plate glass front window. Struck by four .45 caliber slugs in the stomach, elbow, wrist and thigh, Keith immediately fell to the pavement; though seriously wounded and in need of emergency surgery, Keith survived and eventually recovered.

"I got one! I got one!" Nelson shouted.

Alerted to the escalating commotion, bank president, China R. Clarke, soon exited his office, where he was immediately confronted by Dillinger: "You got the combination to the safe?" When Clarke answered no, Dillinger swiftly kicked him in the rear end: "Then get me someone who does!"

Clarke summoned teller, Robert Dargen, who was able to open the safe. Dillinger and Van Meter hurriedly stole $13,000 from the vault. When he spied a second safe, Dillinger ordered Dargen to open it. The teller told him the vault was set to a time lock and could not be opened. Unconvinced, Dillinger ordered Clarke to try anyway, but his efforts proved unsuccessful.

While Dillinger and Van Meter filled their sacks with cash, Gus J. Moen, a customer who had been attending to business on the second floor of the building, strolled into the lobby, unaware that a robbery was in progress. Apparently lost in thought, Moen ignored Nelson's order to halt. The outlaw immediately unleashed a burst of machine gun fire just above Moen's head, raining shards of glass on him, and forcing him to hit the floor.

Once Dillinger and Van Meter had gathered up the available cash, the gang members forced the bank manager and four tellers to lead the way out the front door toward their get-away car. The five hostages were forced to mount the sedan's twin running boards. As the car eased away from the curb, Nelson blasted what was left of the bank's front window with his Tommy gun. Before the get-away vehicle could pick up speed, Patrolman Harley Chrisman managed to fire a shot from his hunting rifle, piercing the Packard's radiator.

The engine-damaged vehicle, overloaded with hostages on the running boards, crept out of town at only 25 miles per hour. While holding onto her arm and steadying a frightened female hostage, one of the bandits tried to reassure her: "Don't be afraid, we don't intend to harm you."

The disabled get-away car managed to get only a few miles out of town before stalling. The fleeing bandits quickly flagged down a passing car, driven by a local farmer, Alfred Muesch. After releasing the hostages, the gang members transferred their possessions, including spare gas cans, into Muesch's Dodge and sped away.

Sheriff Melvin L. Sells, accompanied by three deputies, briefly caught up with the slow-moving bank robbers. Shots were exchanged between the two vehicles, before the outgunned lawmen gave up the chase. Two airplanes also pursued the gang, but lost them after the bandits ditched the stolen Dodge and boarded a black Lincoln they had hidden along their pre-determined escape route.

The witnesses who were questioned by the authorities were inconsistent in their descriptions of the bandits. Only Tommy Carroll was positively identified from the mug shot photographs shown to the customers and bank employees. One witness, however, clearly remembered the robber with the chubby, clean-shaven face, who "chirped with joy" when he shot the motorcycle cop with his machine gun.

The bank robbers made away with $49,000 from the bank in Sioux Falls. Dillinger sorely needed his share of the stolen money to pay his own attorney, help reimburse the attorneys representing the imprisoned Makley, Pierpont, and Clark, and replenish his pocket cash. As the self-appointed leader of the gang, Nelson insisted upon being the one to divide the cash into equal shares. Dillinger was seemingly disinterested in the perceived hierarchy of the gang's leadership, and just wanted his cut of the stolen money.

Indiana State Police Captain, Matt Leach, managed to remain a few steps behind Dillinger, as evidenced by his erroneous assessment of the recent bank robbery: "Dillinger hasn't had time for that job, or I'm badly fooled. That job sounds to me like the work of a Minneapolis gang...If the Sioux Falls job had been pulled next week, I might have suspected Dillinger." The press and the general public, however, were certain Dillinger had orchestrated yet another bank heist. Famed humorist, Will Rogers, chimed in, poking fun at the authorities' difficulty in keeping up with Dillinger: "They had him surrounded in Chicago, but he robbed a bank in Sioux Falls that day. So they wuz right on his trail, just three states behind!" Whether Matt Leach believed it or not, and irrespective of Baby Face Nelson's belief that he was the top dog, what was now known as the *Second Dillinger Gang* was in business.

While the pursuit of John Dillinger would ultimately occupy one of the most prominent places in the Bureau's storied history, J. Edgar Hoover was only reluctantly led into the manhunt. After Dillinger's jail bust in Lima, the Governor and Attorney General of Indiana requested Bureau assistance. In response, Hoover instructed the Chicago, Detroit, and Cincinnati field offices to provide "all available assistance," which amounted to little more than conducting a few interviews and attending a handful of conferences with state and local law enforcement agencies.

Even after Dillinger staged his dramatic jail break in Crown Point, Hoover showed little immediate interest in what he believed was "not a federal case," even though the Bureau was legally empowered to enter the fray once federal laws had been broken. When Dillinger crossed state lines in Sheriff Holley's car, he violated the Federal Motor Vehicle Act (also known as the Dyer Act), which prohibited interstate automobile theft.

When Dillinger committed a bank robbery, just *two days* after escaping from jail, Hoover finally took notice. On March 7, 1934, the day after the Sioux Falls bank heist, Hoover sent a wire to all Special Agents in Charge (SACs) of field offices throughout the country, directing them to "give preferred and immediate attention" to Dillinger.

While he cited Dillinger's violation of the Dyer Act as the impetus for greater involvement by the Bureau, Hoover had other motives. By now, the Dillinger case was generating nationwide coverage, and Hoover could no longer pass up the opportunity for the Bureau to step into the limelight. Ever ambitious, Hoover understood the challenge—this was an opportunity to establish the Bureau as a superior crime-fighting agency and a chance to craft his own enduring legacy. In short order, the Bureau would designate Dillinger as America's first ever *Public Enemy Number One*.

Since Dillinger was believed to be hiding out in the Chicago area, the onus of responsibility was placed on Windy City's SAC—Melvin Horace Purvis, Jr. Twenty-nine years old and standing only five-feet, seven-inches-tall, Purvis' youthful face and high-pitched voice betrayed his youth. A law school graduate from South Carolina, Purvis had joined the Bureau in 1926 and rapidly ascended its ranks.

Hoover, who rarely played favorites among Bureau agents, took an immediate shine to Purvis, likening him to "a slender, blond-haired, brown-eyed" movie star. After promoting Purvis to the SAC of the Chicago office, Hoover privately proclaimed: "All power to the Clark Gable of the service." When Purvis address him as *Mister Hoover*, the Bureau Director went so far as to instruct him to drop the title of *Mister*.

A product of southern privilege, Purvis employed a black manservant to chauffeur him about town in his Pierce Arrow. Impeccably dressed in double-breasted suits, Purvis was so particular about his appearance that he changed shirts up to three times per day. The rakish tilt of the young Bureau agent's hat complemented his cockiness; by appearance and personality, Purvis tended to lure women and often repel other men.

By the early 1930's, Melvin Purvis was Hoover's golden boy—some likened it to a father and son relationship, while those who questioned the Director's sexual orientation suspected something more. The pair regularly exchanged gifts, and Hoover's letters to Purvis lacked the Director's typical stiff formality, often beginning with "Dear Melvin" or "Dear Mel," and closing with "Affectionately, Jayee."

Once John Dillinger became Purvis's top priority, he reassigned five Bureau agents to devote their efforts to the case. Agents travelled to Crown Point, where they interviewed witnesses to Dillinger's jail break, and to the Indiana State Penitentiary to interrogate former gang member, Ed Shouse. The only substantial information gleaned from those interviews was Shouse's disclosure that Dillinger's girlfriend was named Billie Frechette. All the while, Dillinger hysteria abounded, and multiple false sightings of the fugitive sent Bureau agents on wild goose chases.

When Dillinger gang members, Harry Pierpont, Charles Makley, and Russell Clark were tried in March of 1934, rumors abounded that Dillinger was going to swoop into town and set them free. Ohio Governor, George White, activated the National Guard to patrol the streets of Lima, and the Allen County Courthouse was ringed with barbed wire and sandbags. Ten machine gun nests were erected in the perimeter; three contained live .30

caliber guns and the remaining seven held wooden dummy guns. Fearing that Dillinger might kidnap White and ransom him in exchange for Pierpont, Makley, and Clark, two National Guard squads were assigned to protect the Ohio Governor's Mansion.

Under heavy guard, Ed Shouse was transported from the Indiana State Prison to testify in each of the three trials, recounting the course of events leading to the murder of Sheriff Jess Sarber. Ernest Boykin, the Allen County Prosecutor, aggressively went after the defendants, accusing Pierpont of stealing $300,000 from banks since he escaped from prison.

"I wish I had," Pierpont responded, "Well, at least if I did, I'm not like some bank robbers—I didn't get myself elected president of the bank first."

When the courtroom erupted in laughter, Boykin was decidedly unamused: "That's the kind of man you are, isn't it?"

"Yes, I'm not the kind of man you are—robbing widows and orphans. You'd probably be like me, if you had the nerve," Pierpont fired back.

Ed Shouse testified that Pierpont was directly responsible for Sheriff Sarber's murder, which weighed heavily in the defendant's ultimate conviction. Even after Shouse refused to implicate Makley in the murder, the jury still found him guilty. Russell Clark's trial was the last of the three. Flip-flopping, yet again, Shouse testified that Clark had a direct hand in Sarber's death.

While the jury was deliberating Clark's fate, Pierpont and Makley were brought into the courtroom for sentencing. Among those escorting Pierpont was Don Sarber, who had succeeded his father as sheriff. Judge Emmett Everett sentenced Pierpont and Makley to death, fixing their date with the electric chair on Friday July 13, 1934. While also finding Clark guilty, the jury recommended mercy, and Judge Everett sentenced him to life imprisonment.

As he was being led from the courtroom to his jail cell, Pierpont's cool, sociopathic demeanor appeared shaken: "This is the first time I've been nervous in a long time." Later that same day, Pierpont told Makley: "I thought the judge was going to cry, when he sentenced me."

"I guess it's that unlucky thirteen," Pierpont remarked, referring to their scheduled execution date.

"We all have to die sometime," Makley mused.

On Tuesday March 13, 1934, amidst an icy wind and snow flurries, Dillinger, Nelson, Carroll, Hamilton, Van Metter, Chase, and Green rendezvoused at an abandoned quarry just south of Mason City, Iowa. Van Meter and Green had spent the previous few days lodging at the Mason City YMCA, casing the First National Bank.

After a brief conference, the gang members, who had arrived in two vehicles, all boarded a navy blue Buick that had been stolen in Chicago. After driving into Mason City, the wheelman parked the get-away vehicle adjacent to the seven-story, red brick building that housed the First National Bank.

While Mason City was a small town of 25,000 inhabitants, the First National Bank held nearly $250,000 in cash deposits. Dillinger was eager to undertake this high stake's robbery, believing his share of the stolen money would finance an escape to Mexico or South America, where he could "live like a king."

At 2:20 p.m., the gang members, with the exception of John Paul Chase, who remained behind the wheel of the Buick, approached the bank building. Nelson assumed the position of rear tiger in the alleyway behind the bank, while the tiger, Carroll, stood on the sidewalk, next to the front entrance. Dillinger, Van Meter, Hamilton, and Green entered the bank through the front door.

Inside the lobby, the bandits may not have spied the guard stationed inside a steel cage, protected by bullet proof glass with rifle and tear gas ports, elevated 15 feet above the floor, and attached to the building's front wall. Dillinger, who was dressed in a gray suit and overcoat, with a matching fedora, took his position just inside the door, armed with a submachine gun. Van Meter, Green, and Hamilton were assigned the responsibility of emptying the cash drawers and vault.

One of the gang members immediately caught the attention of over 20 customers and employees inside the bank, by firing a burst of machine gun fire into the ceiling. A witness vividly recalled the robbers' dramatic entrance: "I swear they were all doped up on something. Their faces were purple and their eyes were blazing. They never stopped screaming. I had never seen anything like it."

"Down! Down! Everybody on the floor!" Green shouted.

When the bank's president, Willis Bagley, saw Van Meter, armed with a Tommy gun and heading in his direction, he ran into his office and slammed the door shut. As Bagley dove for cover behind his desk, Van Meter splintered the wooden door with machine gun fire. One of the bullets grazed Bagley's chest, but did not seriously wound him. Perhaps thinking he had killed or seriously wounded the bank president, Van Meter made no further efforts to pursue him, and proceeded with the task at hand.

Thirty-three-year-old Tom Walters was the guard assigned to duty inside the raised cage. In the event of a robbery, Walters had been instructed to fire six tear gas canisters into the lobby, such that the noxious fumes would force the bandits to quickly exit the building. The first canister Walters fired through the gun port struck Green in the back, before ricocheting to the floor and emitting its foul smoke.

"Where's the son of bitch who shot me?" and enraged Green shouted, before looking up, "Get that guy with the gas!"

Green and Van Meter immediately opened fire on the bulletproof glass-enclosed cage with their Tommy guns. The burst of machine gun fire splintered the glass, which failed to give way. One bullet managed to pass through the tiny gun port, grazing Walters' chin and right ear. When the bullets failed to penetrate the cage's protective barrier, Green grew more enraged: "Get that son of a bitch with the tear gas!"

Walters' plans went awry when he tried to reload; the now-empty tear gas shell was wedged in the barrel. He vainly attempted to remove the empty shell with his pocket knife, but was forced to give up when the blade broke. Discarding the tear gas gun, Walters grabbed a Winchester rifle, but soon found himself in a helpless position: "Hamilton called me every obscenity in the book, and dared me to shoot. But, I couldn't, because I would've plugged half the people in the lobby."

Bank employee, Tom Barclay, who was working on the mezzanine level, added to the chaos when he tossed a tear gas canister into the lobby. Panicked customers immediately began kicking the smoking canister back and forth across the floor.

After the gas clouds wafted to the mezzanine level, a female switchboard operator crawled to the nearest window and opened it. In the alleyway below, she spied a man dressed in an overcoat: "Hey you! Don't you know the bank is being robbed? Get some help!"

Baby Face Nelson looked up: "Are you telling me, lady?"

Amidst the confusion and gas fumes, Hamilton filled a cloth bag with cash from the tellers' cages. He then ordered the assistant bank cashier, Harry Fisher, to open the vault. Fisher, though frightened, was in no hurry to comply with Hamilton's order, fully aware that the vault held more than $200,000 in cash and securities. When Fisher tarried, Hamilton kicked him squarely in the rear end.

After unlocking the barred door leading to the vault, Fisher propped it open with a bag of pennies. When a greedy Hamilton snatched up the bag of coins, the door shut and locked, leaving the robber and bank employee separated by bars. Complaining that his eyes were watering from the tear gas, Fisher tried to stall: "I don't know whether I can see to work the combination."

"You'd better open it Goddamn quick!" Hamilton threatened.

Taking his time, Fisher eventually opened the vault, but told Hamilton that he could not open the barred door that separated the two men. Hamilton, apparently forgetting that Fisher still had the keys to the door, ordered the assistant cashier to retrieve money from the vault and pass it to him through the bars. A quick-thinking Fisher responded by handing over bags that contained mostly one-dollar bills.

"If you don't hurry up, I'm going to shoot you!" Hamilton warned Fisher.

A small crowd had gathered outside the bank, when Van Meter exited the front door holding 10 hostages at gunpoint. Dillinger, who had made a brief foray outside, stepped back inside the building to gauge Hamilton's progress.

"Give me three more minutes!" Hamilton shouted.

Because of Fisher's delaying tactics, the robbers managed to steal only $50,000 of the First National Bank's $250,000 in deposits. When it was time to go, Dillinger rounded up another half-dozen hostages. As the group exited the front door, Dillinger, who had a submachine gun in one hand and an automatic pistol in the other, instructed the hostages: "Come on, get up around me." When some of the hostages failed to keep their arms raised, Dillinger barked: "Can't you get your hands up any higher than that?"

Van Meter quickly entered a neighboring shoe store and forced another half-dozen people to join the existing group of hostages. An impetuous Nelson soon complicated matters when he fired a burst from his Tommy gun at an approaching automobile, forcing the frightened driver to immediately reverse course and speed away. Manically laughing, Nelson unleashed another rapid-fire volley at a cluster of parked cars and the second floor windows of a nearby hardware store.

When R. L. James, the local school board secretary, unaware that a robbery was in progress, casually approached the bank, Nelson shot him the leg. After James fell to the sidewalk clutching his wounded lower extremity, Nelson berated him: "I thought you were a cop, you son of a bitch!"

"I'm not a cop," the wounded man moaned.

Dillinger hustled down the sidewalk toward the sounds of gunshots, and discovered Nelson standing over the wounded James: "What the hell did you do that for?"

"I thought he was cop!" Nelson snapped.

After Dillinger returned to reposition himself behind the hostages near the front door of the bank, a local judge, John C. Shipley, leaned out his second-floor office window, located directly above the crowd on the sidewalk. Armed with a vintage, long-barreled revolver, Shipley took direct aim at Dillinger and fired. Reacting to the bullet that struck him in the right shoulder, an enraged Dillinger spun around, looked up, and fired a submachine burst at the open window. Shipley immediately hit the floor and avoided being wounded.

Dillinger then spied police officer, James Buchanan, running across the town square toward the bank. When Dillinger aimed his weapon at the lawman, Buchanan immediately took cover behind a stone Civil War marker.

"Come out from behind there, and fight like a man!" Dillinger shouted.

"Get away from that crowd, and I will!" Buchanan replied.

As the gang members hustled their human shield of hostages toward the get-away car, Judge Shipley peeked over the windowsill and caught sight of Hamilton carrying an armful of cash-filled sacks. Taking careful aim with his revolver, Shipley shot Hamilton in the shoulder, who somehow managed to keep his feet, hold onto the bags, and stumble into the get-away vehicle.

The hostages were haphazardly positioned on both running boards, as well as the front and rear bumpers; a few of the women were hurriedly crammed in the backseat. The hostages included bank employees, the white-coated owner of the Mulcahy Prescription Store, and a local scoutmaster. On the back bumper, assistant bank cashier, Ralph Wiley, who Nelson addressed as a "ball-headed son of bitch," found a handhold on the window frame where the bandits had removed the rear windshield.

With nearly two dozen people, either inside the vehicle or mounted on the bumpers and running boards, the overloaded get-away car crept away from the bank at no more than 20 miles per hour. When the car was about to pass Kirk Apartments on the edge of town, elderly hostage, Minnie Piehm, who was clinging to the passenger's side running board, loudly announced: "Let me out! This is where I live." Remarkably, Carroll stopped the vehicle long enough for Piehm to scurry away. When Ralph Wiley tried to slip away with Piehm, one of the gang members halted him: "Get back on, you!"

Amid the chill wind and snow flurries, the slow-moving get-away car exited town, turning south on Highway 18. Two police cars soon caught up with the bandits, one of which was manned by Police Chief E. J. Patton. After spotting the pursuing vehicles, Nelson leaned out of the passenger's side front window and peppered the lawmen with shots from his automatic rifle.

Just outside the city limits, Carroll stopped the car, allowing Nelson to hop outside and continue firing at the police cruisers. Outgunned, the lawmen halted a safe distance behind. After the shooting stopped, Nelson hurriedly spread handfuls of roofing nails on the road. Dillinger was alarmed by Nelson's carelessness: "You're getting tacks under our own car!"

"Let's fight it out with them, here!" Nelson eagerly proposed.

"Get in!" Dillinger shouted to Nelson, unwilling to participate in a shoot-out, unless absolutely necessary.

Another mile further out of town, Carroll turned south on a dirt road. As the car crept way from the scene of the crime, the gang members scarfed down a bag of sandwiches that one of the hostages was about to deliver to a customer, before he stumbled into the middle of a bank robbery. As the get-away vehicle crossed Highway 106, a female hostage complained that she was feeling car sick.

"For God's sake, let her out," a disgusted Dillinger ordered.

"You phone the law. Tell them if they don't stop following us, we're going to kill everyone in this car! That's some law you got!" Nelson instructed the departing hostage.

Clinging to one of the running boards, another female hostage began crying: "I don't want to die this way!" Dillinger, either annoyed or sympathetic to her plea, allowed the woman to leave.

For a time, the twin police cruisers slowly pursued the bank robbers, but eventually gave up the chase. By now, Dillinger was exasperated by how poorly the robbery had gone. When bank teller, Emmet Ryan, offered one of the female hostages his coat, Dillinger glared at him—"the coldest eyes you ever saw—cold eyes and white skin."

Carroll followed a circuitous escape route—traveling south, then east, before turning south again. When the Buick crossed over Highway 65, 45 minutes had passed since the robbery, but the bandits were only three miles distant from Mason City. After stopping yet again, Nelson ordered the hostages from the vehicle. When Emmet Ryan held his gaze too long, Nelson exploded: "Don't look at me, you son of a bitch!"

"Quit gawking at me, you asshole!" Dillinger snapped at another one.

At this point, all but two of the hostages, both women, were set free. When the robbers reached the rock quarry, where their second vehicle lay in waiting, the two women were finally released. It had been a prolonged and harrowing ride for the hostages, who were no doubt traumatized by their unexpected introduction to the Second Dillinger Gang; one of them later contrasted the personalities of the two outlaws who appeared to be in charge of the operation: "The big fellow didn't seem so bad. That little bird was the mean one."

Less crowded in two vehicles, the bank robbers drove north, pausing on one occasion to bandage Dillinger and Hamilton's shoulder wounds. By nightfall, the gang was back in St. Paul. Dr. Nels G. Mortensen, a physician who catered to those requiring discreet medical care, dressed both men's wounds, neither of which proved serious.

After dividing the disappointingly small take from the Mason City bank, the gang members went their separate ways. Aware that it would take Dillinger and Hamilton a period of time to heal from their bullet wounds, Nelson, his wife, son, and mother, accompanied by John Paul Chase, drove west, first stopping in Reno, before moving on to San Francisco.

After driving to Chicago with Billie Frechette, Dillinger met with Art O'Leary and gave him $1,000 for Louis Piquett's attorney's fees, along with $1,000 to be forwarded to Harry Pierpont's parents. Billie then flew from Chicago to Indianapolis, where she was greeted by members of Dillinger's family. At the farmhouse in Mooresville, Billie gave John, Sr. several bundles of cash and the wooden pistol his son had used to escape from the jail in Crown Point, as well as a letter Dillinger had written his sister, Audrey. In the missive, Dillinger indicated that he wanted Audrey's husband, Emmett, to have the wooden gun along with the accompanying letter of authenticity, and bragged about his escape: "I see that Deputy Blunk says I had a real forty-five. That's just a lot of hooey to cover up, because they don't like to admit that I locked eight deputys (sic) and a dozen trustys (sic) up with my wooden gun before I got my hands on the two machine guns, and you should have seen their faces. Ha! Ha! Ha!"

Blunk, the deputy sheriff Dillinger referenced in his letter, while innocent of any wrong-doing, was deeply embarrassed after being hoodwinked by Dillinger. Amidst the post-escape finger pointing and search for scapegoats in Crown Point, both Blunk and janitor, Sam Cahoon, were wrongfully indicted for complicity in Dillinger's jail break.

Dillinger and Billie soon took up residence at the Lincoln Court Apartments on South Lexington Avenue in St. Paul's upscale Hill Section, employing the aliases of *Mr. and Mrs. Carl T. Hellman.* John Hamilton and Pat Cherrington also moved into the one-bedroom apartment, sleeping on the living room couch.

On March 27th, Dillinger employed the *Hellman* alias to secure a Minnesota driver's license. When applying for the license, the fugitive lied about his physical characteristics, identifying his hair color as red and listing his weight at a more robust 170 pounds.

During his period of rest and recuperation, Dillinger, accompanied by Frechette, enjoyed attending movies. On one such occasion, the couple watched the newsreel shown before the main feature, which included an interview with John Dillinger, Sr.: "John isn't a bad boy. They're trying to make a mountain out of a molehill." Dillinger laughed so loudly at his father's comments that Billie feared the other patrons might recognize him.

On March 30th, Dillinger went shopping for a new automobile. At Pottoff Motors, he purchased a Hudson Deluxe Eight sedan. The new car had conspicuous cream-colored wire wheels; the dealer agreed to replace them with black ones at a later date, if the customer so desired.

Dillinger continued to be amused by the national hysteria concerning his whereabouts. Newspaper and radio reporters were falsely blaming him for the recent robbery of a freight terminal. Bogus sightings of Dillinger were reported in multiple locales, including New Jersey, Oregon, Arizona, and Mexico.

In mid-March, J. Edgar Hoover and the Bureau finally caught a break. The manager of the Lincoln Court Apartments, Daisy Coffee, contacted the local U.S. Attorney's office, reporting that her new tenants, *Mr. and Mrs. Carl P. Hellman*, who occupied a third-floor unit, were behaving in a suspicious manner. According to Coffee, the couple always entered the apartment complex from the rear, kept their blinds drawn much of the time, and hosted a number of well-dressed male visitors. Werner Hanni, the Bureau's SAC in St. Paul, was immediately summoned to hear Coffee's story.

Hanni assigned the investigation to Agents Rosser Nalls and Rufus Coulter. Almost immediately, Nalls and Coulter committed a blunder when they presented Coffee a series of photographs of known fugitives. The pictures included Alvin Karpis and members of the Barker family, but *none* of the Dillinger Gang.

After running a license plate check on the mysterious couple's automobile, the Bureau agents learned that it was registered to *Carl Hellman*. At the post office, Nalls and Coulter learned that *Hellman* had no mailing address, suggesting the name was an alias.

The agents soon placed the three-story, U-shaped, red brick Lincoln Court Apartments building under surveillance. During daylight hours, they discovered the blinds to apartment 303 were closed. Returning at night and gazing through a gap in the blinds adjacent to the windowsill, Nalls and Coulter were able to see the movement of at least two people in apartment.

On the morning of March 13th, Agent Coulter, accompanied by St. Paul police detective, Henry Cummings, knocked on the front door of apartment 303;

Agent Nalls remained outside near the car. When Billie Frechette cracked open the door, Detective Cummings identified himself and asked to speak with *Carl.*

"Carl who?" Frechette answered, having apparently forgotten the couple's alias.

"Carl Hellman," Cummings replied.

"He's just left and won't be back until this afternoon. Come back then," Frechette lied.

"Are you Mrs. Hellman?" Cummings asked.

When she nodded yes, Cummings continued: "We'll talk to you then."

"I'm not dressed. Come back this afternoon," Frechette protested.

At this point, Agent Coulter joined the conversation: "We'll wait until you dress."

After informing the lawmen that she would return in a few minutes, Billie closed the door and locked it. She immediately alerted Dillinger, who was still in bed: "It's the cops! What should I do?"

"Keep your shirt on, and get some things into the large bag," Dillinger instructed her, as he quickly dressed.

As Billie frantically dressed and packed, Dillinger began assembling a submachine gun, which he kept stored inside a dresser drawer. Standing in the hall outside the apartment, Agent Coulter and Detective Cummings grew uneasy about the delay. When Coulter suggested they needed back-up, Cummings asked if he wanted federal agents or police officers. After Coulter told him to request additional Bureau agents, the detective walked downstairs to the apartment manager's (Daisy Coffee's) office. When Cummings telephoned the Bureau's St. Paul field office, Inspector W. A. Rorer told him that he would dispatch two agents, and warned the detective to proceed with caution. Minutes later, Cummings returned to the third-floor hallway and joined Agent Coulter.

Outside, Agent Nalls spied a green Ford V-8 coupe parked near the curb. Homer Van Meter, dressed in a newly-purchased overcoat and felt hat, exited the vehicle; he was planning to show off his natty apparel to Dillinger, a fellow clothes horse. Nalls, who did not recognize the stranger, kept a close eye on the Ford.

After climbing the rear stairs to the third floor, Van Meter encountered Nalls and Cummings outside the door to Dillinger's apartment. His suspicions immediately aroused, Van Metter walked past the lawmen toward the front stairwell and started heading downstairs.

"What's your name?" Coulter called out to the stranger.

"I'm a soap salesman," Van Meter answered from the second floor landing.

"Where are your samples?" Coulter challenged him.

"Down in my car," Van Meter replied.

When Coulter asked if the man could produce identification, Van Meter innocently replied: "No, but I have it down in my car."

After the stranger failed to question Coulter's authority to request identification, the Bureau agent suspected that he was dealing with an experienced criminal. Coulter soon followed Van Meter down the stairs to the ground-level foyer. Staring out the glass front door, the agent suddenly realized the man he was pursuing was nowhere in sight. Just then, Van Meter emerged from his hiding place in the basement stairwell to Coulter's rear, armed with a pistol: "You want this, asshole? Here it is!"

Coulter burst out the front door as Van Meter began firing. Struggling to draw his own revolver while running, Coulter managed to dodge the bullets kicking up clouds of snow around his feet. After slipping and sliding down the sloping lawn, the agent finally unholstered his pistol and fired back at Van Meter, who quickly retreated inside the building. Alerted by the sound of gunfire, Agent Nalls rushed to the aid of his G-Man.

"That's the car of the guy who shot at you," Nalls exclaimed pointing to the green Ford parked beside the curb.

Anxious and agitated, Coulter had to fire three shots before he was able to flatten one of the tires on Van Meter's car. Agent Nalls sprinted to a nearby drug store and telephoned the St. Paul Police Department: "We're federal agents in a shootout at Lexington and Lincoln! Send all the squad cars you've got!" Nalls also attempted to phone the St. Paul Bureau office, but discovered that all the lines were busy.

After hearing gun shots outside, Dillinger made his move, firing a machine gun burst through the wooden door of the apartment, and forcing Detective Cummings to seek refuge in an alcove. Billie Frechette, unaccustomed to violence, was frightened: "For God's sake, don't shoot! I'll stay here. I don't care. You go ahead, but don't shoot!"

"Come on baby, it'll be okay. Just stay behind me. Grab the suitcases, we're going out," Dillinger tried to reassure her.

Armed with a submachine in each hand, Dillinger opened the splintered, bullet-ridden door. After quickly scanning the length of the hallway, Dillinger nodded at Billie: "Let's go!"

Before leaving the third floor, Dillinger fired another salvo of machine gun fire in to the now empty hallway; Detective Cummings had already emerged from his hiding place, ran downstairs, and bolted out the front door. Dillinger and Frechette immediately made their way out of the apartment. Amidst the chaos, the lawmen had failed to secure the apartment building's rear entrance. Lugging a large suitcase with both hands, Frechette labored to follow Dillinger downstairs and out the back door.

"Get the car! The keys are in my pocket," Dillinger instructed Billie, when they reached the rear alleyway.

Frantically dragging the heavy suitcase, which was filled with cash and guns, Billie managed to the cover the 200 feet between the rear entrance and the garage where Dillinger's black Hudson was parked. After backing the vehicle out of the garage with the nose pointed east, Billie heard Dillinger shout: "Pull back in. Head out the other way." While hastily repositioning the vehicle, Billie managed to dent the fender against one of the garage walls.

"Head for Eddie's!" Dillinger shouted as he jumped inside the car. The Hudson fishtailed on the icy pavement, as the fugitive couple sped away.

Sitting in the back seat cradling a Tommy gun, Dillinger kept his eyes peeled for further signs of trouble. An anxious Billie kept her foot pressed to the accelerator until Dillinger cautioned her: "Slow down! Slow down! You'll attract attention!"

When Homer Van Meter exited the building and saw the two Bureau agents standing next to his car, he escaped on foot, heading west on Lincoln Avenue. After jumping on the running board of a passing garbage truck, Van Meter jerked opened the passenger's side door, pointed his pistol at the two men in the cab, and ordered the driver to continue heading west. Temporarily discarding his new hat, Van Meter doffed the worn cap of one of the sanitation workers.

During his garbage truck escape, the fugitive informed his shocked travel companions that he had been ambushed by the police. When the driver reached the Minneapolis city limits, Van Meter ordered him to stop. Before disembarking, Van Meter offered each of the sanitation workers $10, but both declined.

After narrowly eluding capture, Van Meter, accompanied by Tommy Carroll, headed to Mankato, Minnesota, 85 miles distant from St. Paul. When Bureau agents impounded Van Meter's Ford, they discovered a submachine gun (the serial number had been filed off) and a fully-loaded magazine inside a leather case, a 100-round Tommy gum drum, and a .351 caliber Winchester automatic rifle.

John Hamilton and Pat Cherrington were at a grocery store during the shoot-out. As they were approaching the apartment complex, Hamilton realized the building was overrun by lawmen and quickly sped away, managing to elude capture.

The Bureau agents and police officers who searched Apartment 303 were unaware of the identity of the escaped couple until they found three photographs of Dillinger and later discovered his fingerprints on a bottle of mouthwash. Drops of blood found in the outer hallway suggested the fugitive had been wounded; Dillinger had indeed been struck in his left calf by one of his own ricocheting machine gun bullets.

Inside the apartment, the authorities discovered two bulletproof vests, Dillinger's newly-acquired machine gun pistol, and an assortment of other weapons, some of which had been modified to accommodate silencers. The machine gun pistol caught the eye of Bureau agents, who had never seen a weapon like this before. Using the serial number on the firing pin, the Bureau was able to trace the purchase of the unusual weapon to Hymie Lebman's gun shop in San Antonio.

The lawmen also confiscated silk lingerie, numerous pairs of shoes, and two bathing suits belonging to Billie Frechette. During his hasty get away, Dillinger left behind slacks, shirts, a leather jacket, and an overcoat. Of greater significance, the authorities discovered a get-away map from a bank in Newton, Iowa, which the gang was planning to rob. A scrap of paper with Eddie Green's telephone number written on it might have proven beneficial, if the Bureau agents had not carelessly waited several weeks before matching the number with the address.

After their escape, Dillinger and Frechette went directly to Eddie Green's apartment. Green then drove them to the office of a Minneapolis physician, Dr. Clayton May—someone local law enforcement agents characterized as "a known abortionist, dope peddler, and associate of hoodlums." Green told May that Dillinger had been wounded by an "exploding still." After examining Dillinger's leg wound, the physician was concerned: "We'd better get you to a hospital."

"To hell with that! Get me some place private!" Dillinger replied, emphasizing the point by aiming his submachine gun at May.

May drove Dillinger to the home of a nurse, who routinely took care of women after their illegal abortions. The doctor patched Dillinger's through-and-through leg wound and administered a tetanus shot. For the next four days, the fugitive remained at the nurse's house until his wound showed signs of healing.

When J. Edgar Hoover learned the details of the shoot-out in St. Paul, he expressed "extreme displeasure" at the "atrocious bungling." He could not understand why only two Bureau agents had been dispatched to Dillinger's apartment, and just one of them had knocked on the door. Allowing both Dillinger and Van Meter to escape made the Bureau look as bad as the bumbling local cops. Hoover also considered it foolish to have involved the notoriously corrupt St. Paul Police Department in the Bureau's operation.

Hoover demanded to know why Agents Nalls and Coulter were armed only with handguns. When Inspector Rorer informed him that some of the agents did not know how to fire a Tommy gun, Hoover was perplexed and angry: "If the agents cannot handle the equipment, they should be instructed immediately in the use of it."

The Director was also unhappy that he had not been informed in advance of the St. Paul raid. Consequently, Hoover established new rules concerning the pursuit of Dillinger—all future raids would be cleared by the Director's office in Washington D.C., and local law enforcement would not be involved, unless Bureau agents "were short of equipment, like machine guns or gas guns." Hoover also dispatched one of his top assistants, H. H. Clegg, to St. Paul to take charge of the Dillinger case.

After Homer Van Meter tried to kill Agent Coulter, Hoover took dead aim at Dillinger and his associates: "In the twenty odd years of the existence of this division, no one has shot any of its agents and got away with it." The Director vowed to "run down the entire gang," and the SACs of field offices were instructed to prioritize Dillinger "over all other pending cases."

Agents were immediately dispatched to St. Paul from throughout the country. Cots were set up in the Bureau office and nearby post office to provide sleeping accommodations for the out-of-town agents. As always, Hoover made sure the Bureau received as much favorable press as possible, and the *St. Paul Dispatch* soon headlined: HOOVER DECLARES WAR ON GANGS HERE—U.S. JUSTICE BUREAU CHIEF HURLS THREAT—EXTRA FORCES TO RUN DOWN ENTIRE MOB.

The night after the shoot-out, Bureau agents located the address of Van Meter's St. Paul apartment by tracking the registration of his abandoned car. Agents immediately converged on Apartment 106, located at 2214 Marshall Avenue. While Van Meter was far too savvy to return to his apartment, the agents did discover a submachine gun stock, a dynamite fuse, road and getaway maps, and ammunition stores. After the raiding party collected evidence and dusted for fingerprints, two Bureau agents remained hidden in the apartment, armed with submachine guns.

Around noon the following day, a black woman named Lucy Jackson used a key to enter the locked door of Van Meter's apartment, where she was confronted by the two armed agents. Jackson explained that she had been asked by her sister, Leona Goodman, who was waiting outside in her car, to clean the apartment. When Goodman was brought inside for questioning, she told the agents that she had been hired by a *Mr. Stevens* (an alias employed by Dillinger gang member, Eddie Green) to clean the apartment. Earlier in the day, *Stevens* had dropped by Goodman's house and given her a dollar bill and the apartment key. She had been instructed to clean the residence and pack up clothes in a suitcase; as extra payment, Goodman could keep 10 silver dollars that were in the apartment. *Stevens* told Goodman that he would drop by her house later in the day to collect the suitcase.

After filling Van Meter's suitcase with wanted posters, three Bureau agents secreted themselves inside Goodman's house. By 3:00 p.m., the agents were lying in wait for *Mr. Stevens'* arrival. Agent George Gross, armed with a submachine gun, positioned himself near a front window. A shot-gun wielding agent named Edward Notesteen was stationed in the kitchen, while a third agent, cradling an automatic rifle, waited in the bedroom. Three other agents waited outside in two cars, prepared to block escape routes. At one point, Agent Notesteen telephoned Inspector Rorer for clarification of his orders.

"If she says 'that's the man,' kill him," Rorer emphatically instructed.

At 5:45 p.m., a green sedan parked in front of Goodman's house. When a man wearing an overcoat approached the front entrance, Goodman cracked the door open wide enough to slide the suitcase out and hurriedly closed it, without speaking to *Mr. Stevens*. The agents immediately asked if this was the man in question.

"It's him," Goodman replied.

"Let him have it!" Notesteen ordered.

Agent Gross fired a five shot burst with his submachine gun through the front window. Green, who was walking away from the house carrying the suitcase, was hit twice—once in the back of the head and a second time in the right shoulder. The wounded man crumpled to his knees and then fell, face first, on the front lawn.

After rushing outside the house, Agent Notesteen shot out one of the rear tires on Green's automobile, while the agent armed with the rifle fired a bullet through the Terraplane's hood and disabled the engine. Green's wife, Bessie, who was sitting in the car reading and listening to the radio, failed to hear any of the gunshots, but soon saw her husband lying in the yard. She ran and knelt beside him, using a handkerchief to try and staunch the blood streaming from his head wound.

"Don't shoot! Don't shoot anymore! We're alone!" she cried, as the agents approached her.

When the gravely wounded Green was quickly searched, the agents failed to discover a weapon in his possession. As the ambulance transporting Green and two Bureau agents departed for Anker Hospital, Bessie cried: "Please get Eddie a priest. He hasn't been to church in a long time and he needs one."

After Bessie Green was taken into custody, agents discovered $105 in her purse and $1,005 sewed in the lining of her coat. They also confiscated two safety deposit box keys; the boxes were stuffed with more than $9,000 in cash. A search of the Green's apartment uncovered a submachine gun, a bulletproof vest, a .45 caliber automatic pistol, a 16 gauge shotgun, and large stores of ammunition.

As expected, the wounded man was carrying fake identification. By the next day, however, the Bureau had positively identified him as Eddie Green.

At Anker hospital, Green was discovered to have a .45 caliber slug embedded in his scalp. The impact of the bullet had driven skull fragments into his brain, and the doctors were certain the wound would prove fatal. The semi-comatose patient, however, managed to linger for eight days.

A rotating pair of Bureau agents was assigned to Green's hospital room around the clock—one to interrogate the patient and the other to transcribe his words. The agents role-played, hoping to get as much information as possible out of Green before he died; one agent assumed the role of a doctor and the other a gangster. A delirious Green was never informed of their true identities. Coupling inhumanity with deception, the *doctor* agent sometimes bartered morphine injections in exchange for information.

Lapsing in and out of consciousness, Green revealed the name of at least one Dillinger gang member, Tommy Carroll, who was currently hiding out in Wisconsin. He also told the agents that the Dillinger Gang planned to rob a bank in Newton, Iowa, and had already staged heists in Sioux Falls and Mason City.

As the interrogation progressed, Green disclosed that Dillinger had been wounded in the leg during the St. Paul shoot-out. He also provided the address of the apartment where Dr. Clayton May had treated Dillinger's gunshot wound, but did not reveal the physician's actual name. The apartment number proved erroneous, and ended with gun-wielding Bureau agents confronting an innocent and unsuspecting couple at their front door. Even if the agents had discovered the right apartment, Dillinger remained one step ahead of them, having fled that location five hours earlier.

Eddie Green died on April 11, 1934. Bureau agents had literally executed an unarmed man, forcing the agency to rationalize the necessity of shooting Green in the back. The agency's official report explained that Green was "running in leaps" instead of walking, and accused him of making "threatening" and "menacing" gestures. Adding to their official embellishments, the Bureau's report claimed that the suspect had been ordered to "stop," after he reached into his pocket, as if he was drawing a weapon.

Many of those closest to the action viewed the Bureau's explanation with skepticism. The *St. Paul Dispatch* demanded a formal inquest into the shooting. A handful of St. Paul police officers derided the Bureau agents as little more than "lawyers armed with guns."

In damage control mode, J. Edgar Hoover went on the offensive. The names of the agents involved in Green's take-down were withheld, which prevented them from being served with subpoenas. Wielding power from his self-proclaimed *seat of government*, Hoover succeeded in blocking the inquest. Consequently, the Bureau's inaccurate and self-serving report became the only official record of Green's shooting.

Green's widow, Bessie, who refused to cooperate with the Bureau agents in St. Paul, was transported to Chicago for interrogation by Melvin Purvis. Surrendering to unrelenting pressure, Bessie eventually identified the names of various Dillinger gang members, including a diminutive, fair-haired, light-complexioned man named *Jimmie*, who had a wife named Helen and two young children. It did not take long for the Bureau to discover that *Jimmie* and Baby Face Nelson were one in the same.

On April 4th, Dillinger and Billie Frechette departed St. Paul; still recuperating from the gunshot wound to his leg, Dillinger allowed his girlfriend to drive. Shortly after midnight on April 6th, the couple arrived in Mooresville, parking on a dirt road, one-quarter mile from the Dillinger farmhouse.

At this point in time, the Bureau had not yet placed the Dillinger farm under surveillance. Earl Connelley, the SAC in charge of the field office in Cincinnati, whose territory included central Indiana, had been actively involved in the Dillinger case for only a week.

John Dillinger, Sr. clearly recalled the night his son arrived at the farm: "I was in bed. I heard someone knock on the back door...A woman was there. I'd never seen her before. She was young and pretty and she looked foreign—dark, with olive skin and black, flashing eyes. She whispered, 'Johnnie's out by the barn. Is it all right?' 'Yes, it's all right,' I told her." John Sr.'s recollection was either faulty or disingenuous; he had met Billie Frechette on at least one occasion prior to that evening.

When Dillinger walked inside the farmhouse, he placed a submachine gun on the kitchen table, before shaking his father's hand. The elder Dillinger was apprehensive: "I told John it wasn't safe for them there. 'Probably not, Dad, but I just wanted to see you before—well, you know, before anything happens'."

Dillinger enjoyed the rendezvous with his family, proudly introducing Frechette, as *Anne*, his "wife." The morning after his arrival in Mooresville, Dillinger's half-brother, Hubert, arrived at the farm. He was surprised to see Johnnie, who snuck around a corner and pointed his finger: "Stick 'em up!" The brothers later went out to the barn where Dillinger's Hudson was hidden, and carefully painted the automobile's cream-colored wire wheels black.

That same night, Dillinger and his half-brother drove to the town of Liepsic, to visit with Harry Pierpont's parents, and make sure they had received the money he forwarded to them through his attorney. During the three-hour trip, Dillinger told Hubert that he was limping because of a bullet wound suffered in the St. Paul shoot-out. He also recounted his escape from the Crown Point jail, describing the odds as "one chance out of a hundred."

After arriving in Liepsic and learning that Pierpont's parents had moved to another town, the brothers immediately headed back to Mooresville. At 4:00 a.m., during the return leg of their trip, Hubert fell asleep behind the wheel, and rear-ended a Model T Ford transporting an elderly couple. After impact, Dillinger's Hudson ran off the road, plowed through a wire fence, and traveled 300 feet into a neighboring field. While no one was injured in the collision, the Ford lost a rear wheel and Dillinger's Hudson was totaled.

Dillinger apologized to the couple, agreed to pay for the damages to their automobile, and quickly removed the front and back license plates from his own wrecked vehicle. After the man and woman departed on foot to seek assistance, Dillinger, armed with a submachine gun wrapped in a blanket and accompanied by Hubert, began walking cross country. By the time they had hiked through the woods and farmlands to reach the next paved highway, Dillinger's injured leg was throbbing. At this point, he instructed Hubert to hitchhike back to their father's farm, fetch another vehicle, and return to pick him up. After tying a handkerchief around a fence post to the mark his present location, Dillinger hid in a hay crib, cradling his Tommy gun, until Hubert returned.

When the Indiana State Police investigated the scene of the accident and discovered a machine gun clip inside a wrecked car lacking license places, the officers notified Captain Matt Leach. The Hudson, which registered only 1,400 miles on its odometer, was traced back to the Pottoff Brothers dealership in St. Paul. The authorities discovered the vehicle had been purchased by *Carl Hellman*, one of John Dillinger's known aliases. At the crash site, Leach informed reporters that the vehicle most likely belonged to Dillinger. He also pointed out to the newsmen how the car had narrowly missed hitting any trees when it ran off the road: "Just look at that. There is some more Dillinger luck. Nobody could have been so fortunate but Dillinger."

Later on the day of the accident, Dillinger sent Hubert and Billie Frechette to Indianapolis to purchase a replacement vehicle. At Frank Hatfield Ford, they bought a black V-8 Ford for $722. To avoid attracting undue attention, the new car was temporarily garaged in Mooresville.

The Bureau shifted its focus to Indiana, dispatching 10 additional agents to the state. Earl Connelley, SAC of the Cincinnati office, set up a temporary office at the Spink Arms Hotel in Indianapolis. Connelley immediately assigned agents to keep watch on the family farm, Audrey Dillinger's house, and the gas station in Indianapolis, where Hubert was employed. Lacking the manpower to maintain 24-hour surveillance on a single target, the agents were instructed to drive back and forth between the three locations.

On Sunday April 8th, the Dillinger family staged a reunion of sorts at the farm. An outdoor picnic lunch included two of Dillinger's favorite dishes— fried chicken and coconut pie. Over the course of the late morning and early afternoon, family members flew kites and posed for individual and group pictures, including gag shots with Johnnie's now famous wooden pistol. While Dillinger's 18-year-old niece, Mary, a beauty school student, was giving her uncle a manicure, she accidently bumped into his wounded leg. Dillinger grimaced, but immediately reassured her: "Forget it, kid. It was nothing." John Sr. later recalled that his son was "carefree and laughing," but at the same time, "sensed he was going to die" soon.

While Dillinger enjoyed bragging about his exploits, he was careful about exposing family members to information the authorities might use as leverage. When his brother-in-law, Emmett Hancock, asked for details about the

Crown Point jail break, Dillinger cautioned him: "Big boy, let me tell you something—if you don't know anything, you can't tell anything, can you?" While talking with his niece, Mary, Dillinger downplayed his reputation: "You believe what's in the papers if you want to, but take it from me, I haven't killed anyone, and I never will."

The mood of the Sunday picnic changed dramatically when an airplane flew overhead. While Dillinger correctly surmised that it was a military aircraft (National Guard training flight from nearby Stout Field), he was still a bit unnerved. A short while later, his niece reported seeing a "suspicious" car occupied by two men, passing slowly by the farm. The sudden appearance of the airplane and the mysterious automobile were enough to convince Dillinger that it was time for him to go. He immediately instructed Hubert and his nephew, Fred Hancock, to drive into Mooresville and retrieve his newly-purchased car from its garage hiding place.

That same Sunday afternoon, a number of people were traveling by car on Route 267; many of them were hoping to catch a glimpse of the Dillinger farm. One of those cars contained Bureau agents, J. L. Geraghty and T. J. Donegan. Mid-afternoon, the agents spied three vehicles parked outside the Dillinger farm house—one of them resembled a Chevrolet coupe belonging to Hubert Dillinger—a man they had been instructed to watch closely.

Because the farm house sat atop a slight hill, the agents concluded that it would be less conspicuous for them to engage in passing surveillance, rather than stopping beside the road. After traveling two miles past the Dillinger farm, Geraghty and Donegan reversed course and drove past the house again. This time, they saw two men and several children standing outside. When the agents turned around and made a third pass, they noticed the Chevrolet coupe had disappeared.

Determined to locate the car, and perhaps Hubert Dillinger, Geraghty and Donegan drove into Mooresville. Just after arriving in town, the agents saw Hubert's car, led by a black Ford, passing in the opposite direction.

When Hubert arrived at the farm, he informed Dillinger that he had spotted a car occupied by two suspected lawmen. Dillinger instructed his half-brother and nephew to leave and drive away from Mooresville. When the bureau agents made their fourth pass and observed that Hubert's car had not returned to the farmhouse, they sped past the Dillinger homestead, hoping to catch up with the Chevrolet. After driving as far as the next town, Plainfield, without spotting the vehicle in question, the agents reversed their course.

While Geraghty and Donegan were being led on a wild goose chase, three cars departed the Dillinger farm. The first vehicle, driven by Audrey and her husband, turned left and headed toward Mooresville. John Dillinger, Sr. drove the second automobile and turned right. Car number three, the new Ford, was driven by Billie Frechette, accompanied by two of the fugitive's teenage nieces; Dillinger hid under a blanket on the rear floorboard with his submachine gun in hand.

As they motored toward Plainfield, Dillinger told Billie to pull over to the side of the road. Dillinger stepped out of the car just as Geraghty and Donegan were passing by; even though both agents had a clear view of the fugitive, who was dressed in a gray suit and hat, neither recognized him as John Dillinger! Once again, America's most-wanted fugitive had slipped past the authorities, and was soon on his way back to Chicago.

The newspapers soon learned from Dillinger's sister, Audrey, about the fugitive's visit to Indiana. Embarrassed yet again by Dillinger's elusiveness, the Bureau never made mention of having agents in the Mooresville area.

Dillinger's return home was no secret among local residents, and a number of Mooresville's citizens soon circulated a petition asking Governor Paul McNutt to pardon the fugitive, in exchange for his surrender. When the *Indianapolis Star* featured a front page story about Dillinger's recent visit to Mooresville, Indiana's Commissioner of Public Safety expressed puzzlement: "It's mighty queer that people would tell a newspaper about Dillinger's visit before they told the police or other law enforcement agencies..."

After returning to Chicago from Indiana, Dillinger told Billie that they should move to a distant locale, perhaps implying that he was ready to give up a life of crime. Around that same time, Dillinger asked Louis Piquett's investigator, Art O'Leary, if the attorney was acquainted with a plastic surgeon: "I'd like to have him work on me. I want to live like other people. Billie and I would like to be married and settle down somewhere."

On Monday, April 9th, Billie met with Larry Strong, the ex-boyfriend of one of her long-time friends, asking for his assistance in locating a place to live in the Chicago area. Strong agreed to make some inquiries, and then meet back with her that night at the U-Tavern, located at 416 North State Street.

Unbeknownst to Billie, Strong had previously been questioned by Bureau agents about his association with John Dillinger. After meeting with Frechette, Strong telephoned SAC Melvin Purvis.

Shortly before 8:00 p.m., Dillinger parked his car outside the U-Tavern and watched as Billie entered the building. Inside the tavern, Agent Purvis was already seated at the bar. Agent James J. Metcalfe, who was stationed just down the street, observed a Ford parked outside the tavern. After watching a woman exit the vehicle, Metcalfe decided to take a closer look, and walked along the sidewalk, to within five feet of the car. The agent was unable to get a clear look at the driver, and had no way of knowing that Dillinger had a Tommy gun resting in his lap.

Purvis recognized Billie Frechette when she entered the tavern, and unsuccessfully tried to position himself close enough to overhear her conversation with Larry Strong. Afterwards, Purvis briefly exited the building, nodding to the other agents who were stationed nearby. Dillinger watched as the agents, one of whom was armed with a submachine gun, entered the tavern.

Once inside, Purvis and his fellow agents arrested both Frechette and Strong, and then searched for Dillinger in the tavern's basement. The agents did not give any thought as to how Billie arrived at the meeting site, until it was too late. When they rushed outside, Dillinger had already sped away.

Dillinger later admitted that Frechette's arrest made him "cry like a baby." Later that evening he telephoned Art O'Leary: "The G's just picked up Billie."

"How did it happen?" O'Leary inquired.

"I was sitting in my car around the corner. There were too many of them for me to take her away. It was that rat, Larry Strong..." Dillinger lamented, before asking the investigator to telephone Piquett and inform him about Billie's predicament.

While Frechette remained largely uncooperative with Purvis and the other agents who interrogated her, the Bureau had finally made a meaningful arrest in the Dillinger Case. J. Edgar Hoover was delighted and praised his favorite agent, Purvis: "Well, son, keep a stiff upper lip and get Dillinger for me, and the world is yours."

While he was devastated by Billie's arrest, Dillinger knew that the Bureau's Chicago field office, located in the high-rise Banker's Building, was an impossible location to target for a jail break. From the newspapers, Dillinger learned that his girlfriend would be extradited to St. Paul to stand trial for *harboring a fugitive*. Aware that the authorities were hot on his trail, Dillinger hid out for several days in Fort Wayne, Indiana, accompanied by Homer Van Meter. All the while, he was formulating a plan to rescue Billie during her transfer from Chicago to St. Paul.

On Wednesday April 11th, Dillinger and Van Meter rendezvoused with Nelson, Carroll, and Hamilton, at which time the group discussed plans to free Frechette. Such a daring operation would most likely involve gunplay, and the gang members realized they needed additional protective armor. Van Meter soon suggested a location where bulletproof vests might be procured.

Two days later, at 1:15 a.m., police officer, Judd Pittenger, was walking his normal beat in the small town of Warsaw, Illinois, when he was accosted by two men wearing raincoats and armed with Tommy guns. While he did not recognize Van Meter, Pittenger immediately identified Dillinger from his wanted posters.

"We want your vests, and we mean business," Dillinger announced.

Pittenger initially resisted, grabbing the barrel of Dillinger's submachine gun. After Van Meter jammed his Tommy gun in the officer's back, Dillinger warned him: "Leave loose—we don't want to kill you."

Never one to favor peaceful negotiations, Van Meter grabbed Pittenger's service revolver from his holster and clubbed the officer twice in the head. Pittenger instantly capitulated: "Don't hit me anymore!"

"Don't hit him," Dillinger instructed his partner.

At gunpoint, Pittenger led the fugitives to the police station, where Dillinger saw pictures of himself tacked to the wall, accompanied by the caption: *IF YOU SEE THIS MAN, TELEPHONE THE POLICE AT ONCE.* Dillinger ordered the officer to lead him to the room where the department's weapons were stored.

"I don't have a key," Pittenger protested.

"Who has the key?" Dillinger replied.

"I don't know," Pittenger lied.

"Don't be a fool. We don't want to be forced to kill you," Dillinger warned.

"I don't want you to kill me. I have a couple of kids at home," Pittenger replied.

"That's the reason we don't want to kill you," Dillinger advised him.

Pittenger reluctantly fished the key from his pocket and led his captors to the second-floor weapons closet. After gaining access to the room, Dillinger and Van Meter stole three bulletproof vests and two pistols. On their way back to Chicago, the fugitives managed to elude the state police's hastily-constructed road blocks.

In the Chicago field office, Bureau agents relentlessly questioned Billie Frechette. During the marathon interrogation sessions, she was often sleep-deprived, handcuffed to a desk, and forced to stare into bright lights: "They kept me up, talking to me until I didn't know what I was saying. They'd leave me alone for a long time. I was nearly crazy. They thought John was coming to rescue me."

Frechette remained either tight-lipped or fed her interrogators with misinformation. On one occasion, Agent Harold Reinecke grew so frustrated that he slapped her across the face. In return, a tearful Billie offered up a tall tale, informing Reinecke that Dillinger was planning to meet her at an apartment where the couple once lived; agents were immediately dispatched to the location to investigate the fabricated rendezvous.

On Friday, April 13th, Frechette was arraigned by federal court commissioner, Edwin K. Walker, on charges of *conspiracy to harbor a federal fugitive*. Her bail was set at $65,000 ($900,000 by modern-day standards). Afterwards, Frechette was transported to the Chicago House of Corrections, pending extradition to St. Paul.

Like Billie Frechette, Dillinger's family members provided Bureau agents with little in the way of useful information. Throughout the state of Indiana, agents pursued a multitude of fruitless leads. In other parts of the Midwest, false sightings of Dillinger tied up valuable Bureau man hours. Melvin Purvis, however, remained undeterred: "Sometime, one of those tips is going to be true. And, then we're going to catch Dillinger. That time is going to be soon.

We'll get him." On April 17th, based on information provided by Eddie Green's widow, Bessie, the Bureau arrested Dr. Clayton May, charging him with *harboring John Dillinger and performing illegal procedures.*

All the while, the Bureau was beset with near-misses. On Saturday April 14th, Dillinger drove to Louisville, Kentucky to obtain an X-ray of one of his knees, which was causing him significant discomfort. Dr. David Wilmouth, who recognized the fugitive, told him that the X-ray office was closed for the weekend, and scheduled Dillinger's appointment for the following week; afterwards, the physician informed police that the outlaw would be returning in three days.

At 11:00 a.m. on that Tuesday, four Bureau agents and two Louisville Police Department detectives lay in wait in a back room of the X-ray clinic, while 22 other lawmen were stationed at various points outside the building. By then, Dillinger had already returned to Chicago, with no intention of keeping his scheduled doctor's appointment.

When an eager Melvin Purvis suggested posting a $5,000 reward for information leading to Dillinger's capture, J. Edgar Hoover refused, still convinced that the fugitive could be apprehended without directly relying on the help of private citizens. Hoover soon exerted tighter control over the Dillinger manhunt. On April 18th, the Director ordered Purvis to remain in Chicago, rather than chase down leads in neighboring cities and states. Determined to streamline the chain of command, Hoover order all SACs to phone Purvis with daily updates. In addition, all field offices were instructed not to investigate any leads related to the Dillinger Gang without first clearing them with Purvis.

While the Dillinger case proved frustrating to the Bureau, the authorities' relentless pursuit began to unnerve some of the gang members. John Hamilton developed a sense of foreboding, convinced that he would be killed in the near future. Unable to talk a morose Hamilton out of travelling to his sister's house in Sault St. Marie, Michigan, Dillinger decided to accompany him. On April 17th, Hamilton and Pat Cherrington drove to Michigan's Upper Peninsula, while Dillinger followed in a separate vehicle.

Hamilton's sister, Anna Steve, welcomed the trio with open arms, preparing a home-cooked meal and cutting both men's hair. Hamilton confided his feeling of impending doom to his sister, predicting the entire Dillinger

Gang would soon be captured or killed. At the conclusion of their brief visit, Hamilton gave Steve his V-8 Ford. By the time Dillinger, Hamilton, and Cherrington reached Lake Michigan on their return trip to Chicago, the last ferry of the evening had departed, forcing them to spend the night in a hotel in St. Ignace.

Alerted to Dillinger's visit by one of Anna Steve's neighbors, Bureau agents arrived at her house after the fugitive's had departed. Hoover was determined to make an example out of anyone who was friendly to the Dillinger Gang—part of his newly-adopted "zero tolerance policy." Anna Steve and her 17-year-old son, Charles, were arrested for *harboring fugitives*. While her son was ultimately acquitted, Mrs. Steve was convicted and sentenced to four months in jail and fined $1,000. The Bureau also confiscated the automobile Hamilton had given to his sister as a parting gift.

While the Bureau's successes in rounding up the Dillinger Gang were greatly outnumbered by their failures, J. Edgar Hoover firmly believed that persistence would eventually prevail. When his agents finally succeeded in capturing or killing *Public Enemy Number One,* Hoover was certain that he and the Bureau would reap the benefits.

CHAPTER ELEVEN

Little Bohemia

In mid-April of 1934, the Second Dillinger Gang reunited for the first time in nearly three weeks, meeting at the Fox River Grove Inn. The resort, located just outside Chicago, was owned by Louie Cernocky, a friend and acquaintance of many underworld figures. The gang members, concerned that about the heightened vigilance of Chicago and St. Paul authorities, wanted to find an out-of-the-way, temporary hiding place. Cernocky suggested a country inn and resort in northern Wisconsin, operated by a man he considered to be a trusted friend.

The Little Bohemia Lodge, a 400-mile drive from Chicago, was located near the small town of Manitowish, Wisconsin. During the off-season for tourism, the vacation spot was situated well off the beaten path. Constructed in 1931, the lodge was owned and operated by Emil Wanatka. The short but stocky Wanatka, who had immigrated to the United States from Bohemia in 1916, had previously owned a restaurant and saloon in Chicago, where he became well-acquainted with gangsters, bootleggers, and crooked politicians. Wanatka and his wife, Nan, moved to Wisconsin in the early 1930s, where a number of her relatives already resided. By the time he opened Little Bohemia, Wanatka believed that his association with shady characters was a thing of the past.

On Friday morning April 20th, the Second Dillinger Gang left Chicago, bound for northern Wisconsin. In cautious fashion, the outlaws traveled in three separate vehicles, departing at staggered intervals. The first car, occupied by Homer Van Meter, his 21-year-old girlfriend, Marie Conforti, and her Boston Bull Terrier puppy, was chauffeured by gang lackey, Pat Reilly, and arrived at Little Bohemia in the early afternoon.

The sign at the lodge's Route 51 entrance was welcoming: *DINE, DANCE, & SWIM AT LITTLE BOHEMIA* and promised *STEAK, DUCK, & CHICKEN DINNERS.* The two-story log structure, located at the end of a 200-yard, pine tree-line driveway, housed a bar, kitchen, and dance floor on the first floor, with 10 bedrooms located on the second story. A free-standing cottage stood behind the main building, only 30 yards from the shore of Little Star Lake.

Reilly backed Van Meter's car into the parking area, ever-prepared for a quick get-away. Van Meter greeted Emil Wanatka and asked if the lodge could accommodate 10 guests for a several-day stay. Wanatka was initially delighted to host the unexpected guests; particularly during the off-season, when winter was still hanging on in the northern Midwest. Van Meter promised that one of the later-arriving guests would bring a formal letter of introduction from one of Wanatka's old friends.

The others arrived over the course of the afternoon and early evening. The second car contained John Dillinger, John Hamilton, and Hamilton's girlfriend, Pat Cherrington. The last to arrive were Baby Face Nelson, his wife, Helen, Tommy Carroll, and Carroll's girlfriend, Jean Delaney. Nelson brought with him the letter Cernocky had written, identifying the newly-arrived guests as "friends who should be well treated."

Early on, tension arose over the gang members' choice of rooms. Dillinger, Hamilton, Van Meter, and Cherrington occupied rooms on the second floor of the main building, while the late arrivers, Nelson, Carroll, and their wives were assigned to the free-standing cabin. Already smarting over the fact that the media and authorities had designated Dillinger as the gang leader, Nelson complained about being housed in the cabin. Dillinger, annoyed by Nelson's pettiness and belligerence, confided to Pat Cherrington: "I'd have let the little bastard have the place, if hadn't been such an asshole about it."

Ever vigilant, the gang members identified themselves only through aliases—*Johnnie* (Dillinger), *Jimmy* (Nelson), and *Wayne* (Van Meter). Twenty-six-year old George Bazo and 23-year-old Frank Taube, the lodge's bartenders/waiters/bellhops, were confused by the heaviness of the guests' luggage, unaware the bags contained guns and ammunition.

It did not take long for Little Bohemia's owner to ascertain the true identity of one the guests. The night of the gang's arrival, Emil Wanatka recognized Dillinger from his front page-picture in a recent edition of the *Chicago Tribune*. During an after-dinner poker game, Wanatka noticed that Dillinger had a pistol concealed inside his coat. The observant lodge owner soon realized the other male guests were wearing shoulder holsters. When Emil and Nan went to bed at the end of the night, she complained to her husband: "I hope they don't stay."

"Shut up and don't talk," he whispered, "but I think the man with the dyed hair is Dillinger."

The following morning, Wanatka confronted his infamous guest: "You're John Dillinger."

"You're not afraid, are you?" Dillinger asked.

"No, but everything I have to my name, including my family, is right here, and every policeman in America is looking for you. If I can help it, there isn't going to be any shooting match," Wanatka replied.

"Emil, all we want is to eat and rest for a few days. We'll pay you well and get out. There won't be any trouble," Dillinger tried to reassure him.

Uncertain if Wanatka could be trusted, Dillinger informed the other gang members that the owner was aware of their true identities. For the remainder of the day, both Dillinger and Nelson listened closely whenever anyone used the lodge's telephone.

That Saturday, the gang members were cautious, but managed to enjoy their leisure time. Dillinger, Van Meter, Nelson, and Wanatka took target practice with rifles and pistols. Dillinger and Nelson also played catch with eight-year-old, Emil Wanatka, Jr. In the afternoon, Dillinger dispatched Pat Reilly to St. Paul, with instructions to collect $4,000 owed to Van Meter by restaurant owner, Harry Sawyer, as well as purchase additional ammunition for the gang. Pat Cherrington, who was not feeling well, accompanied Reilly, hoping to see a doctor.

By the next morning, Nan Wanatka, who had read a newspaper account about the arrest of John Hamilton's sister, Anna Steve, on charges of *harboring fugitives*, was determined to disassociate her family from the outlaw guests. When a local fishing guide, Lloyd LaPorte, visited the lodge, she handed him a package of Marvel cigarettes, which contained a note addressed to her brother-in-law, Henry Voss. After receiving the smuggled message, which revealed that the Dillinger Gang was staying at Little Bohemia, Voss was uneasy about using the local party line telephone and drove to the nearby town of Rhinelander. From there, Voss telephoned a police officer he knew in Milwaukee, who directed him to contact the U.S. Marshall's office in Chicago.

Voss's telephone call was eventually routed to Melvin Purvis, who was at his apartment, enjoying a rare day off since assuming responsibility for the Dillinger manhunt. At 1:00 p.m., when Purvis spoke with Voss, he was startled by the Wisconsin man's message: "The man you want most is up here."

"You mean Dillinger?" Purvis stammered.

Voss confirmed that Dillinger and four other men were staying at the Little Bohemia Lodge near Manitowish. When Purvis asked for the location of the closest airport, Voss told him Rhinelander, located 50 miles south of Little Bohemia. After explaining that he expected to arrive at the airport by 6:00 p.m., Purvis told Voss to wear a handkerchief around his neck, as a means of ready identification.

Purvis immediately telephoned J. Edgar Hoover in Washington D.C. The Bureau Director instructed Purvis to take as many agents as possible to Wisconsin, and ordered him to coordinate his operation with the St. Paul field office, located only 185 miles from Little Bohemia.

Purvis chartered two airplanes for himself and 11 other agents to make the three-hour, 275-mile flight to Rhinelander. Assistant Bureau Director, Hugh Clegg, who had been temporarily assigned to the St. Paul office, chartered an aircraft for himself and several agents, while also dispatching additional agents by automobile; even though the agents were allowed to carry their weapons aboard the planes, tear gas grenades were prohibited and had to be transported by car.

At Little Bohemia, Dillinger was growing antsy. On Sunday nights, the lodge restaurant offered one-dollar-per-plate dinner specials, which drew a large number of local customers, particularly workers from the Civilian Conservation Corps camp in nearby Mercer. Earlier in the day, Dillinger had informed Wanatka that the group would leave Little Bohemia the following morning. He eventually hastened the departure time to that evening, just as soon as Reilly and Cherrington returned from St. Paul.

Shortly after 5:00 p.m., Assistant Director Clegg, accompanied by four Bureau agents, landed at the airport in Rhinelander. The two planes containing Purvis and his agents arrived an hour later. The trip from Chicago had been prolonged and turbulent—the pilots had to rely on roadmaps to guide them to Rhinelander, and the flight was so bumpy that several passengers and one of the pilots suffered from air sickness.

Once the Chicago and St. Paul agents were on the ground, Henry Voss drew a map of the Little Bohemia Lodge and its surrounding area. By virtue of his seniority, Clegg would be the leader of the operation, with Purvis designated as second in command. At the end of their strategy session, Clegg and Purvis agreed to launch the raid at daybreak, hoping to catch the gang members still in bed.

The plan quickly changed when Voss' wife arrived in Rhinelander. She had been at the Little Bohemia lodge earlier in the afternoon, and after learning from Wanaka that Dillinger and his gang members planned to leave that night, she rushed to notify her husband. Now in hurry-up mode, Clegg and Purvis were forced to borrow and rent cars for the 50-mile drive to Little Bohemia. One of the borrowed vehicles that would ultimately play an unexpected role in the operation was a 1934 Ford Deluxe coupe, owned by a local citizen, 22-year-old Isidor "Izzy" Tuchalsky. The sleek coupe, black with cream-colored wire wheels, had been modified by Tuchalsky, and was now equipped with a more powerful engine and customized rear suspension, enabling the vehicle to reach speeds of 100 miles per hour.

At 7:15 p.m., a five-car caravan, consisting of 17 Bureau agents, departed Rhinelander. The mostly unpaved roads, slick and muddy from melting snow, slowed their progress. Along the way, one vehicle broke down and another had a flat tire; with no time to spare, the agents occupying those cars were forced to complete the trip mounted on the running boards of the other three automobiles.

Shortly before 9:00 p.m., the agents arrived at Henry Voss's home, Birchwood Lodge, located on Route 51, just a mile from Little Bohemia. They were greeted by Nan Wanatka and her daughter, who an hour earlier had snuck away and driven to her sister and brother-in-law's house. Nan informed the group that Dillinger and his associates were still at Little Bohemia, but were planning to leave that night.

In Washington D.C., J. Edgar Hoover was enthusiastic. He had already alerted reporters to a forthcoming "major development in the Dillinger case." Hoover soon revealed that Bureau agents had the Dillinger Gang "trapped in a remote roadhouse," and the outlaws' capture or death was imminent.

The attack plan formulated by Clegg and Purvis called for five agents, clad in bulletproof vests, to enter the front door of the lodge, while 10 other agents would take positions in the woods, covering both sides of the building. It was thought the lake would serve as a natural barrier against anyone attempting to escape from the rear, and required no additional coverage.

Unbeknownst to the agents, Voss's crude map of Little Bohemia exposed them to unanticipated pitfalls. At the rear of the property, a 10-feet steep bank provided cover for anyone moving along the shoreline of Little Star Lake. On the lodge's left flank, a waist-deep ditch served as a natural barrier, while a barbed-wire fence ran along the right side.

It was cold, dark, and moonless when the agents arrived at Little Bohemia. Clegg and Purvis made sure to leave their vehicles parked end-to-end at the bottom of the driveway, not only to prevent engine noise from alerting the occupants of the lodge to their arrival, but also to block other vehicles from escaping. The agents were immediately unnerved by barking sounds; Voss had also failed to inform them that Wanatka owned dogs. While the barking dogs spurred the raiding party to an even greater sense of urgency, those lodging at Little Bohemia, including the Dillinger Gang, took little notice.

When the G-Men arrived on the scene, Dillinger, Van Meter, and Hamilton were in their upstairs rooms. Nelson's wife, Helen, was also on the second floor of the lodge, visiting with Hamilton's girlfriend, Jean. Carroll's exact whereabouts has never been established; he was thought to be either in the cabin with Nelson, or in the lodge's first-floor bar.

Earlier in the evening, around 75 locals had flocked to Little Bohemia to enjoy the dollar-per-plate dinner special. By the time the Bureau agents arrived at the lodge, only three remained on the premises—35-year-old CCC camp foreman, Eugene Boisneau, 28-year-old gas station owner, John Huffman, and 59-year-old John Morris, a cook at the CCC camp.

From his position in the driveway, SAC Purvis observed "four or five men" standing on the lodge's dimly-lit porch. He mistakenly assumed that at that the small group included Dillinger gang members. In reality, the porch-dwellers were the three customers, Boisneau, Huffman, and Morris, the lodge's two employees, George Bazo and Frank Taube, as well as owner, Emil Wanatka. After saying goodnight, Boisneau and Morris climbed into a Chevrolet coupe driven by Hoffman.

As the car made its way down the long driveway, the radio was playing so loudly that the driver and two passengers were oblivious to sounds coming from outside the vehicle. The Chevrolet's approaching headlights soon illuminated Purvis and Clegg, who were standing in its path.

"Police! Stop! Federal agents!" Purvis or Clegg shouted; in the tension of the moment, neither could recall exactly who said what.

When the driver failed to heed the verbal warning, either Purvis or Clegg ordered: "Fire!"

Purvis and Clegg later claimed that they directed the agents to shoot only the vehicle's tires. In the heat of moment, no one apparently heard Frank Taube shout from the porch: "Don't shoot! Those are customers of ours!"

Agents on both sides of the car opened fired with pistols, shotguns, and submachine guns. Nearly 30 shots were fired at the vehicle, shattering glass and flattening all four tires.

The Dillinger gang members were immediately alerted by the gunfire. Nelson was the first to react, running outside the cabin and firing his machine gun pistol in the direction of the driveway. After his wild shots kicked up dirt around Purvis's feet, Nelson ran through the piney woods on the left side of the lodge, slid down the bank, and continued his hurried flight along the lakeshore. Nelson's quick exit, coupled with the difficulty of negotiating the ditch, prevented any of the agents from pursuing him.

Bureau Inspector, William Rorer, and two other agents were approaching the lodge from the left when they spied a man in a second-floor window, preparing to jump. "Police, stop!" Rorer ordered, before firing a shot at the presumed fugitive.

When the man in the window fired back, the Bureau agents answered with three shotgun blasts. During the exchange of gunfire, Rorer thought he saw another man emerge in the window. Once the shooting stopped, Rorer saw no one, and mistakenly assumed the men had retreated inside the lodge.

In reality, Dillinger, Van Meter, and Hamilton, armed only with pistols, had crawled out of the second floor window onto the roof of the rear porch.

After jumping into a snow pile, they ran 75 feet to the lake, slid down the bank, turned right, and escaped along the shoreline. Moments later, Carroll exited the same window and escaped, following the same route as his three fellow gang members. Unbeknownst to the Bureau agents, every one of the male fugitives had fled the premises, right under their noses. Only the women, Helen, Jean, and Marie, remained inside the lodge.

Unaware that the subjects of their manhunt had already escaped, Purvis and Clegg were now focused on the three men who were still inside the bullet riddled Chevrolet. Once the vehicle came to a complete stop, gas station attendant, John Hoffman, who had been shot in the right arm and right leg (and cut on the face and both arms by glass shards), sprinted out of the vehicle. After dodging two shotgun blasts from a Bureau agent, Hoffman disappeared into the woods.

A second man, John Morris, who had been shot twice in the right shoulder with .45 caliber machine guns and wounded by buckshot pellets in his right hip, stumbled out of the car. After identifying himself as "John," Morris slumped to the ground in a sitting position and took a long swallow of whiskey from his pocket flask.

Before Purvis and Clegg could search the automobile, another vehicle arrived on the scene. Pat Reilly and Pat Cherrington, who were late arriving from their sojourn to St. Paul, tried to pull into the driveway, but found it blocked by the cars the Bureau had appropriated in Rhinelander.

"We're federal agents. Identify yourself," Agent Samuel Hardy shouted.

Reilly immediately jammed the car in reverse, backed onto Route 51, and sped away. At least two Bureau agents opened fire, flattening a rear tire and puncturing the radiator, but it was not enough to keep Reilly and Cherrington from escaping the area. While planning the hastily organized raid, the Bureau had neglected to set up roadblocks and failed to notify local law enforcement of their presence in the area, making it much easier for the gang members and their associates to escape. The misadventure at Little Bohemia was life changing for Reilly; arriving in St. Paul, nearly 24 hours later, Reilly informed his wife that he was severing all ties with the Dillinger Gang.

While the Bureau agents were dealing with the suspicious vehicle that had suddenly arrived and departed, a bleeding and intoxicated John Morris staggered up the driveway and entered the lodge. Morris immediately called

Alvin Koerner, who operated the local telephone exchange: "Alvin, its Johnny Morris. I'm at Emil's. Somebody's held up the place. Boiseneau's dead and everybody's knocked out!" After completing the distress call, Morris slid to the kitchen floor and passed out.

While Morris was using the phone, Emil Wanatka and his employees were hiding in the cellar. George Bazo, certain a robbery was afoot, hid his wallet, which contained $50 in tips given to him by Dillinger gang members, in the coal bin.

Inside the shot-up car, the third occupant was not moving. When Clegg leaned inside the vehicle and checked Eugene Boiseneau's pulse, he discovered the man was lifeless. The CCC camp foreman, who had been in the wrong place at the wrong time, was fatally wounded in the head and chest.

"I don't know who that young fellow is, but he's dead," Clegg informed Purvis and the other agents.

Not yet able to separate Dillinger gang members from innocent bystanders, Purvis and Clegg were uncertain about what do next. Consequently, they decided not to storm the lodge until the teargas grenades and additional bulletproof vests arrived by car from St. Paul. For nearly an hour, the idle agents shivered in the cold.

Alerted by John Morris's phone call, an ambulance and physician were dispatched from the nearby CCC camp. When he saw the ambulance arriving on the scene, wounded car passenger, John Hoffman, emerged from the woods.

"Is it all over?" Hoffman shouted.

A Bureau agent quickly frisked the bleeding man, who protested that he was not a criminal. The agent, however, remained unconvinced: "Why did you run from us then?"

"Because you were shooting at me!" Hoffman replied in an incredulous tone.

The camp doctor and Hoffman loudly called out John Morris' name, encouraging him to come out of the lodge. Moments later, Morris, who awakened from his drunken slumber, along with Emil Wanatka, George Bazo, and Frank Taube emerged from the building with their hands raised.

Purvis immediately peppered Wanatka with questions. How many gang members were inside the lodge and cabin? Which rooms were they occupying?

What kinds of weapons did they have? Wanatka, who found Purvis arrogant and overbearing, told him that he was certain the gang had already escaped, and the only people still inside the building were the three young women hiding in the basement.

"Did you see them run off?" Purvis inquired.

"I was too busy running, myself," Wanatka answered.

"We know for a fact that some of Dillinger's men are still in there," Purvis snapped, without any evidence to support his assertion.

Believing that Wanatka was being evasive, Purvis suggested the lodge owner was aiding and abetting the Dillinger Gang. An incensed Wanatka immediately pointed out that he and his wife were the ones who notified the authorities about Dillinger's presence at Little Bohemia.

While Purvis and Clegg were contemplating their next move, Dillinger and his gang members were well on their way to escaping. Tommy Carroll, who was separated from the others, eventually hiked to the town of Manitowish, stole an automobile, and headed to St. Paul.

Dillinger, Van Meter, and Hamilton made their way out of the woods onto Highway 51, one-quarter mile distant from Little Bohemia. After unsuccessfully trying to flag down a passing car, the trio walked to Mitchell's Rest Lake Resort, which consisted of the owner's house and several rental cabins. When the 70-year-old owner, Edward J. Mitchell, answered the knock on his door, the fugitives forced their way inside. Hamilton immediately ripped Mitchell's telephone off the wall, cutting off contact with the outside world.

"You couldn't be Dillinger, could you?" Mitchell's wife inquired, having heard rumors that the infamous bank robber was lodging at Little Bohemia.

"You couldn't have guessed better," Dillinger calmly replied.

Aware that Mr. Mitchell was frightened, Dillinger tried to reassure him: "Now don't worry old man, I'd never harm a hair on your head." When Mitchell explained that his wife, who was lying on the couch, was sick with the flu, Dillinger gently covered her with a blanket: "Here you are, mother."

When Dillinger demanded access to a vehicle, Mitchell informed him that his Model-A Ford was on blocks. Instead, the trio stole a Ford coupe belonging to Robert Johnson, a carpenter, who lived in one of the rental cabins. They also forced Johnson to accompany them on the first leg of their escape;

when the fugitives later stopped for gas, the carpenter was set free, along with seven dollars that Dillinger gave him. Once the felons had left his house, Edward Mitchell reflected on the brief, but unforgettable encounter: "For an outlaw, that Dillinger was a gentleman. He made the others behave—no foul language and cool as a cucumber." Mitchell's gentleman outlaw and his two associates were soon well down the road from Little Bohemia.

Baby Face Nelson, who also fled the lodge on foot, headed in the opposite direction from his fellow gang members. After 30 minutes of traveling along the lakeshore and negotiating the piney woods, he happened upon a cabin, a half-mile south of Little Bohemia. Without knocking, a pistol-wielding Nelson burst in on an unsuspecting couple, Mr. and Mrs. George W. Lange: "Now don't get excited. I won't harm you, but this is a matter of life and death."

Nelson ordered the couple to drive him away from the immediate area in their aging Chevrolet. After traveling less than a mile on Route 51, the automobile's headlights stopped working, aborting the fugitive's immediate escape plan. When Nelson spied the lights of a nearby house, owned by the local switchboard operator, Alvin Koerner, he headed in that direction. After spotting a suspicious vehicle parked in front of his house, Koerner telephoned the Birchwood Lodge, where he communicated his concerns to two Bureau agents, Jay Newman and Carter Baum.

Forty-five minutes earlier, Melvin Purvis had instructed Newman and Baum to drive to the Birchwood Lodge to telephone the agents still in Rhinelander and check on the progress of the tear gas grenades en route from St. Paul, as well as belatedly notify the local authorities about the raid on Little Bohemia. When they left the Birchwood Lodge to investigate the mysterious car parked outside Alvin Koerner's residence, the agents took Izzy Tuchalsky's souped-up Ford.

Accompanied by Constable Carl C. Christensen, the three lawmen were squeezed tight in the front seat of the Ford coupe—Newman was behind the wheel, Baum occupied the middle, and Christensen sat on the passengers' side. When they arrived at Koerner's residence, Nelson was in the process of kidnapping the owner and his car. Easing the Ford to a stop, Newman rolled down the window: "Hold on there. We're federal agents."

"I know who you are—a bunch of fucking government cops with vests on! I can give it to you bastards, high and low!" Nelson angrily announced.

The next few seconds would remain indelibly etched in Constable Christensen's memory: "He was on us with the gun, before we could move. The little jackrabbit flew right out of nowhere. Our car wasn't even stopped, when his gun came through the window." Christensen was amazed by Nelson's odd-looking weapon, "a .45 Colt converted into a machine gun, with a long clip and pistol grip."

Agent Newman, who was armed with a .45 caliber automatic and a .38 caliber revolver, reached inside his coat. Nelson immediately confronted him: "Don't touch that gun or I'll blow your brains out!" He then ordered Newman to exit the vehicle. Nelson would later wonder why Agent Baum, armed with a submachine gun, failed to react: "The big agent (Baum) had me cold. I could never figure out why he didn't pull the trigger on me. I should have been dead, right there."

Unlike Baum, Constable Christensen did not freeze, and drew his pistol. In a split second, Nelson opened fire inside the vehicle, seriously wounding Baum and Christensen, and causing the constable to drop his handgun. Agent Newman, who was in the process of exiting the vehicle, tried to grab Nelson's weapon; during the ensuing struggle, Nelson fired, grazing Newman on the right side of his head and knocking him to the ground.

While Newman was crawling for cover and trying to unholster his pistol, Christensen managed to open the passenger's side door and dive outside the vehicle, but not before another bullet struck him in the back. As he tried to run away, the constable was hit yet again, before falling into a ditch.

Briefly trapped in the middle of the front seat, Agent Baum was struck in the throat by a bullet, which entered above his bulletproof vest, spiraled into his chest cavity, and struck his heart. Mortally wounded, Baum tumbled out of the car, somehow managed to regain his feet, and staggered a short distance, before crumpling sideways over a rail fence.

Lying in the ditch, Constable Christensen managed to grab the submachine gun Baum had dropped, but was unable to release the safety mechanism and fire it. Nelson hopped inside the Ford coupe, and before driving away, fired another burst from his machine gun pistol at Christensen, striking the constable in the foot. As the outlaw sped away, a wounded Agent Newman vainly fired his .45 caliber pistol at the departing vehicle. Christensen later recalled the fugitive's hurried exit: "Nelson gave us a look like he'd like to kill us, but didn't have the time."

Just after 11:00 p.m., SAC Werner Hanni and three other agents from the St. Paul office were speeding north toward Little Bohemia, when they encountered a fast-moving vehicle headed in the opposite direction. Unbeknownst to the Bureau agents, Baby Face Nelson, who had just murdered one of their colleagues, was behind the wheel of the powerful Ford. Using a spotlight, Nelson temporarily blinded the driver of the Bureau car, nearly forcing him to run off the road. Eager to reach the lodge, Hanni decided not to pursue the spotlight-wielding driver of the mysterious vehicle.

Newman, Baum, and Christensen were rushed to a nearby hospital. Newman suffered a concussion from the wound to his scalp and several superficial lacerations from splintering glass, but was stable enough to be discharged after several days. Constable Christensen had eight gunshot wounds—two in the chest, one in the back, one in the left hip, one in the right arm, one in the left leg, one in the left arm, and one in the right foot. When Christensen arrived at the hospital, one of the nurses offered a dismal prognosis: "This one's a goner." In spite of a punctured lung and liver, as well as fractures to his hip, arm, and foot, Christensen ultimately survived. After remaining in the hospital for nearly a year, he was discharged and lived for another 60 years.

Agent Baum was dead on arrival at the hospital. His body was taken to the hospital morgue, where he occupied a table next to the corpse of CCC camp foreman, Eugene Boisneau.

Back at Little Bohemia, the Bureau agents were joined by the local sheriff and several of his deputies. Purvis and Clegg still believed the Dillinger Gang was trapped inside the lodge and were eager to roust them. Even though the tear gas grenades had finally arrived from St. Paul, the agents encountered unexpected difficulties; the lone tear gas gun could not generate enough muzzle velocity to propel the grenades through the lodge's window screens. Under the cover of diversionary gunfire, Agent John McLaughlin was forced to run to the side of the building and toss several grenades through the open door.

At 4:00 a.m., as the noxious fumes wafted throughout the lodge, a woman's voice could be heard: "We'll come out, if you'll stop firing."

"Come out and bring everyone with you, with your hands up," Purvis shouted back.

Jean Delaney, Helen Gillis (Nelson), and Mickey Conforti soon emerged from the building and were placed under arrest. While searching the premises, agents discovered a .351 caliber Winchester rifle hidden under the bed in Dillinger's room and a .45 caliber pistol in the cabin where Nelson had been staying. Inside Carroll's Buick and Hamilton's Ford, they found six submachine guns, two shotguns, a rifle, and five bulletproof vests.

To the dismay of Purvis, Clegg, and the agents under their command, they failed to locate a single member of the Dillinger Gang. By now, Dillinger and the others were well on their way to making Little Bohemia a distant memory.

CHAPTER TWELVE

Shoot to kill, then count to ten

Little Bohemia was a disastrous affair for Melvin Purvis and Hugh Clegg. Bureau agents under their command shot two men named *John*—killing one and wounding the other—but, neither was *John Dillinger*. Adding to their woes, Agent Carter Baum had been killed by Baby Face Nelson.

The press immediately went on the attack. The *Chicago American* featured a damning headline: *DEMAND PURVIS QUIT IN DILLINGER FIASCO*. On Tuesday April 24, 1934, a civic council in Northern Wisconsin began circulating a petition calling for Purvis' suspension. Citing the "irresponsible conduct of federal officers," the petition accused the Bureau agents of "wanton recklessness and disregard of human life in firing upon a car bearing three unarmed and respected citizens," and condemned them for "criminal stupidity." J. Edgar Hoover, who considered any criticism of the Bureau loathsome, managed to exercise considerable restraint. He instructed Inspector W. A. Rorer to "not try to suppress the petition or interfere with it."

The Vilas County Coroner's Office held a formal inquest into the deaths of Agent Baum and Eugene Boisneau. When Melvin Purvis and six other agents were called to testify, they unanimously defended their actions, explaining that the driver of the car transporting Boisneau had been ordered to halt. At the same time, the agents disingenuously claimed that Boisneau was caught in a cross fire between the lawmen and the Dillinger Gang.

The agents' testimony was enough to convince the coroner that their actions were justified. The inquest found Boisneau's death was "a result of gunshot wounds inflicted by federal agents in the act of apprehending the

Dillinger Gang." The names of the agents who fired the shots at the vehicle, including the deceased Carter Baum, were not disclosed, and they were all exonerated of any wrong-doing.

The debacle at Little Bohemia had national political ramifications. For a time, rumors circulated that Hoover would be relieved of the Bureau directorship. A reporter for the *Chicago Tribune* speculated that Hoover would be fired unless the Bureau captured Dillinger "real soon."

The *Associated Press* reported that the federal government had spent two million dollars trying to capture Dillinger—four times the total amount of money the fugitive had stolen from banks. Attorney General Homer Cummings, however, offered an opposing argument, laying blame on inadequate funding. Testifying before a congressional subcommittee, just one day after the failed raid, Cummings shared his concerns: "If we had had an armored car up there in Wisconsin, our men could have driven up to the house where Dillinger was. The terrible tragedy then would not have happened." Cummings' appeal was poorly received by some lawmakers. Senator Royal S. Copeland, Chairman of the Committee on Racketeering, was particularly harsh: "There has been a pathetic failure of cooperation between federal, state, and local authorities."

The national press made Hoover and Purvis the scapegoats. The *Milwaukee Sentinel* featured a scathing headline: COMIC OPERA COPS. Another newspaper headline parodied the failed raid as Custer-like, labeling it the *Battle of Little Bohemia*. The *Chicago Times* lambasted the Bureau for transforming the manhunt for Dillinger into a "farce comedy" that "turned to tragedy in killing innocent bystanders rather than the hunted desperado." The *Chicago Herald and Examiner* headlined: U.S. AGENTS IN DILLINGER HUNT CALLED STUPID. Humorist, Will Rogers, added his own satirical commentary: "Well, they had Dillinger surrounded, and was all ready to shoot him when he came out. But, another bunch of folks came out ahead; so they just shot them instead. Dillinger is going to accidently get in with some innocent bystanders some time, then he will get shot!" A few Bureau agents even managed to join in the fun, nicknaming the SAC of the Chicago office as "Nervous Purvis."

Attempting to mask his embarrassment, Purvis initially avoided reporters. When he finally made a formal statement, Purvis tried to be encouraging: "We've got more evidence to work on than we ever had before in hunting Dillinger. We'll have him before long. His trail is getting broader every minute." Attorney General Cummings echoed Purvis' statements: "...We have had a setback. We have been touched by sorrow. That is the part which makes all of us the more determined to go on. We will go on. This campaign against predatory crime will be finished."

In spite of its public display of optimism and bravado, the entire Bureau was traumatized by the murder of Agent Baum and the wounding of Agent Newman. The death of the likeable Baum caused many of his fellow agents, most of whom were young men, to contemplate their own mortality, and soberly reminded them of the risks associated with chasing down gangsters.

J. Edgar Hoover was shaken by the events at Little Bohemia and appalled when the press lampooned the Bureau's folly—he wanted triumphs, not tragedies. In a memorandum to Purvis, the Director instructed him to engage in "less raiding," and rely on "more confidential informants."

When Purvis offered to resign and assume the lion's share of the blame, the Director turned him down. Instead, Hoover defended the actions of his agents in a memorandum to the Attorney General: "...They were approaching a known gangsters' hide-out, and they saw three men leaving this hide-out. These three men were called upon to halt, but instead of doing so, they entered an automobile and proceeded to drive away, and consequently, the agents fired."

Had he accepted Purvis' resignation, the Director would have been forced to publicly acknowledge the Bureau's failure; and failure was not an option for Hoover. Instead, Hoover saw to it that the wounding and killing of innocent citizens at Little Bohemia was excised from the Bureau's history. For now, Purvis remained Hoover's pet, but the affectionate relationship was showing signs of strain. Deflecting criticism from Purvis, Hoover informed the Attorney General that Assistant Director Clegg was "in charge of the detail at all times." Hoover soon found another target for his frustration, accusing SAC Werner Hanni of an "inexcusable" lapse in judgment, when he failed to stop the car driven by the murderous Baby Face Nelson. In the eyes of the Director, Hanni had missed an excellent opportunity to partially negate the disaster at Little Bohemia.

That Monday, as Dillinger and his fellow gang members were fleeing Little Bohemia, state and local authorities set up roadblocks in Wisconsin and

Minnesota, hoping to snare the fugitives. A number of citizens, armed with shotguns and hunting rifles, formed vigilante bands, patrolling the smaller highways and country roads, but their efforts went for naught.

Tommy Carroll was the first gang member to escape northern Wisconsin. In a stolen Packard, he drove furiously, until the vehicle slid off a muddy road into a ditch. From there, he hitched rides the remainder of the way to St. Paul.

After freeing the stolen Ford coupe's owner near Park Falls, Wisconsin, Dillinger, Van Meter, and Hamilton stuck mainly to country roads during the drive to St. Paul. At 10:30 a.m., the trio crossed the Mississippi River in Hastings, Minnesota, 20 miles south of St. Paul. Four local police officers were parked at the south end of the river bridge checking license plates, comparing the numbers and letters on the tags of passing vehicles to a list of stolen vehicles from the Little Bohemia area, which had been supplied by the Bureau in a flash bulletin. When the fugitives' Ford coupe passed by, the lawmen were stunned to discover the Wisconsin license plate, B92652, was on their list.

The policemen immediately gave chase across the bridge, but were delayed by a slow-moving cattle truck. The cruiser also lacked a two-way radio, making it impossible for the officers to notify the authorities in St. Paul. Ten miles after crossing the bridge, the lawmen finally caught up with the fugitives, who were driving at a leisurely 40 miles per hour.

Leaning out the window of the police car, one of the officers opened fired with his 30-30 rifle, unsuccessfully attempting to flatten one of the stolen vehicle's rear tires. As Van Meter accelerated, Dillinger, who was sitting in the back seat, shattered the rear windshield with the butt of his automatic rifle and started returning fire.

The running shoot-out progressed for nearly 50 miles, at speeds of up to 80 miles per hour. Van Meter followed such a circuitous route, that by the time the pursuit had ended, the fugitives were only two miles distant from its starting point. Some 30 to 40 shots were exchanged between the two vehicles. Dillinger managed to shatter the front windshield of the cruiser, but failed to hit any of the police officers. In contrast, a bullet fired by one of the police officers managed to pass through the body of the Ford, between the rear fender and spare tire; Hamilton, who was seated in the passenger's side front seat, was struck in the lower back and gravely wounded.

After rounding a blind curve, Van Meter cleverly exited the highway onto a dirt road. When the pursuing police car sped past, the chase was over. For the next two hours, the gang members slowly made their way north, sticking to unpaved roads. Hamilton was bleeding profusely and in immediate need of medical care. The fugitives were also searching for a less recognizable vehicle.

Nearing the noon hour, Van Meter eased to the shoulder of a gravel road, three miles south of St. Paul. Before long, an automobile driven by Roy Francis, a district manager for the Northern States Power Company approached; Francis was enjoying a leisurely midday drive with his wife, Sybil, and their 19-month-old son, Robert. Francis' blissful excursion came to a screeching halt when Van Meter, armed with a pistol, stepped into the middle of the road.

"I'm sorry to trouble you, but I've got to have your machine," Van Meter informed the couple.

After Francis exited the vehicle with his arms raised, and his wife, cradling the baby, stepped out the passenger's side door, Van Meter tried to reassure them: "Keep your hands down. We won't shoot you."

"What do you do?" Van Meter asked the driver.

"I work at the power company," Francis replied.

"You're lucky to have a nice job and family," Van Meter opined.

Before stealing Francis' 1934 Ford V-8 Deluxe, Dillinger smiled and gently caressed the baby's head: "Don't worry, we like kids."

Dillinger sped away in the stolen vehicle, while Van Meter and Hamilton followed in the Ford coupe. After hiking to a gas station, two miles away, Francis telephoned the police.

Realizing federal, state, and local law enforcement agents would now be focused on St. Paul, Dillinger and Van Meter transferred their weapons and the injured Hamilton into the stolen car, and headed for Chicago. Along the way, they abandoned the bloodied Ford, and also made a brief stop in Dubuque, Iowa, purchasing a first aid kit, in a vain effort to treat Hamilton's wound.

In the wake of the raid at Little Bohemia, Baby Face Nelson finally achieved national recognition. The Justice Department characterized him as "John Dillinger's top trigger man," and "the gang's vicious machine gunner."

Hoover's focus on Nelson was a calculated choice—by shifting attention to Agent Baum's murderer, the public's focus would be diverted from the murder of the innocent John Boisneau.

It took Nelson much longer to escape from northern Wisconsin than his fellow fugitives. Just 12 miles west of Little Bohemia, the hotrod Ford Nelson hijacked from the Bureau agents broke down. Armed with his machine gun pistol, a .45 caliber handgun, and Constable Christensen's .38 caliber revolver, the fugitive continued his escape on foot. Bypassing the highways, where law enforcement officers might be patrolling, Nelson walked cross country for nearly 20 miles, until he reached the Lac du Flambeau Indian Reservation.

Nelson eventually stumbled upon a three-room cabin occupied by a young woman named Mary Schroeder and her two daughters. A full-blooded Chippewa Indian, Schroeder was staying in the cabin owned by her aunt and uncle, Maggie and Ollie Catfish, while her husband was on a trapping expedition. When Nelson first arrived, Schroeder's aunt and uncle were on an overnight visit to a nearby town.

"Hello, mother, could I buy some lunch from you? Your baking smells good," Nelson greeted Mary.

After she fed the stranger breakfast, Schroeder accepted two dollars in payment. She also gave Nelson a pair of khaki pants and a sleeveless plaid shirt that belonged to her husband, which he slipped over his existing clothing for added warmth, and then settled down for a long nap.

Later in the day, when Ollie and Maggie Catfish arrived home, Nelson quizzed them about the local geography, and learned the closest town was six miles away. The remote cabin, lacking a telephone or radio, appeared to be an ideal temporary hiding place for Nelson.

Nelson lodged with his adopted family for four days, during which time he helped with chores, including splitting fire wood and making syrup. Mary Schroeder later recalled that their mysterious guest, who kept three guns hidden beneath his cot, was "nice and polite" and "very friendly with the kids."

On Thursday April 26th, after paying Schroeder $70 for expenses related to his three-night stay, Nelson asked Ollie Catfish to guide him to the nearest highway, located three miles away. When they finally reached the highway,

Nelson encountered Adolph Goetz, a postal worker and local deputy sheriff, who was parked adjacent to a lake.

"Whose car is that?" Nelson asked.

"Mine," Goetz replied.

"I want the keys," Nelson demanded.

"Who are you? What's your authority for this?" Goetz challenged.

"Never mind—I want the keys," Nelson repeated, drawing a pistol.

Once Goetz handed over the keys, Nelson explained why he was taking the vehicle: "I'm in trouble. I need a car to get out of this country. I want to get out right away."

After disabling the only other car parked in the area, by ripping out the engine's distributor cap, Nelson offered to purchase Goetz's vehicle. When Goetz informed him that he did not have the title in his possession, Nelson asked if the automobile was insured. After Goetz answered in the affirmative, Nelson quipped: "You'll get paid for it then."

Nelson gave Goetz $20 "to take you home," and then ordered Ollie Catfish to join him in the car. The fugitive drove south, then west, until he was a safe distance away, before freeing Ollie. Some 140 miles distant from Little Bohemia, the stolen Plymouth burned out a connecting rod, and Nelson was again forced to travel by foot. Arriving at a farmhouse along the way, Nelson told the owner, Joseph Gregorich, that he was a CCC employee. In exchange for $20, Gregorich agreed to drive Nelson to the closest town, Marshfield, Wisconsin.

"What are you looking at me for so much?" an amused Nelson asked the farmer during their drive into town, "Are you scared? Maybe you think I'm Dillinger."

An unsuspecting Gregorich never considered the youthful stranger to be a threat; in fact, he thought Nelson was still a teenager. The farmer, however, was curious. How could a CCC worker afford to pay $20 for a short car ride?

"I've been doing a little bootlegging on the side," Nelson replied.

Just outside Marshfield, Nelson instructed Gregorich to stop. Nelson paid the farmer an additional $10, before watching him drive away. After shedding the outer layer of clothing given to him by Mary Schroeder, Nelson hiked the rest of the way into town. At Marshfield Hardware and Auto Company, Nelson told the salesman that he wanted to purchase a car with "a good motor and good rubber." He then negotiated a price of $165 for a 1929 Chevrolet; on the bill of sale, Nelson listed his name as *Harold Aaron*, a resident of Greenwood, Wisconsin. From Marshfield, Nelson drove to Chicago and became the last member of the Second Dillinger Gang to escape rural Wisconsin.

Dillinger, Van Meter, and the gravely wounded Hamilton arrived in Chicago on Tuesday morning, one day after the Little Bohemia raid. Dr. Joseph Moran examined Hamilton and cleaned his wounds; by this time, however, gangrene had set in, and he was clearly dying. The three fugitives took immediate refuge in an apartment rented by Barker/Karpis gang member, Volney Davis, located in Aurora, 45 miles southwest of Chicago.

Hamilton died on Thursday April 26th, three days after being shot. That night, Dillinger, Van Meter, and two Barker/Karpis gang members took Hamilton's body to a quarry, six miles south of Aurora. Before placing Hamilton's body in a freshly-dug grave, Dillinger took rather extreme precautions to make it difficult for the authorities to identify the remains. He severed the corpse's right hand, which was distinctively marked by two amputated fingers, and disposed of it in a separate location. He also poured lye on Hamilton's head, to obliterate his facial features. In the process of mutilating the corpse, Dillinger mournfully addressed his long-time friend: "Red, old pal, I hate to do this, but I know you'd do the same for me."

Before filling the grave, Dillinger placed a horse shoe on Hamilton's chest— a symbol of "good luck" in the afterlife. Before leaving, Dillinger positioned a roll of barbed wire over the grave, to serve as a make-shift tombstone.

For several days, Dillinger and Van Meter hid in Volney Davis' apartment. While grieving Hamilton's death, Dillinger grew increasingly paranoid, believing Louis Cernocky, the tavern owner who directed the gang to Little Bohemia, had also notified the Bureau of their ultimate destination. For the next few days, Dillinger and Van Meter kept guns at their sides, around the clock, and wore bulletproof vests when they slept.

The Bureau continued to be flooded with bogus sightings of Dillinger, as far away as California and Canada. On May 4th, the Chicago Police Department asked Scotland Yard to carefully search for Dillinger among the guests and crewmembers departing all ships that sailed to the United Kingdom from the United States and Canada. The Department of Justice requested that Canadian officials be on the look-out for Dillinger, who was rumored to be fleeing North America aboard a British vessel. The captains of all Canadian Pacific steamships were advised to search their ships before taking to the seas. In Glasgow, Scotland, the *Duchess of York*, which had steamed across the Atlantic from Halifax, was thoroughly searched for anyone fitting Dillinger's description.

The Bureau continued to generate encouraging and often disingenuous press releases. Melvin Purvis informed an *Associated Press* reporter that he had received reliable information that Dillinger had died from gunshot wounds sustained at Little Bohemia. The fictional tidbit was largely based on blood stains found in the vehicle outside St. Paul, which originated from the now-deceased John Hamilton.

The three women who were arrested at Little Bohemia, 21-year-old Helen Gillis (Nelson), 22-year-old Jean Delaney, and 19-year-old Marie Conforti, were largely uncooperative with the authorities. After initially being incarcerated at the jail in Eagle River, Wisconsin, the prisoners were transferred to Dane County Jail, located in the capital city of Madison. The attractive young women garnered considerable attention from the press, who christened them the "Mollettes."

Bureau agents, Sam Hardy and R. G. Gillespie, informed the county sheriff that the Mollettes were *federal prisoners*, who should be incarcerated in isolated cells and deprived of routine inmate privileges. The arrestees persistently refused to cooperate with their G-Men interrogators. Nelson's wife, Helen, identified herself as the newly-married *Marion Virginia Marr*. The defiant *Mrs. Marr* claimed that Little Bohemia was a scheduled stop on their honeymoon trip.

At midnight on the first day of the Mollettes' incarceration, the sheriff's office received a tip that the Dillinger Gang was poised to stage a jail break. Reacting to yet another hysterical rumor, 12 armed guards took the three female prisoners to a nearby church, where they were hidden away until the following morning.

The luggage the fugitives left behind at Little Bohemia offered little in the way of meaningful information about their future plans. Bureau agents did discover a business card for Father Philip Caughlin, a priest and friend of Baby Face Nelson's family. Agents soon interrogated Caughlin, who lived just outside of Chicago. The priest revealed nothing about Nelson's current whereabouts, but did disclose the names and locations of the fugitive's family members. Afterwards, Melvin Purvis placed Nelson's mother and sister under surveillance.

Earl Connelly, the SAC of the Bureau's Cincinnati office, whose territory included Mooresville, Indiana, exerted pressure on Dillinger's family. On at least one occasion, Connelly's efforts proved embarrassing. After establishing a relationship with Dillinger's nephew, Norman Hancock, Connelly enlisted him as a spy. While Connelly and six other Bureau agents hid near the farm, Hancock entered the Dillinger's house under the auspices of helping John, Sr. build a fence. Hancock had been instructed by Connelly to wipe his face with a handkerchief if he discovered the fugitive inside the house. When Hancock emerged from the house with John, Sr., he twice wiped his face with the handkerchief. As the two men began walking to the spot where the fence was to be erected, Bureau agents stormed them.

Much to Connelly's dismay and embarrassment, Hancock's supposed signal meant nothing—John Dillinger was nowhere near Mooresville. Adding insult to injury, Captain Matt Leach proclaimed that Connelly's ill-conceived raid had jeopardized the chances of any law enforcement agency capturing Dillinger in Indiana. Leach's rant further poisoned the deteriorating relationship between the Bureau and the Indiana State Police. Bureau agents continued to keep the Dillinger farm under surveillance, but their efforts proved fruitless.

A few days after burying John Hamilton, Dillinger and Van Meter left their hide-away in Aurora and rendezvoused with Tommy Carroll in Chicago. On the night of May 2nd, the trio travelled to the Fort Wayne, Indiana home of Audrey Russ—a long-time friend of the Van Meter family. Russ, his wife, and their 11-year old-daughter were less than enthusiastic about hosting the wanted men, but agreed to let them to stay the night. While the fugitives were unpacking, Russ was appalled to see Dillinger carrying four submachine guns, an armload of bulletproof vests, and a stack of stolen license plates into his house.

Russ later told authorities that Dillinger regaled him with stories about his Crown Point jail break and the Bureau's raid on Little Bohemia. Dillinger also told Russ that he would never be taken alive; if he was cornered, Dillinger promised that "several" lawmen would also die. While ridiculing state and local authorities as "a lot of clucks," Dillinger informed Russ that he was far more concerned about the "feds," whose money and resources enabled them to engage in relentless pursuit, to the extent of being able to rent airplanes.

Around this same time, Dillinger indulged his mischievous sense of humor, writing Henry Ford a letter complimenting him on the quality of the manufacturer's new V-8 models: *Hello Old Pal: Arrived here at 10 a.m. today. (I've) been driving it for three weeks. It's a treat to drive one. Your slogan should be, drive a Ford and watch the other cars fall behind you. I can make any other car take a Ford's dust. Bye-bye, John Dillinger.* The legendary automobile maker reportedly kept Dillinger's letter on display for years to come. Aside from its humorous overtones, Dillinger's missive may have been a ploy designed to trick authorities into believing that he was hiding out in the Detroit area.

On the morning of Wednesday, May 3rd, Dillinger, Van Meter, and Carroll departed the Russ's house and drove to Toledo, Ohio, where they stole a black V-8 Ford adorned with yellow wire wheels. Their funds nearly exhausted, the trio drove to Fostoria, a small town located 40 miles south of Toledo, which Van Meter had previously scouted. At 2:30 p.m., Dillinger and Van Meter, armed with submachine guns hidden underneath their overcoats, entered the bank lobby via a connecting drug store, while Carroll remained behind the wheel of their stolen get-away car.

"Stick 'em up!" Van Meter announced, pointing his Tommy gun at the tellers.

Van Meter soon forced the bank president, Andrew Emerine, and assistant cashier, William Daub, to open the vault. Dillinger strolled through the swinging doors into the area behind the tellers' cages and began filling his sacks with cash, while Van Meter kept the bank employees clustered at gunpoint.

"Don't kill me!" a tearful female employee begged.

"You be quiet, and I won't," Van Meter replied.

When a handful of customers on the mezzanine level stared down into the lobby, Van Meter scattered them with a burst of fire from his submachine gun. Not yet done, he fired several more shots at the partition separating the lobby from the cages, shattering the glass. While Van Meter was blasting away with his Tommy gun, one of the bank tellers, Frances Hillyard, managed to slip out of the building and notify Chief of Police Frank Culp that a robbery was in progress. While the 67-year-old Culp may have been past his prime, he remained an excellent marksman, who had gunned down his share of felons.

Culp cautiously entered the bank lobby through the same drug store entrance the robbers had used. The police chief planned to take the elevator to the mezzanine, where he could get a drop on the bandits. Van Meter, however, spotted Culp immediately, and fired a single shot from his Tommy gun, which sent the lawmen reeling back into the drug store. The bullet entered Culp's chest and penetrated his lung; though seriously wounded, he eventually recovered from the shooting.

After hearing another shot coming from inside the bank, Carroll exited the get-away car and fired several bursts from his submachine gun, shattering the plate glass windows of neighboring businesses. By now, Dillinger had bagged more than $17,000 in cash and bonds. Eyeing the growing commotion outside the bank's front entrance, Van Meter shouted to Dillinger: "It's too hot out there. Let's go through the drug store."

Forcing bank employees William Daub and Ruth Harris to lead the way, the bandits exited the bank through the drug store. Once outside the building, Van Meter impulsively fired a machine gun volley at the elk's head hanging above the entrance of the local lodge, located just across the street from the bank.

After ordering the hostages to mount the get-away car's twin running boards, the bank robbers raced out of town, scattering roofing nails in their wake. Two miles outside of town, the hostages were set free.

"Thanks," Dillinger smiled to Daub and Harris, as the Ford raced away.

Carroll took leave of his two partners soon after the heist, presumably returning to St. Paul. For several days, Dillinger and Van Meter hid out in a ramshackle house in Lake County, Indiana, not far from Crown Point—the site of Dillinger's infamous wooden gun jail break.

On May 7th, gang member, John Paul Chase, purchased a red-paneled, Ford V-8 delivery truck from Rimes Motor Company in East Chicago, employing the alias of *Addie James*. The truck, which cost $637, was similar to those used by many grocery stores. The vehicle became a mobile hide-away for Dillinger and Van Meter, who traveled the back roads of Indiana and the outlying areas of Chicago. At night, the pair slept on a mattress in the rear of the truck.

On the night of May 9th, Dillinger and Van Meter, desirous of a home-cooked meal and at least one night's rest in a real bed, returned to Audrey Russ' house in Fort Wayne. Aware of their forthcoming visit, an anxious Russ informed his boss at the Western Gas Company, who in turn notified the Bureau's South Bend, Indiana office. However, when Melvin Purvis was notified, for reasons unknown, he chose to ignore this very solid lead.

After enjoying a one-night stay at Russ' residence, Dillinger and Van Meter departed the next morning. Russ once again contacted his boss, who put his employee in touch with Bureau agents. While he was able to describe the fugitive's paneled truck, a panicked Russ had neglected to write down or memorize the vehicle's license plate. Yet again, Purvis was just hours behind Dillinger, and belatedly assigned agents to place Russ' house under surveillance.

The agents who manned the stake-out found it decidedly unpleasant, describing Mrs. Russ as "demented" and possessing a "mean and avaricious disposition." The presence of Bureau agents inside her house infuriated Mrs. Russ; so much so, that she accused the G-Men of numerous transgressions, including spitting on her floor.

On Thursday May 10th, one week after the bank robbery in Fostoria, Dillinger briefly visited the LaSalle Street gas station in Indianapolis, where his nephew, Fred Hancock, was employed. Unshaven and wearing eyeglasses, Dillinger wore an odd disguise, donning overalls, a blue shirt, blue tie, sleeveless jacket, and brown hat. The fugitive delivered four packets of cash to his nephew: $550 for John, Sr., $500 for his sister, Audrey, $100 for his half-brother, Hubert, and $100 for Fred. Dillinger instructed Hancock to inform John, Sr. that if anything happened to him (Dillinger), Billie Frechette was entitled to a portion of the stolen cash hidden away at the family farm.

Bureau agent, Lish Whitson, who had the gas station under surveillance that day, actually witnessed Dillinger's visit. At first, Whitson thought the oddly-dressed visitor was merely a "bum." After managing a closer look at the man and observing the distinctive cleft in his chin, Whitson decided to follow Dillinger on foot. Whitson was within 100 feet of the stranger, when Dillinger made an abrupt turn onto Washington Street. By the time Whitson reached the intersection, the supposed bum was nowhere in sight.

Throughout May of 1934, the general public remained enthralled by the Dillinger case. The hysteria led to multiple false sightings of the fugitive in Chicago, Omaha, Mooresville, New York City, Montreal, the Yucatan Peninsula, and Charleston, South Carolina. A *Time* magazine reporter shared his witty observations: "If John Dillinger has really been at all the places he was reported to have been in the last month, he must leap along the central plains like a demented Indian's ghost." *Time* satirically featured the manhunt in a board game called *Dillinger Land*, with the "game starts here" position centered over Crown Point, Indiana.

A byproduct of the media frenzy was the romanticizing of Dillinger as an underdog, who was being pursued by powerful, yet inept, local, state, and federal law enforcement agencies. When asked about Dillinger, a Boy Scout in Indiana summed up the feelings of many Midwesterners: "Personally, I'm for him." *Detective* magazine featured the results of a poll taken by movie theater owners: "In point of popularity, they ranked, in order, Dillinger first, President Roosevelt second, and Colonel (Charles) Lindbergh third, thereby actually making this notorious thief, thug, and cold-blooded murderer the outstanding national hero of the hour!"

Many of Dillinger's home town citizens viewed him as anything but threatening. A Mooresville bank clerk echoed the prevailing sentiments: "I wouldn't be afraid if John walked in here right now. He's a town boy, and I don't think he would hurt any of us. We don't even take precautions against him."

A group of Indiana citizens actually circulated a petition to the Governor, asking him to pardon Dillinger in exchange for the fugitive's promise that he would no longer engage in criminal activities. John Dillinger, Sr. agreed with the idea of a pardon, even suggesting that his son had the makings of a good law enforcement officer! Some Hoosier State residents suggested that Dillinger should run for Governor—once elected, he could pardon himself.

Dillinger's father was offered $500 per week, a fortune during the Great Depression, to travel the vaudeville circuit and lecture about his son's life. Now 70 years old and uncomfortable speaking in public, John, Sr. declined the offer. *Universal Newsreel Company* promised a $5,000 reward to anyone

THE WAR ON CRIME

who could alert them in advance of Dillinger's capture. Clarence Darrow, the defense attorney in the famed Scopes Monkey Trial, used the media to send a "call me" message to Dillinger; it was Darrow's opinion that Dillinger had received a harsh prison sentence as a result of his original felony conviction (the mugging of Indianapolis grocer, Frank Morgan).

The Dillinger case continued to influence the national legislative process. On May 5th, the House of Representatives passed 10 of the 12 anti-crime bills submitted by Attorney General Cummings. One of the new laws, which J. Edgar Hoover had long championed, made the murder of a Bureau agent a federal crime. Interstate flight and robbing federally insured banks were also added to the federal crime code.

On May 19th, President Roosevelt signed six of those bills into law. Roosevelt used the bully pulpit of the presidency to take dead aim at the wanted fugitives and scold many of his unenlightened countrymen: "Law enforcement and gangster extermination cannot be effective while a substantial part of the public looks with tolerance upon known criminals, or applauds efforts to romanticize crime."

For the better part of two weeks, Dillinger and Van Meter lived in their red-paneled truck. The pair took baths at tourist camps and occasionally spent a night or two at those same camps, to escape the narrow confines of their mobile hide-away.

On May 19th, Dillinger met with his attorney's investigator, Art O'Leary, on the outskirts of Chicago. While Dillinger drove and O'Leary sat in the passenger's seat, Van Meter stared out the back window of the delivery truck, armed with a submachine gun. Sick with a respiratory infection and fever, Dillinger was in dismal spirits as he inquired about Billie Frechette's case. He instructed O'Leary to remind his attorney, Louis Piquett, that he was still interested in undergoing cosmetic surgery.

The following evening, when O'Leary visited again, he brought Dillinger a bottle of cough medicine, a pint of whiskey, and a letter from Frechette. In the missive, Billie warned Dillinger against trying to break her out of jail in St. Paul, and expressed a willingness to serve out her sentence. Once she had completed her jail time, Frechette wrote, the two lovers could reunite. At the conclusion of this visit, Dillinger gave O'Leary $600 to pass along to Piquett for legal fees.

Around this same time, Dillinger sent a letter to Pat Cherrington informing her of John Hamilton's death. Cherrington was angry and hurt that her
lover had left no money for her. To placate a disappointed Cherrington, who
might have been tempted to take out her frustrations by contacting the
authorities, Dillinger sent her a packet of cash, drawn from his share of the
money stolen in the Fostoria bank robbery.

On May 21st, Dillinger, Van Meter, and a third man (perhaps Carroll)
robbed a small bank in Galion, Ohio, located just 40 miles southeast of their
most recent heist in Fostoria. In jackrabbit fashion, Dillinger vaulted over the
eight-feet-high partition to gain access to the tellers' cash drawers. The robbers managed to steal $5,400, before the alarm rang. At this point, Dillinger
and Van Meter bypassed the vault and exited the bank through its rear windows, hoping to avert a shoot-out. This change in tactics signaled a newfound
urgency, and may have been the direct result of newly-adopted federal government policies. In attempt to stem the tide of bank robberies, the government had shipped surplus World War I weapons to Federal Reserve banks. The
bank presidents were authorized to issue the guns to neighboring business
owners. The prospect of encountering well-armed civilians in areas surrounding banks exposed the bank robbers to even greater risks.

In the latter half of May, Billie Frechette, along with three others accused
of aiding and abetting the Dillinger Gang, were tried in St. Paul. On day one
of her trial, during a midday recess, Frechette managed to meander into the
hallway, and was briefly hidden among the crowd of courtroom spectators.
Just before Frechette reached an exit door, a police officer nabbed her.

"I was just going to have lunch with the other folks. I was coming back,
really," Billie smiled.

Throughout her incarceration and trial, Frechette remained unrepentant.
Just prior to her extradition from Chicago to St. Paul, she once again taunted
Bureau agents: "Watch out for John. He's the big, bad wolf, you know."

On May 23rd, the jury found Frechette guilty of *harboring a fugitive*; she
was sentenced to a two-year term at the Women's Federal Penitentiary in
Milam, Michigan and fined $1,000. That same day, Dr. Clayton May was found
guilty for failing to report his treatment of Dillinger's gunshot wound, and

was sentenced to two years at the federal penitentiary in Fort Leavenworth. May's nurse, however, was acquitted. Eddie Green's widow, Bessie, who had been the Bureau's most cooperative witness, was sentenced to 15 months in prison (the sentence was later reduced to nine months).

The three Mollettes, Helen Gillis (Nelson), Marie Conforti, and Jean Delaney, who had been arrested at Little Bohemia, appeared before Federal Magistrate Patrick T. Stone on May 25th. After pleading guilty to *harboring*, they were each sentenced to probation for one year. Stone explained his rationale for the seemingly lenient punishment: "The court is satisfied that while the girls are technically guilty, they didn't do anything to aid in the concealment of Dillinger. It is doubtful a jury would have convicted these girls."

J. Edgar Hoover, who had vowed to make an example of anyone associating with John Dillinger, was furious. Stone tried to reassure the Bureau Director, explaining that the Dillinger gang members "would attempt to contact" the newly freed women. If Bureau agents kept the three under surveillance, baiting and watching the trap, the outlaws might be lured into capture.

The Mollettes were allowed to serve their probationary sentences in Chicago. Prior to departing Wisconsin, Marie Conforti, who had grown weary of her media moniker, confronted reporters outside the courtroom: "Don't call us Molls. We hate that!" Nelson's wife, Helen, made an effort to exploit the tension between the Bureau and state/local law enforcement: "Everyone in Madison has been very nice to us. The federal men are the only ones who acted rough."

On May 23, 1934, law enforcement achieved a long-awaited victory in the War on Crime, when a posse gunned down the infamous Bonnie (Parker) and Clyde (Barrow), just outside Gibsland, Louisiana. The Bureau, which had not been directly involved in the case, was unable to share in the accolades. John Dillinger was decidedly unimpressed, referring to Bonnie and Clyde as a "couple of kids stealing grocery money."

Just a day after Bonnie and Clyde were killed, Dillinger was implicated in another high-profile felony. Two East Chicago Police Department detectives, Martin O'Brien and Lloyd Mulvihill, were found shot to death in their automobile. Before leaving the police station for their final time, the detectives reportedly told a fellow officer that they were en route to investigate a tip concerning Dillinger's whereabouts.

When the two bodies were discovered, the lawmen's pistols were still holstered, suggesting an ambush. The detectives had been shot multiple times at point blank range with a submachine gun and a .38 caliber pistol. East Chicago Police Chief, Nick Makar, immediately accused Dillinger of murdering the two detectives. The case, however, was far from open and shut, and the police department closed a blind eye to the conflict within its own ranks. Detective Mulvihill and a notoriously corrupt East Chicago cop, Detective Martin Zarkovich, were known to detest one another. Mulvihill was believed to possess information linking Zarkovich with Dillinger, even suggesting that he (Zarkovich) had aided the fugitive in his escape from the jail in Crown Point. Rumors arose that Zarkovich and an accomplice had been the ones who gunned down the detectives, or had made arrangements for Dillinger and Van Meter to carry out the ambush, in exchange for future protection from local authorities.

Now accused of a double homicide, Dillinger felt even more pressure. Fearing that it was no longer safe to hide out in their delivery truck, Dillinger and Van Meter met with Tommy Carroll and Baby Face Nelson at a cottage in Wauconda, Illinois, just north of Chicago, on the night of May 24th. From there, Nelson drove the pair to the nearby Rain-Bo Inn, owned and operated by one of his acquaintances, Jimmy Murray. For the next three days, Dillinger and Van Meter took refuge in the tavern's attic.

On Sunday, May 27th, Dillinger and Van Meter relocated to a residence at 2509 North Crawford Avenue in North Chicago. The two-story house was rented by Jimmy Probasco, an acquaintance of both Jimmy Murray and Dillinger's attorney, Louis Piquett. The 76-year-old Probasco had his own shady past, running a speakeasy during Prohibition and fencing stolen goods. Even though he had been arrested several times, Probasco had somehow avoided conviction, all the while maintaining close connections to the underworld. Hoping to save enough money to purchase a tavern, Probasco agreed to house Dillinger and Van Meter for $35 per day. Probasco introduced Dillinger to his live-in girlfriend, 33-year-old Margaret "Peggy" Doyle, as *Mr. Harris*, who hailed from Naperville, Illinois, and would be staying with them for a few weeks.

The night after Dillinger and Van Meter settled into Probasco's house, Art O'Leary arrived with the two physicians Louis Piquett had recruited to perform plastic surgery on Dillinger and Van Meter. The lead surgeon, 58-year-old Wilhelm Loeser (also known as *Ralph Robiend*), had previously served a three-year prison term for selling drugs. Piquett was Loeser's attorney, and earlier in the year had recruited the physician to perform cosmetic surgery on another one of his unsavory clients.

The doctor assisting Loeser, 32-year-old Harold Cassidy, happened to be Art O'Leary's cousin and had once practiced with Dr. Charles Eye, the physician who previously treated Dillinger for skin inflammation. Cash-strapped and a heavy drinker, Cassidy was no stranger to vice, often performing illegal abortions.

Loeser had agreed to perform the desired cosmetic surgeries on Dillinger and Van Meter for a fee of $5,000, each. Dillinger had already made an upfront payment of $3,000 through his lawyer. Cassidy would be paid $600 to assist Loeser during the operations.

A cot set up in the front bedroom of Probasco's house served as the operating table. Van Meter, who was less enthusiastic about subjecting himself to the surgeon's knife, allowed Dillinger to serve as the test case. After stripping off his shirt, Dillinger laid supine on the cot, while Cassidy administered general anesthesia through an ether-soaked rag. When Cassidy dosed the patient with too much of the anesthetic, Dillinger swallowed his tongue and went into respiratory failure. While O'Leary opened a window to vent the noxious ether fumes, Dr. Loeser used forceps to reposition the patient's tongue and then pressed Dillinger's arms against his sides to stimulate breathing.

After the patient nearly died from an ether overdose, Loeser switched to a local anesthetic. Further difficulties soon arose. Dillinger had lied to the doctors about not having eaten that day; in fact, he had consumed a full meal, just an hour earlier. As a result, Dillinger vomited several times during the course of the surgery.

In spite of potentially life-threatening complications, Loeser excised three moles from Dillinger's face, made incisions behind each ear and pulled his skin tight (a face lift), and filled his chin cleft with skin transplanted from his cheeks. When Dillinger fully awakened after the surgery was completed, O'Leary explained how close he had come to dying.

"It might just as well have been now, as some other time," Dillinger grog-gily laughed.

By now, the presence of two strange men in their house, one of whom was undergoing cosmetic surgery, had Probasco's girlfriend, Peggy Doyle, questioning their true identities. Probasco ultimately promised to purchase Peggy a new outfit, if she would "keep her mouth shut" about the real name of one of the men—John Dillinger.

Less than a week after the operation, Dr. Loeser removed Dillinger's bandages. Staring at his bruised and swollen face in the mirror, Dillinger was appalled, and accused Loeser and Cassidy of "botching the job." Louis Piquett, who was present for the unveiling, quickly intervened: "John, you look wonderful." The attorney explained that a few "tune-ups" were needed in most cases of cosmetic surgery, and the end product would be more pleasing. That same evening, under local anesthetic, Loeser performed a touch-up procedure on his unhappy patient's face. An impatient Dillinger would have to wait a while longer to judge the ultimate outcome of Loeser's handiwork.

In the frustrating manhunt for John Dillinger and his gang members, J. Edgar Hoover reluctantly concluded that his clean-cut, college-educated agents were ill-prepared to engage in gunplay with gangsters. He soon transferred two Texans, 38-year-old Charles Winstead and 55-year-old J. C. "Doc" White, to the Chicago field office. The so-called "Cowboys," armed with their own Colt .45 and .357 Magnum handguns, wore traditional boots and Stetson hats. Winstead and White were both excellent shots and seasoned veterans in shoot-outs. White, a former Texas Ranger, became the oldest agent on the Dillinger Squad.

Another Texas Ranger, the famed Frank Hamer, who days earlier had orchestrated the murderous ambush of Bonnie and Clyde, after trailing them for several weeks, offered to assist the Bureau in tracking down Dillinger. The Texas lawman was pragmatic about the likelihood of his becoming involved in the Dillinger case: "The government men may not give me a chance to kill him. There's a lot of jealousy in this man-hunting game." Hamer understood politics all too well—J. Edgar Hoover was not about to share the credit with an outsider.

Hoover made another crucial decision when he transferred 31-year-old Herman "Ed" Hollis from Tulsa to Chicago. Even though he was a college boy and an attorney, Hollis was a gifted marksman, who had qualified as a sharpshooter with the Thompson submachine gun.

Hoover also raided police departments in the Southwest to augment the Dillinger Squad. Dallas Chief of Detectives, R. L. "Bob" Jones, Waco Detective, Buck Buchanan, and two members of the Oklahoma City Police Department pistol team (Detective Jerry Campbell and Night Police Chief Clarence Hurt) were recruited to join the Bureau.

In spite of his long-standing favoritism toward Melvin Purvis, Hoover was growing impatient over the Chicago SAC's lack of progress and the repeated blunders committed by agents under his command. The mistakes continued when Purvis placed Baby Face Nelson's sister's (Juliette Fitzsimmons') house on Marshfield Avenue under surveillance. On May 29th, Nelson, who had been hiding out in a variety of places in the Chicago area since his escape from Little Bohemia, drove to within a few blocks of his sister's house. From there, he dispatched a messenger, perhaps a teenager looking to make a fast buck, to Fitzsimmons' house where his wife, Helen, along with Jean Delaney, had been staying since their release from jail. The messenger passed a note to Helen, instructing her to walk north on Marshfield Avenue. Nelson eventually pulled abreast of Helen in his car, and for the next hour the couple drove around the neighborhood. Nelson informed his wife that he was in the process of securing an appropriate hide-away for them, and would return in a few days.

Nelson's visit with Helen had occurred while an undercover Bureau agent was positioned at a gas station, located across the street from Fitzsimmons' house. The agent, who later claimed to have seen Nelson circle the block four times in his car, failed to notify the Chicago Bureau headquarters. When Hoover learned of this egregious error, he sent Purvis a scolding letter: "I am becoming quite concerned over some of these developments in the Chicago District. We have had too many instances where surveillances have not been properly conducted, and where persons under surveillance have been able to avoid the same." The Director issued Purvis an uncharacteristically terse warning: "I cannot continue to tolerate the action of investigators that permit leads to remain uncovered, or at least improperly covered. It is imperative that you exercise the proper supervision over the handling of this case." Hoover also reprimanded the self-promoting Purvis for talking freely with reporters about the Dillinger case.

When Purvis adopted a new strategy, the outcome proved disastrous. After employing a prison parolee, whose name happened to be *George Nelson*, as paid informer, he instructed the man to establish a relationship with Nelson's wife. The informant, an experienced swindler, conned Purvis into believing that he had known Dillinger in prison, and falsely claimed that Baby Face Nelson had appropriated his name.

On Thursday night, May 31st, informant Nelson was sent to Fitzsimmons' house. Just as he was arriving, Helen and Jean Delaney were departing the residence. Earlier in the day, Helen had received a note from her husband, and was en route to another rendezvous with him. When the informant approached the two women, he told them that he was carrying a personal message from John Dillinger and Baby Face Nelson. Neither woman recognized the stranger and correctly surmised that he was working at the behest of the Bureau.

Agent Ed Hollis, who was in charge of the surveillance, watched as Helen and Jean, trailed by the informant, walked around the corner from Fitzsimmons' house and entered a movie theater. Rather than follow the women inside, Hollis and his fellow agents remained outside the front entrance. Fifteen minutes later, the two women snuck out the theater's rear entrance, crept down an alleyway, and hopped into a car driven by Nelson. The automobile raced into the night, bound for a hide-away at the Lake Como Inn, three miles west of Lake Geneva, Wisconsin. In the wake of the failed surveillance, the Bureau's inept informant was sent packing.

The following morning, Purvis explained to Hoover that agents under his command had bungled yet another operation. For Hoover, it was the last straw; he immediately dispatched one of his principal aides, Sam Cowley, to Chicago, to assume leadership of the Dillinger case.

Cowley, a 34-year-old Utah-born Mormon, was a graduate of Utah Agricultural School and Hoover's alma mater, the George Washington University Law School. At age 29, Cowley had joined the Bureau, and soon made his mark working in the Detroit, Chicago, Butte, Salt Lake City, and

Los Angeles field offices. His hard work, coupled with an innate understanding of Hoover's treasured filing system, soon caught the Director's eye, and Cowley was promoted to a higher ranking position at Bureau headquarters in Washington D.C.

Standing five-feet, nine-inches-tall and weighing 170 pounds, Cowley was undistinguished in appearance. He was, however, a tireless worker, who frequented the office seven days per week and on holidays. While Cowley was a desk jockey, who had yet to qualify on the Bureau's pistol range, his dedication and efficiency were the traits Hoover most admired. Cowley's stellar 1934 job performance rating included a notation that he had "a habit of consistently doing things right."

While it was well-known at Bureau headquarters that Cowley was assuming command of the Dillinger Squad, Purvis was told the newly arriving supervisor was making an "inspection tour." Before he departed Washington D.C., Cowley received explicit orders from Hoover: "Stay on Dillinger. Go everywhere the trail takes you." The Director also provided the new squad leader with a take-no-prisoners edict: "Take him alive, if you can, but protect yourself." Cowley accurately summarized Hoover's mandate as "shoot to kill, then count to ten."

On Sunday June 3rd, when Cowley arrived at the Chicago field office, he immediately confronted the four agents who had been assigned to the surveillance of Baby Face Nelson's wife. Disregarding Purvis' defense of all four men, Cowley reassigned three of the agents.

Cowley's arrival coincided with a profound decline in office morale. Many of the agents assigned to the Dillinger Squad were openly questioning if their job satisfaction was worth the risk of being gunned down by machine gun-wielding gangsters. Purvis' secretary, Doris Rogers, later recalled that the Chicago office had been deemed a failure by Hoover: "There was a sense Melvin had been betrayed. We all felt betrayed—defeated."

On the afternoon of Cowley's arrival in Chicago, he and Purvis drove to Fort Wayne, Indiana to evaluate the surveillance of Audrey Russ's house. After learning that the disagreeable Mrs. Russ had insisted the G-Men move to a hotel 12 miles away, promising to telephone them if Dillinger returned to her residence, Cowley ended the stake-out and ordered the agents to return to Chicago.

The next day, Cowley drove to Indianapolis and Mooresville to review the surveillance on the Dillinger farmhouse and other family members' residences. After learning SAC Connelly had 16 agents assigned to the Indianapolis area, Cowley made no immediate changes, even though he doubted their efforts would amount to much. Hoover was impressed by Cowley's take-charge attitude, informing Purvis: "I want Cowley to take complete charge."

On June 3rd, Homer Van Meter underwent his own cosmetic surgery. Having witnessed Dillinger's near-death experience after inhaling ether, Van Meter opted for local anesthesia. For a fee of $5,000, Dr. Loeser, assisted by Cassidy, flattened Van Meter's nose, thinned his lower lip, and removed a scar from his forehead. Using an acid preparation, Loeser also removed a tattoo from the patient's right forearm.

After completing the operation on Van Meter, Loeser used a formula, consisting of two parts hydrochloric acid and one part nitro hydrochloric acid, to try and obliterate both outlaws' fingerprints. Loeser charged $100-per-finger to perform the intensely painful procedure, which he had actually tested on himself. At the end of the day, Loeser left behind a large supply of morphine tablets for both men; while Dillinger used the narcotic pain killer sparingly, Van Meter ingested the opiates like candy.

Later that same day, Baby Face Nelson paid a visit to Dillinger and Van Meter. Nelson couldn't resist the urge to poke fun at his partners' cosmetic procedures: "So you two decided to go out and buy yourselves a pair of new mugs? Maybe you needed them."

"At least I'll be able to go out on the street and get around," Dillinger replied.

"You weren't all that pretty to begin with," Nelson needled Van Meter.

"If you hadn't killed that Fed, Johnnie and I wouldn't have had to get our faces cut," Van Meter angrily protested.

Placed on the defensive, Nelson indicated that when he killed the Bureau agent at Little Bohemia, he had "no choice in the matter." Louis Piquett, hoping to defuse the tension, suggested that Nelson might want to consider cosmetic surgery. Nelson made it abundantly clear that he would never trust "a quack with a knife."

When the time came for his bandages to be removed, Van Meter was more dissatisfied than Dillinger had been. He damned Dr. Loeser as a "butcher," who had transformed his face into a "fucking mess." Van Meter was so angry that he retrieved his submachine gun, planning to "drill" the physician, but found his acid-treated fingers were too sore to pull the trigger. Dillinger managed to step in and cool Van Meter's murderous temper, but neither man would ever be content with the outcomes of their respective cosmetic surgeries.

During a follow-up visit, Louis Piquett informed Dillinger that he needed money to reimburse the attorneys who had represented Billie Frechette during her recent trial. Dillinger soon dispatched Art O'Leary to Indiana to retrieve a portion of the money he had stashed with his father. In Mooresville, O'Leary retrieved a packet containing $3,000—money Dillinger had given his father after the bank robbery in Fostoria. If the Bureau was aware of O'Leary's visit to the Dillinger farm, it went unrecorded. Either way, the Feds missed yet another opportunity to follow a trail that would have taken them directly to Dillinger.

The *Indianapolis News* soon featured a story reporting that the Bureau had offered Dillinger's father and sister $10,000 to convince their wayward son and brother to surrender. If the Bureau made such an offer, it was never revealed to outsiders. Either way, it is doubtful the fugitive's family would have betrayed him for money, as reflected in the statement John, Sr. gave to an *Associated Press* reporter: "It's up to John as to what he wants to do, and I don't think anyone would expect me to turn against him. Life is just as precious to John as to anyone else..."

On Thursday June 7th, another Dillinger gang member met a violent end. While Tommy Carroll and his lover, Jean Delaney, were driving through Iowa, en route to her parents' house in St. Paul, their automobile developed engine problems. In Waterloo, a garage mechanic contacted the local police, after discovering a stack of license plates beneath one of the Hudson's floor mats. The mechanic told the cops that the man who owned the car had the appearance of a "tough customer."

Waterloo Police Department Detective, Emil Steffen, along with police officer, P. E. Walker, rushed to the garage, only to find that the man and automobile in question had already departed. After searching the city streets, the lawmen located a bronze-colored Hudson; ironically, Carroll had parked across the street from the police station. Steffen and Walker discovered the vehicle was empty and locked, but gazing through the windows, they saw what appeared to be a submachine gun, partially concealed by a bathrobe, in the backseat; it was actually an automatic rifle, accompanied by 300 rounds of ammunition.

Waiting and watching, the two cops noticed a well-dressed couple approaching the Hudson. After Carroll opened the passenger door for Delaney and was making his way around the car, Officer Walker called out: "Hey, just a minute! Who are you?"

"Who are you?" Carroll replied.

"Police officers," Walker announced.

When Carroll stepped back from the car and reached inside his coat to draw his pistol, Walker punched him in the face, knocking the fugitive to the pavement. Carroll quickly got up and ran down the sidewalk, pistol in hand. Detective Steffen drew his service revolver and fired, hitting the fleeing suspect in the left arm. Stunned, Carroll dropped his pistol and staggered into a nearby alley. This time, Steffen took careful aim and fired three times; two of the bullets found their mark, dropping Carroll in his tracks. Standing over the gravely wounded man, Steffen asked his name.

"Tommy Carroll," the fugitive moaned, before continuing, "I've got 700 dollars on me. Be sure the little girl gets it. She doesn't know what it's all about."

After Carroll was taken to a local hospital, two Bureau agents from St. Paul rushed to Waterloo. Carroll refused to disclose any information to the agents before he died in the early evening. While another Dillinger gang member had been eliminated, the Bureau still could not take credit for the triumph.

Jean Delaney was arrested for violating her parole and was transported to Madison, Wisconsin. On June 11th, Judge Patrick Stone sentenced her to 366 days at the Federal Institution for Women in Alderson, West Virginia. A day later, Stone revoked Helen Gillis' (Nelson's) probation, whose whereabouts were currently unknown.

Delaney would later claim that she suffered a miscarriage of Carroll's child in the wake of his death. While insisting she was Carroll's wife, Delaney was found to have a legal spouse in Chicago, as well as another boyfriend. Carroll was also married, and his wife, Viola, was understandably angry at Delaney. The real Mrs. Carroll shared her displeasure in an interview with a reporter: "They just turned that woman loose so she would get Tommy and lead him into a police trap. If I ever see here, it will be just too bad for her!"

Dillinger and Van Meter were still living at Jimmy Probasco's house when they learned of Tommy Carroll's demise over the radio. Van Meter's reaction was predictable, vowing that he would never be shot down in an alley. Dillinger, who had learned that same day about Billie Frechette's transfer to a federal prison, was uncharacteristically morose. Confiding in Van Meter, Dillinger complained that he had brought bad luck to his friends—they were either in prison or dead.

Dillinger's depression was coupled with anger, and he quickly added the names of the two Waterloo police officers responsible for Carroll's death to his expanding "death list," which included, among others, Matt Leach, Sargent Frank Reynolds, and Melvin Purvis. Not willing to be outdone in the pursuit of vengeance, Van Meter vowed to kill the garage mechanic who had ratted out Carroll.

Baby Face Nelson, along with his wife and John Paul Chase, were at their hide-away in Lake Como, Wisconsin when they received word of Carroll's death. Nelson took the news hard, as he felt closer to Carroll than any of the other gang members. Helen was equally distraught, considering Jean Delaney to be "like a sister."

For the next six weeks, Nelson was more cautious than ever, moving from one tourist camp to another, all of which were located within easy driving distance to Chicago. Given the fact that the authorities were in the mood to shoot before asking questions, Nelson vowed to never stay "two nights in the same place."

In spite of his paranoia, Nelson still visited with his sisters, Amy and Juliette, as well as Dillinger and Van Meter, all of whom were residing in

Chicago. Those clandestine meetings invariably occurred after dark, on the back roads outside the Windy City.

Chase soon travelled to California to visit with his girlfriend. At the same time, he hoped to recruit another of Nelson's former colleagues, Joseph "Fatso" Negri, to return east and help fill the void left by Hamilton and Carroll's deaths.

Now that his face had been surgically altered, Dillinger was determined that he would no longer live like a hermit. To augment his cosmetic surgery, the fugitive colored his hair black, grew a mustache (dyed to match his hair) and purchased a pair of gold-colored wire rim spectacles. On Friday June 8th, just one day after Tommy Carroll was killed, Dillinger attended a Chicago Cubs baseball game at Wrigley Field. Among the stadium crowd, Louis Piquett, who had accompanied Dillinger to the game, caught sight of John Stege, a member of the Chicago Police Department's Get Dillinger Squad.

"Fuzz—big fuzz," Piquett reminded Dillinger.

After he seemingly went unrecognized at a crowded Wrigley Field, Dillinger began to venture out more, visiting nightclubs and dining out at restaurants. He also met a new love interest—an attractive young waitress named Polly Hamilton.

Like Billie Frechette, Rita "Polly" Hamilton was of Native American ancestry. At age 13, she had run away from her Fargo, North Dakota home and started working as a dancer in a travelling show. Hamilton eventually met Anna Chiolak (also known as *Anna Sage*), who ran a brothel in Gary, Indiana, and for a time, she worked as a prostitute. In 1929, she married a Gary police officer, Roy O. Keele, but divorced him four years later.

In mid-1934, Hamilton was working as a waitress at the S & S Sandwich Shop in Chicago. She maintained a close relationship with Anna Sage, who was also living in Chicago. In June of that year, Hamilton first met John Dillinger at the Barrel of Fun night club in Chicago.

"What would happen if I called you up some night?" the well-dressed man asked.

"Try and see," Hamilton answered, before giving her number to the man, who identified himself as *Jimmy Lawrence*, an employee of the Board of Trade.

Dillinger did not have to wait to telephone Hamilton; the pair went out dining and dancing the same night they met. Polly was impressed with *Mr. Lawrence*: "He was one of the shyest fellows I ever met, but I liked him a lot." Since the adjective *shy* was rarely ever used to describe John Dillinger, the fugitive may have effected a change in his personality to accompany the alterations in his personal appearance. As always, Dillinger was disingenuous, telling Hamilton that the scars on his face were the result of an automobile accident.

With her dark complexion and striking features, Polly Hamilton resembled Billie Frechette, leading some to believe that Dillinger had merely found a substitute for his one true love. Dillinger, however, appeared infatuated with Hamilton, nicknaming her "Countess" and "Cleopatra." Hamilton was equally smitten: "He was better to me than any other man I ever knew."

Whether deceived, naïve, or blinded by love, Hamilton claimed that she never learned the true identity of her new boyfriend. Moreover, she seemed unfazed when a fellow waitress commented that her beau "looks just like John Dillinger."

Even under Sam Cowley's leadership, the Bureau's Get Dillinger Squad continued to be plagued by blunders and oversights. Shortly after Cowley ended surveillance on Mickey Conforti, she disappeared and reunited with her lover, Homer Van Meter. In spite of Louis Piquett's dubious reputation as a stock swindler and defender of known criminals, Cowley failed to keep Dillinger's attorney under surveillance. Consequently, Piquett and Art O'Leary were able to visit Dillinger at Probasco's house, two to three times per week, without Bureau agents on their tail.

While the Bureau may have underestimated Piquett, the lawyer remained an ambitious schemer. Hoping to cash in on Dillinger's popularity, Piquett offered a *Chicago American* newspaper reporter the unprecedented opportunity to interview the infamous bank robber, in exchange for a fee of $50,000. The newspaper's publisher refused to consider Piquett's offer, but Dillinger remained keenly interested in having his autobiography written, and to have his life story captured on the big screen.

Piquett suggested that Dillinger purchase cameras and recording equipment to produce a documentary of sorts. Dillinger's and Van Meter's ideas about the purpose of such a film were vastly different.

"I'll give out a message to the youth of America," Van Meter proposed.

"No, that's not the idea, Van. We just want to tell them that crime does not pay," Dillinger asserted.

"Well, you tell them that crime does not pay, and I'll give my talk to the youth of America," Van Meter argued.

While the two fugitives, particularly Van Meter, remained hidden away inside Probasco's house, they were forced to look for ways to fill their idle hours. Dillinger occupied much of his time reading newspapers, while Van Meter listened to a police band radio, paying particular attention to broadcasts related to the Dillinger Gang. Dillinger was continually amused by his fictitious sightings throughout the country. When he read that the Attorney General had authorized Bureau agents to shoot rather than capture him, Dillinger's mood darkened. Shortly thereafter, Dillinger provided Art O'Leary with the home addresses of Melvin Purvis and Agent Harold Reinecke, the latter of whom had berated Billie Frechette during her interrogation: "I want you to check up on these addresses and see that they're right."

After O'Leary passed along Dillinger's request to Piquett, the attorney confronted his client: "Just what are you planning to do, Johnnie?"

"They're out to kill me, aren't they? Why should I sit around and wait for it? We're going to be parked outside their houses one of these nights and get them before they get us," Dillinger threatened.

"Don't you realize what a stunt like this would mean? They'd call out the Army and place the town under martial law, and hang me form a lamppost," Piquett argued.

Piquett eventually convinced Dillinger of his folly, but not before the two had a heated argument. During their acrimonious exchange, Piquett warned his client that if he continued to talk about killing Bureau agents, "you and I will be through."

Both Van Meter and Piquett thought Dillinger was foolish to push his luck by venturing into public. Dillinger ignored their concerns and continued to attend Cubs' games and visited the World's Fair. The longer he went unrecognized in crowds, Dillinger grew more confident that the transformation in his appearance had been successful. Van Meter, who opted to remain a hermit, warned Dillinger: "You're going to get it one of these days, running around so much."

On June 22, 1934, Dillinger's sister, Audrey, purchased a classified ad in the *Indianapolis Star*: "Birthday greetings to my darling brother, John Dillinger, on his 31st birthday. Wherever he may be, I hope he reads this." The announcement garnished further attention, when other newspapers ran copies of it. That same day, Dillinger received an unwelcome birthday gift from the Department of Justice; Attorney General Homer Cummings announced the reward for the fugitive's capture had been upped to $15,000.

"Looks like my price is going up," Dillinger quipped to Van Meter, pointing out that Baby Face Nelson's bounty was only $7,500, "Watch Jimmy burn when he finds the government put a cheaper price tag on him than me. And you, Van, you don't rate at all."

"Nuts to you. You just better watch out that someone doesn't cash in on that reward," Van Meter retorted.

Polly Hamilton's 25th birthday followed just one day after her boyfriend's. Hamilton's beau presented her with two dozen red roses, an amethyst ring, and a date to the French Casino nightclub. Polly later remembered the back-to-back birthdays as "just about the most important thing that ever happened to me." She was now convinced that her beau was smitten: "He must have been in love with me. Lots of times, he talked about a home and kids of his own."

On June 26th, Dillinger pushed his luck even further, when he recognized Robert Volk, a mail carrier from Crown Point, Indiana, among the spectators at Wrigley Field. Perhaps hoping to test the effectiveness of his cosmetic surgery and disguises, Dillinger changed positions, moving to within two seats of Volk.

"This is getting to be a habit," Volk announced, after immediately recognizing the fugitive.

"It certainly is," Dillinger smiled.

Volk contemplated alerting a deputy sheriff sitting in a lower row, but was talked out of it by a friend. Dillinger wisely left the ball park before the end of the game, eluding another potential threat to his freedom.

During one of his periodic, late night visits, Baby Face Nelson warned Dillinger about taking unnecessary risks. Nelson was particularly concerned about Dillinger's cavorting with Polly Hamilton and his public flirtations with other women: "Your dick is going to do you in."

Dillinger was courting danger at a time when his face was on wanted posters throughout the country—one photograph was taken straight-on, and the other in profile. Based on information recently relayed to them by Jean Delaney, the Bureau attached a detailed description to the wanted posters: *Height 5 feet, 7-1/8 inches; Weight 155 pounds; Build medium; Hair medium chestnut; Eyes gray; Complexion medium; Marks and scars: 1/2-inch scar back left hand, scar middle upper lip, brown mole between eyebrows.*

In spite of his recent demotion, Melvin Purvis remained encouraged by the gradual disintegration of the First and Second Dillinger Gangs—Harry Pierpont and Charles Makley were on death row, Russell Clark was serving a life sentence, and Eddie Green, Tommy Carroll, and John Hamilton (suspected, but not confirmed) were dead.

More than ever, the Bureau was keeping close watch on the Dillinger's family members. A temporary Bureau field office was set up inside Indianapolis' Fletcher Savings and Trust Building. Dillinger's half-brother Hubert's gas station was kept under surveillance, while agents, equipped with binoculars, hid in a barn adjacent to the Dillinger family farm. When the fugitive's uncle, James H. Dillinger died, Bureau agents attended the funeral in Knightsville, Indiana, just in case the deceased man's notorious nephew made an appearance.

The Bureau also kept tabs on those gang members already imprisoned. Harry Pierpont and Russell Makley's attorney, Jessie Leavy, who had succeeded in delaying her clients' scheduled executions, was unaware that the Bureau had installed secret wiretaps to monitor her confidential communications.

As the month of June progressed, Dillinger was in need of additional funds. By now, he was seriously contemplating a permanent move to Mexico or South America; Dr. Loeser had promised to obtain a forged birth certificate to facilitate his escape from the country. To relocate outside the United States, Dillinger calculated that he would need a minimum of $35,000.

Van Meter soon provided his fellow gang members with a prospective target—the Merchant's National Bank in South Bend, Indiana. Van Meter understood that the unpretentious bank regularly received large Post Office deposits, which translated into significant cash stores.

Shortly after 11:00 a.m. on Saturday, June, 30, 1934, a tan, four-door Hudson sedan, which had been stolen from Butler Motors in Chicago two days earlier, arrived in South Bend. In the sleepy city of 85,000 residents, best known as the home of Notre Dame University, five men exited the vehicle in front of the Merchant's National bank, while the wheelman waited inside the get-away car. Only three of the bank robbers were ever positively identified—Dillinger, Nelson, and Van Meter. Two of the others were thought to be Nelson's associates, John Paul Chase and Jack Perkins. To date, the sixth man remains a mystery—possibly another Nelson crony, "Fatso" Negri, or the infamous Arthur "Pretty Boy" Floyd.

After entering the bank lobby, Dillinger loudly announced: "This is a stick-up! Everybody stand still!"

When only a few customers heeded his initial warning, Dillinger dropped the pillow case covering his Tommy gun and fired a burst of shots into the ceiling; a few of the .45 caliber slugs completely penetrated the hardwood floor of a second floor conference room, and a white-colored cloud of plaster dust descended on the lobby. At least one of the bullets ricocheted off the ceiling, striking and non-fatally wounding a customer, Bruce Bouchard, in his left side.

In short order, the bandits filled three pillow cases with a bit over $28,000 in cash. As the robbers exited the front door of the bank, a nearby jewelry store owner, Harry Berg, emerged from his business, armed with a pistol. Firing once, Berg hit Nelson in the chest. While the slug did not penetrate his bulletproof vest, the painful impact enraged Nelson, who chased Berg back into his store with a machine gun burst that shattered a portion of the front window.

Patrolman Howard Wagner was among the first lawmen to arrive at the scene, and was immediately greeted by machine gun fire from Nelson and Van Meter. Struck in the abdomen by several bullets, Wagner fell to the pavement; he would later die in the hospital. Three other policemen crouched behind parked cars, seeking protection from the outlaws' Tommy guns. One of the officers grazed Van Meter's head with bullet—a non-fatal, but profusely bloody wound.

Adding to the mayhem, a 16 year old boy, Joseph Pawlowski, sprinted out of his parents' car and jumped on Nelson's back. As Nelson tried to shed the unexpected piggy-back rider, Pawlowski shouted to the crowd: "Shoot him! Grab him!"

Nelson finally managed to strike the teenager in the head with the barrel of his Tommy gun, before tossing him through the plate glass window of a nearby business. Brave yet foolhardy, a bleeding Pawlowksi brushed himself off and prepared to make another run at the bank robber. Nelson answered with a burst of machine gun fire; one of the bullets passed completely through Pawlowski's hand, forcing him to hit the deck, where he wisely remained.

As the get-away car sped out of town, Nelson sprayed store front windows and the movie theater marquee with machine gun fire, much to the annoyance of Dillinger, who considered it purposeless and reckless. A motorcycle cop, Bert Olmstead, pursued the bandits until his Harley engine burned out: "I was doing 80 miles per hour, all the cycle had, and they just walked away from me." Two South Bend Police Detectives, Lucius LaFortune and Fred Miller, gave chase for 45 miles, until their patrol car ran over roofing nails, flattening two tires.

Among the bank employees and customers, there was considerable confusion about who they saw and what they witnessed. Many could not identify Dillinger from the photographs provided by the Bureau and the Indiana State Police—perhaps a by-product of the fugitive's recent cosmetic surgery. Captain Matt Leach was so unimpressed with the witness identifications that he believed the South Bend robbery had been the work of "Italian gangsters," rather than Dillinger and his associates. Others, however, were certain the Second Dillinger Gang had struck again. One newspaper reporter shared his prosaic observations: "The Midwest has come to look on this machine gun-armed, modern Jesse James as an incredible wraith who will go on forever."

At least two residents of South Bend emerged as heroes. Baby Face Nelson's attacker, Joseph Pawlowski, grew up to become a respected attorney, concert violinist, and symphony conductor. Jeweler, Harry Berg, seemed unfazed by his brief gun battle with Nelson, and before the end of the day of the bank robbery posted a sign in what was left of his store front window: "Not Hurt, open for business."

None of the bank robbers were happy. Dillinger was fed up with the unwanted attention drawn by Nelson's loud mouth and itchy trigger finger. The two men argued loudly when they returned to their rendezvous spot, a schoolhouse in the southwest suburbs of Chicago. Nelson was disgusted with Van Meter, who had recommended robbing a bank with so little cash. An unhappy Van Meter, whose head had been grazed by a bullet, was unable to locate a physician, and had to depend on Jimmy Probasco, a one-time veterinarian, to dress his wound. Perhaps Dillinger was the most disappointed. His share of the stolen money amounted to less than $5,000, far less than what he needed to escape the country.

Dillinger might have been more distraught had he known this would be the last bank robbery of his infamous career.

CHAPTER THIRTEEN

The Lady in Red

On Wednesday, July 4, 1934, after spending more than a month under Jimmy Probasco's roof, John Dillinger relocated to a different residence. By now, Dillinger had grown wary of the hard-drinking Probasco, who was a conspicuous loud mouth, particularly when intoxicated. That same day, the fugitive moved into an apartment at 2420 North Halstead Avenue in Chicago's North Side. Dillinger shared the dwelling with two roommates—his girlfriend, Polly Hamilton, and brothel-proprietor, Anna Sage. His association with Sage would ultimately prove fateful.

The 42-year-old Sage, a long-time friend of Hamilton's, was easily recognizable by her stout, five-feet, three-inch, 165-pound fame, black eyes, eight gold teeth, and thick Slavic accent. A newspaper reporter once described her as "a woman of the extra sizes, with a metallic jaw and quick adjusted eyes."

Rumanian-born, Sage immigrated to the United States with her husband in 1909, under her married name of Anna Chiolak. Even though she learned to speak Rumanian-accented English, Sage never learned to read or write the language of her adopted land, and signed her name with the letter X. In 1921, after separating from her husband, Anna purchased part interest in the People's Hotel in Gary, Indiana. For two dollars, the hotel's male customers could rent a room and a romp with Sage or one of her other prostitutes. While in Gary, Sage was twice arrested for prostitution; the first case was dismissed and the second resulted in a $25 fine.

In May of 1929, Anna married another Rumania immigrant, Alexander Sage, who operated a cigar store. Even in marriage, Anna continued to operate brothels. After divorcing a second time in 1932, she became engaged to Holger Burglam, a Scandinavian native. The relationship ended after Sage discovered that Burglam was stealing money from her.

In July of 1934, when Dillinger moved into her apartment, Sage was managing the Harbor Bay Inn in East Chicago, after its proprietor had been jailed for violating state liquor laws. Two dollar prostitutes were among the amenities offered by the Harbor Bay under Sage's management.

As a career criminal, Dillinger enjoyed a comfortable relationship with Sage, and mistakenly believed that he could trust her. In a letter to his father, Dillinger alluded to his newfound living arrangements: "I still have some friends who won't sell me out." In that same letter, he made reference to his ultimate plan to flee the country: "I will be leaving soon and you will not need to worry anymore."

How Dillinger first met Sage is not entirely clear; perhaps through her friendship with Polly Hamilton. It is also possible that a mutual acquaintance, the notoriously corrupt Detective, Martin Zarkovich, introduced the pair.

Zarkovich, a Yugoslavian immigrant, had cleverly managed to advance his rank within the East Chicago Police Department while maintaining ties to the underworld. During the Prohibition-era, he fattened his wallet with bribes from bootleggers and speakeasy owners. Zarkovich eventually became closely associated with Anna Sage, so much so, that when his wife divorced him, she referenced his affair with the brothel operator. Sage's relationship with the corrupt detective had been beneficial in more ways than one; it is believed that Zarkovich used his influence with prosecutors to either drop prostitution charges against his lover, or reduce the severity of the penalties.

In 1930, Zarkovich, the Chief of Police, Mayor, and 13 other city officials were convicted for accepting illegal payoffs. An appeals court eventually overturned their convictions and ordered retrials. After the Mayor died suddenly of a heart attack, the cases were dismissed. Zarkovich not only avoided going to jail, but also maintained his position with the police department.

Zarkovich's connection with Dillinger remains cryptic. Outlaws were known to bribe corrupt law enforcement officers for protection, and Zarkovich may well have received discreet payments from Dillinger to keep him apprised of developments in the ongoing manhunt for the fugitive and his gang.

Unconfirmed rumors suggest that Zarkovich was somehow involved in assisting Dillinger with his escape from the Crown Point jail.

Unbeknownst to Dillinger, who might have chosen another place to live, Anna Sage's life was in crisis. After Sage was arrested and convicted, yet again, on prostitution charges, the authorities reported her to federal immigration officials, recommending deportation. In a most uncomfortable and uncertain position, a desperate Sage was willing to use any available bargaining chip to remain in the United States.

Dillinger's romance with Polly Hamilton marked his first serious relationship since Billie Frechette's arrest and imprisonment. When Hamilton was not working at her waitressing job, the couple was inseparable, dining and dancing, as well as frequenting movie theaters, amusement parks, and baseball parks. Hamilton, who still knew her lover by the name of *Jimmy Lawrence*, was clearly smitten. She soon presented him with a gold ring, featuring personalized engraving on the inside: *WITH ALL MY LOVE, POLLY.*

Dillinger's determination to abandon the life of a recluse grew more reckless. On three separate occasions between mid-June and mid-July, Dillinger accompanied his girlfriend to the Chicago Police Building, where Hamilton was trying to obtain a health permit to work at the Loop Hotel (the permit became mandatory after an outbreak of amoebic dysentery). While he waited for Polly to complete her business, Dillinger roamed the halls and ventured into the police department's squad room.

Those who met Hamilton's bespectacled beau viewed him as quiet and unassuming. At restaurants and nightclubs, Dillinger was affable and chatty, but rarely consumed more than one alcoholic beverage, and many times drank only orange juice. In Polly's eyes, her boyfriend was ideal—he was chivalric, rarely cursed, and was a graceful dancer.

Dillinger proved to be an amiable roommate, and Anna Sage gave him a set of keys to the apartment and access to a private closet, where he stored his weapons, ammunition, and bulletproof vest. Without being asked, Dillinger helped with household cleaning chores and post-meal dish washing.

Sage's 24-year-old son, Steve Chiolak, frequently visited his mother's apartment to play cards with Dillinger. On occasion, Dillinger and Polly double dated with Chiolak and his girlfriend. Steve, who knew Dillinger only by his alias, considered him a refined gentleman, who "didn't act tough" or "talk tough." Chiolak later remembered that his mother's roommate never behaved as if he were fugitive: "He didn't pay much attention out in public to the people around him, but he talked a lot and laughed." Dillinger enjoyed watching Steve play in sandlot baseball games, loudly applauding the team's success and sometimes jeering the umpires; after one contest, Dillinger bought beers for both teams.

During the short-lived period of domestic bliss, Dillinger enjoyed Polly's home cooked meats and vegetables. Other times, he ordered in meals for himself, Polly, and Anna, indulging his taste for frog legs, ice cream, and fresh strawberries. When the two (or three, if Sage came along) of them went out to dinner, one of Dillinger's favorite destinations was Steven's, located at 2604 Southport Avenue. Owner and chef, Steve Jankovich, had won two World's Fair awards for his cuisine, which Dillinger came to fancy. Neither Jankovich nor his wife, Millie, who worked as a waitress, had any idea their frequent, generous-tipping customer was John Dillinger. One evening, as Jankovich was tallying his receipts, Dillinger kidded him: "That's a big wad of money, Steve. Aren't you afraid John Dillinger might drop in and take it away from you?"

"No. He just robs from crooked banks. If Dillinger knew I needed money, he'd probably give it to me," Jankovich replied.

"Yeah, he probably would," Dillinger smiled.

While Dillinger was settling into Anna Sage's apartment, Homer Van Meter and Mickey Conforti were living together in nearby Calumet City. Baby Face Nelson and his wife continued to move frequently between various hide-outs. While Dillinger and Van Meter visited on a regular basis during the daylight hours, less frequent meetings with Nelson were nighttime occurrences, conducted on the roadsides just outside of Chicago. By now, Van Meter had grown comfortable enough to make occasional excursions outside of his hide-away. On July 10th, Dillinger and Van Meter took their girlfriends to the World's Fair.

Palpable tension existed between Van Meter and Nelson, both of whom complained about the other to Dillinger. During a July 12th meeting with Dillinger and Art O'Leary, Van Meter shared his frustration about Nelson's division of recently-stolen bonds: "I had it out with Jimmy. I told him I wasn't

226

going to pay any 2,500 dollars. I never did care a hell of a lot for that guy, anyway."

"He was always complaining about you, too," Dillinger responded.

"We had it pretty heavy there for a while. I thought we were going to draw guns on each other," Van Meter added.

"Forget it Van. We're through with Nelson, anyway. He's out of the gang," Dillinger asserted.

During that same conversation, Dillinger informed O'Leary that he and Van Meter were planning a train robbery: "It'll be one of the biggest jobs in the world—just me and Van. We're not cutting anybody else in on this. We've got it spotted—we've been watching it for weeks—we know all its stops. We've got the 'soup' (nitroglycerin) to blow the door of the mail car. We know how much money it will be carrying, and it is plenty. We'll have enough to last us the rest of our lives, and right after it's over, we're lamming it out of the country."

Unbeknownst to Van Meter and Nelson, Dillinger was skillfully playing both sides against the middle, maintaining a fragile peace among his associates. Dillinger made no effort to tell Nelson that he had been expelled from the gang, and continued to include him in the planning of the proposed train robbery.

On July 14th, Dillinger met with O'Leary and Dr. Harold Cassidy, the latter of whom had not yet been paid his share of the fee for assisting in Van Meter's cosmetic surgery. Dillinger gave Cassidy $500 from his own pocket, but told the doctor that the money had come from Van Meter; Dillinger's arrangement satisfied the doctor and kept his partner, who was still unhappy with the outcome of the surgery, from erupting, yet again.

Trouble invariably found Baby Face Nelson, or perhaps it was the other way around. On the night of July 16th, Nelson hosted a meeting of gang members (Dillinger, John Paul Chase, and the newly-recruited Fatso Negri and Jack Perkins) on a side road just northwest of Chicago. While Nelson's wife sat in the car and read with a flashlight, the five outlaws talked outside their vehicles. Negri later recalled that the gang members discussed the planned robbery of the Chicago, Milwaukee, St. Paul, & Pacific Railroad, which was thought to be transporting more than one million dollars.

At 2:00 a.m., two Illinois State Troopers, Fred McAllister and Gilbert Cross, were cruising the main highway when they noticed three vehicles parked on a secondary road. After stopping their cruiser, McAllister and Cross approached the men clustered around their cars.

"What's the trouble here?" McAllister asked.

"No trouble at all," one of the men replied.

Suddenly and without warning, a burst of machine gun fire interrupted the stillness of the night. Cross was struck by six bullets, while McAllister was wounded once. The gunman was likely Baby Face Nelson, who may have been using his machine gun pistol.

As the outlaws sped away, McAllister vainly fired his service revolver at the departing vehicles. McAllister was stable enough to drive the cruiser to the Des Plaines Emergency Hospital, where both patrolmen were treated and ultimately survived their gunshot wounds.

The following day, the shooting of two state troopers dominated the headlines in Chicago-area newspapers. As usual, Dillinger was considered the most likely culprit. The investigation, however, turned in a different direction when a bootlegging operation was discovered in a farmhouse, only one-quarter of a mile from the site of the shooting. Among the eight people arrested there, a 19-year-old man fit the description of the shooter provided by McAllister, and the bootleggers were ultimately held responsible for the attack.

Dillinger's relative anonymity was rapidly coming to an end. When the Bureau raised the reward for his apprehension from $15,000 to $25,000, potential betrayers started finding the temptation nearly irresistible.

On Tuesday July 17th, Art O'Leary stopped by Jimmy Probasco's house to retrieve a radio and rifle that Dillinger had left behind. Much to O'Leary's surprise, Probasco said that he had been recruited by Louis Piquett to rat out Dillinger and kill O'Leary. According to Probasco, once O'Leary was dead and could not testify that he (Probasco) and Piquett had aided and abetted Dillinger, both men would be viewed as heroes and pocket the reward money.

Later that same day, O'Leary met with Dillinger at a local park. Probasco had apparently told Dillinger the same story about Piquett's proposed betrayal.

"Have you seen Probasco?" Dillinger asked.

"I was up there this afternoon," O'Leary replied.

"Did he tell you about Piquett?" Dillinger inquired.

"Yes, but I don't believe any of that bunk," O'Leary answered.

"Well, I believe it," Dillinger responded.

"Oh, don't pay any attention to Probasco. You know he's drunk practically all the time. He doesn't know what he's talking about," O'Leary opined.

Dillinger was not convinced, and while remaining on good terms with O'Leary, he no longer confided in his lawyer. No longer trusting Piquett, Dillinger was also angry that the attorney had allegedly pocketed money that he had given him to distribute to others. Dillinger, whose paranoia was escalating, gave O'Leary $500 and suggested that the investigator leave town for a while. Realizing that further contact with Dillinger was risky, O'Leary soon fled to Wisconsin with his wife and children, "to go fishing."

On July 19th, Anna Sage telephoned her lover, Detective Martin Zarkovich, requesting a face-to-face meeting. Later that day, when the two met, the wheels were set in motion for John Dillinger's ultimate demise.

Shortly after 4:00 p.m., on Saturday July 21st, Melvin Purvis was in his office when he received a telephone call from Captain Timothy O'Neil of the East Chicago Police Department. O'Neil reported that he and Detective Martin Zarkovich had information concerning John Dillinger's whereabouts and wished to meet with Purvis as soon as possible.

Two hours later, Purvis escorted O'Neil and Zarkovich to Special Agent Sam Cowley's room on the seventh floor of the Great Northern Hotel. Zarkovich told Purvis and Cowley that a female informant he had known for many years informed him that Dillinger and his girlfriend would be attending a movie the following evening. Zarkovich told them the informant was willing to reveal the location of the movie theater to Bureau agents. Aware that J. Edgar Hoover and the Bureau wanted the lion's share of credit for apprehending Dillinger, O'Neil and Zarkovich asked only for a portion of the $25,000 reward.

Fooled too many times by bogus tips, Cowley insisted that a representative of the Bureau meet personally with Zarkovich's informant. The detective indicated that the woman in question, Anna Sage, was prepared to talk with them that very night. In short order, the four men drove in two cars (Purvis and Zarkovich inside one vehicle, with Cowley and O'Neill travelling in the second automobile) to a prearranged meeting site at 707 West Fullerton Street in North Chicago, just across from the Children's Memorial Hospital.

At 9:30 p.m., Anna Sage boarded one of the automobiles for a face-to-face discussion with Purvis. The agent and informant drove to an isolated area overlooking Lake Michigan, while Cowley followed closely behind in the second car. After insisting that Purvis display his badge to prove his identity, Sage told him she would share what she knew about Dillinger in exchange for assistance in revoking her pending deportation. Purvis and Sage had differing recollections about what transpired next. According to Purvis, he told her that he would lobby officials in the immigration department on her behalf. Sage, however, recalled that Purvis made a binding commitment: "Your case is nothing compared to getting Dillinger. We'll take care of it."

Sage's revelations were not entirely truthful. Rather than admitting that she was *harboring* a fugitive, Sage claimed that Dillinger only *visited* her residence to see Polly Hamilton. Sage's partial admission was savvy; had she told Purvis that Dillinger was living with her, the Bureau could have launched a raid on the apartment, without owing Sage anything in return. Sage also lied when she said that she had not known *Jimmy Lawrence* was actually John Dillinger until *two weeks* after she first met him. In reality, Sage had long known Dillinger's true identity and had been driven to betray him soon after receiving the deportation letter from the U.S. Immigration Service.

Sage informed Purvis that she would be accompanying Dillinger and Hamilton to see a movie the following night. She believed they would attend the Marbro Theater on West Madison Street, but would notify Purvis once their plans were final. She also told him that she would be wearing an orange dress, which would make it easier for the Bureau agents to spot her at the theater. At the conclusion of their meeting, Purvis provided Sage with his private telephone number—*Andover 2330*.

That same night, unaware that Sage was in the process of betraying him, Dillinger drove to the northwest suburbs of Chicago to meet with Nelson, Van Meter, Murray, and Negri, presumably to discuss plans for the forthcoming train robbery. If Dillinger had really intended to exclude Nelson from the train heist, he had not yet informed him of that decision. When Van Meter failed to show up for the meeting, an angry Nelson advised Dillinger to locate their missing partner and "kick his skinny ass." Since Van Meter was unavailable, the group agreed to meet again in two days.

Sunday, the 22nd of July, marked the third straight day of an oppressive heat wave. By day's end, the temperature would climb into triple digits. The day before, 17 Chicago residents died from heat-related complications; 23 more would die on Sunday.

That morning, Melvin Purvis and Sam Cowley met with Zarkovich, O'Neil, and two other East Chicago Police Department officers. Cowley reiterated that the take down of Dillinger would be executed by Bureau agents. Nineteen hand-picked members of the Dillinger Squad, along with a handful of other agents from the Chicago office were told to stay near telephones for the remainder of the day. Cowley decided not to place Sage's apartment under surveillance, fearing such a move might attract the wily Dillinger's attention. By 3:00 p.m., all of the agents involved in the case were assembled and waiting in the field office.

Dillinger spent that Sunday in Sage's third-floor apartment, reading and playing cards in front of an electric fan. When Hamilton returned from working the breakfast-to-lunch shift at the S & S Sandwich Shop, she was overheated and exhausted. Dillinger insisted that she lie down on the bed in front of the fan, and then walked downstairs to the ground-floor delicatessen and purchased her ice cream.

Shortly after 5:00 p.m. Sage began preparing dinner. After informing Dillinger and Hamilton that she had to go to the market to buy butter, Sage used a downstairs pay phone to call Melvin Purvis. Once again, Sage was less than truthful, reporting that Dillinger had *just arrived* at her apartment. She also told Purvis that the three of them planned to see a movie after dinner, and would likely leave her apartment around 8:00 p.m. Before hanging up, Sage promised to call back with additional information.

Purvis and Cowley nervously waited at headquarters for Sage's next phone call. Shortly after 7:00 p.m., she telephoned again: "He's here. We'll be leaving in a short while. I still don't know if we are going to the Biograph or Marbro." Proving that she was less than a reliable informant, Sage hung up before Purvis could ask for further details.

Purvis was in a quandary. Until now, Sage had made no mention of the Biograph Theater, which was located at 2433 North Lincoln Avenue, within easy walking distance of her apartment. Purvis and Cowley immediately dispatched Agents Earle Richmond and Jim Metcalfe to survey the Biograph and its surrounding area. Their report was troublesome; the theater had multiple rear exits, which fed into four different alleyways—two ran parallel to Lincoln Avenue and the other two ran at 45-degree angles to the street, forming a letter *K* configuration. In order to cover both theaters, Purvis and Cowley were forced to recruit additional agents.

At 7:15 p.m., nearly 30 agents crowded inside Purvis' office. Detective Zarkovich spoke first, informing the agents of Dillinger's post-surgical and dye-job physical features—a rounder face, no moles, a reduced chin cleft, black hair, and a mustache. He explained that the fugitive would be accompanied by two women, one of whom was "heavy-built" and would be dressed in a white blouse, a bright orange shirt, and a wide-brimmed, white hat. The second woman, "Dillinger's lover," would appear younger and thinner.

Nattily dressed in white plants, a blue jacket, and straw boater hat, Melvin Purvis addressed the assembled agents before they departed for their assignments: "Gentlemen, you all know the character of John Dillinger. If he appears at either of the picture shows and we locate him and he affects his escape, it will be a disgrace to our Bureau. It may be that Dillinger will be at the picture show with his woman companions without arms; yet, he may appear there armed and with other members of his gang. There, of course, will be an undetermined element of danger in endeavoring to apprehend Dillinger. It is the desire that he be taken alive, if possible, without injury to any agent of the Bureau. Yet, gentlemen, this is the opportunity we have all been awaiting, and he must be taken. Do not unnecessarily endanger your own lives, and if Dillinger offers any resistance, each man will be for himself, and it will be up to each of you to do whatever you think necessary to protect yourself in taking Dillinger." In essence, Purvis, with the blessings of J. Edgar Hoover, had given the agents permission to gun down Dillinger, with minimal provocation.

Purvis explained that he would lead a five-man team to apprehend Dillinger. The group of five would include two of the Bureau's best marksmen—Agents Charles Winstead and Clarence Hunt. Stationed outside the box office, Purvis would function as a sentry. After spotting Dillinger, Purvis would light a cigar, signaling the remaining members of the capture team to close in on the fugitive.

J. Edgar Hoover had issued explicit orders from Washington D.C. concerning the forthcoming operation. Determined not to repeat the fiasco at Little Bohemia, the Director ordered the agents to carry only pistols. Each agent was instructed to exercise "extreme caution" and warned against "hasty opening of fire on any particular car and its occupants, merely from its description."

Sam Cowley would remain at the field office to communicate with both teams and the Washington D.C. headquarters, until Dillinger's exact location was ascertained. Since it was not yet known which of the two theaters Dillinger would be attending, both the Marbro and Biograph had to be placed under surveillance. Once Dillinger's arrival was confirmed, all agents would converge on that one theater.

Purvis correctly surmised that Dillinger would choose the Biograph, where a gangster movie, *Manhattan Melodrama*, was playing, rather than see the Shirley Temple musical at the Marbro. Consequently, Purvis and Agent Ralph Brown drove to the Biograph, arriving at 7:40 p.m. and parking 60 feet south of the theater's front entrance. Detective Zarkovich, who knew Dillinger by sight, accompanied the agents assigned to the Marbro Theater.

While Brown stood watch just outside the car, Purvis walked to the box office, where the ticket collector informed him the next showing of the movie would begin at 8:30 p.m. Purvis and Brown were now left to wait inside the car until Dillinger's anticipated arrival time. At five minute intervals, Brown hustled to a nearby bar and used a pay phone to call the field office and update Cowley. At the Marbro, Agent Winstead and Detective Zarkovich were positioned where they could keep their eyes on the ticket booth and front entrance.

At 8:15 p.m., customers started arriving at the Biograph and purchasing tickets for the next feature. Purvis anxiously kept his eyes trained for Dillinger. By 8:25 p.m., Purvis feared this might turn out to be yet another failed attempt to corner America's Most Wanted Man.

Dillinger had no reason to hurry; Sage's apartment was less than two blocks from the Biograph Theater. As he dressed, Dillinger concluded that it was too hot to wear a coat, which would normally conceal his shoulder holster. Instead, he slipped his automatic pistol inside his pants pocket. Ever prepared for a sudden escape, Dillinger stuffed $3,000 in his wallet and pants pockets. At 8:30 p.m., Dillinger and his two female companions left the apartment; he did not inform Hamilton and Sage of their ultimate destination until after they had walked out the door.

At 8:36 p.m., Purvis and Brown spotted a man and two women walking down the sidewalk, approaching the theater. Under the glow of the marquee lights, Anna Sage's orange skirt appeared red, earning her a lasting moniker— *The Lady in Red.*

While Brown ran to telephone Cowley about Dillinger's arrival, Purvis remained inside the car, watching as Dillinger, dressed in gray pants, a white broadcloth shirt, a gray necktie with red polka dots, white buckskin shoes, a fashionable straw boater hat, and sunglasses, purchased tickets from the box office. Purvis was relieved to see that the fugitive was accompanied by no male companions and was not wearing a coat, which meant he could only be carrying a single pistol.

Because of their late arrival, the trio found that the theater was already quite crowded. Unable to locate three seats together, Dillinger and Hamilton took seats on the third row, while Sage sat alone, near the back of the auditorium. Purvis immediately purchased his own ticket and entered the theater. While the plan called for Dillinger to be confronted outside the theater, minimizing the risk of catching innocent bystanders in a cross fire, Purvis briefly entertained an alternative strategy. If there were open seats in the row directly behind the fugitive, Purvis believed that he and two other agents could pin Dillinger's arms and disarm him, without any shots being fired. In the semi-darkness of the theater, however, Purvis could not locate Dillinger in the crowd.

Exiting the theater, Purvis returned to the car, where Brown informed him that agents assigned to the Marbro Theater were en route to the Biograph. An impatient Purvis soon walked to the box office and spoke with the ticket collector, who informed him that the movie would run for two hours and four minutes.

If Dillinger had any morbid premonitions, they were not evident. During the course of the movie, Dillinger laughed heartily and occasionally stole a kiss from Polly. His longtime nemesis, Melvin Purvis, was anything but relaxed as he waited in the car, but was somewhat relieved when Cowley and the agents assigned to the Marbro arrived on the scene. Together, Cowley and Purvis positioned the additional agents at strategic locations surrounding the theater.

Two East Chicago police officers were stationed on the sidewalk, just north of the theater's front entrance. Sharp-shooting Bureau Agents, Charles Winstead and Clarence Hurt occupied similar positions on the south side, which was the direct route to Anna Sage's apartment. Four agents were stationed at the convergence of the four back alleyways, covering the building's rear exists. The remaining agents and police officers, teamed in pairs, were positioned at intervals on the sidewalk, to the left and right of the theater's front entrance.

By 9:30 p.m., with an hour to kill, the ambush was set. Purvis stood inside the theater's recessed front entrance, chewing on an unlit cigar, anxiously wondering if the Bureau had finally set an inescapable trap for Dillinger.

At 10:20 p.m., the entire operation was nearly jeopardized when two District 37 Chicago Police Department cruisers suddenly pulled into one of the alleyways behind the theater. While the Bureau had enlisted the help of a small number of East Chicago police officers, the police department, as a whole, had not been informed about the planned take down of Dillinger.

"Police! Put up your hands!" one of the officers shouted.

"Federal agents," Agent E. J. Conroy countered, producing his badge as identification.

The other Bureau agents also presented their badges and explained that the Feds were on a stake-out. Conroy, however, refused to provide the name of their suspect. The police officers explained that they were answering a complaint about suspicious characters congregated in the alleyway. Instructed that their assistance was not needed, the local cops soon drove away.

Ten minutes later, just as the movie was about to end, two plain clothes East Chicago police detectives confronted Agent Jerry Campbell and the two local officers, who were stationed with him on the sidewalk. The detectives were responding to a call from the Biograph's manager, who feared the suspicious-looking men gathered outside the building were planning to rob the theater. After proffering identification, Campbell informed the detectives about the stake-out and sent them away.

At 10:35 p.m., as theater patrons began exiting the building, Melvin Purvis stood outside the main entrance, eyeing each departing face. It took nearly five minutes for Dillinger to come into view. As the trio walked out the front door, Polly Hamilton was holding onto the fugitive's left arm, while Anna Sage was a step back and to his right. When Dillinger passed through the door, Purvis distinctly remembered making brief eye contact with the infamous outlaw: "He looked into my eyes. Surely he must have seen something more than casual interest in them, but apparently he didn't recognize me, and I struck the match and lit my cigar."

Twenty feet to the south, Agents Winstead and Hunt saw Purvis light his cigar, and observed a man and two women walking toward them. Hurt immediately whispered to Winstead: "That's Dillinger, with the straw hat and the glasses."

Across the street, Agent Jerry Campbell watched intently as Purvis lit his cigar, informing the agent paired with him: "There they go." The two agents immediately began walking south on the opposite side of the street, paralleling the movements of Dillinger, Hamilton, and Sage.

While Purvis was trailing Dillinger down the sidewalk, he suddenly realized that a number of his agents had failed to recognize the signal. Quickly lighting another match, Purvis was frustrated by the inattentiveness of the agents, whispering: "Damn it! Come on!"

After Dillinger and his female companions passed the recessed doorway where Winstead and Hurt were stationed, the two agents stepped out behind him. By now, the fugitive was even with one of the Bureau's parked cars, where Agent Ed Hollis was standing. When he spied Hollis, Dillinger paused to turn around, and came face-to-face with Agent Winstead. By now, Purvis was in position to make eye contact with the fugitive: "I was about three feet to the left and a little to the rear of him. I was very nervous; it must have been a squeaky voice that called out, 'Stick 'em up, Johnnie—we have you surrounded'."

Agent Jack Walls, who was standing on the opposite side of the street, remembered that Dillinger "appeared to realize that he was trapped," and a "tense look" passed over his face. After letting go of Hamilton's arm, Dillinger made brief eye contact with Agent Hollis, as he hurriedly surveyed the area for an escape route. Eyeing the nearby alley, the fugitive crouched and ran, reaching into his right pants pocket to draw his .380 caliber automatic pistol. At the opening of the alleyway, Dillinger bumped into a woman and spun away.

Agent Winstead took dead aim at the fugitive with his .45 caliber pistol and fired three times. Almost instantaneously, Agent Hollis discharged his handgun twice. Two of the shots found their mark. One bullet entered Dillinger's right side, spiraled downward though his chest, and exited the opposite side of his body, adjacent to a rib. One of Winstead's .45 caliber slugs entered the back of the fugitive's neck, tore through his brain stem, and exited below his right eye. Neither Winstead nor Hollis had identified themselves or offered a verbal warning before shooting Dillinger.

An eyewitness later recalled that Dillinger "spun like a top," before falling face down on the pavement, shattering one lens of his spectacles and crushing the brim of his straw hat. As he collapsed, Dillinger was clutching the Colt .380 in his right hand, but the safety was still locked in the *on* position. Dillinger's lips briefly trembled as Purvis bent down and grabbed the pistol out of his hand.

"He mumbled some words that I couldn't understand. That was the end," Purvis remembered.

"Don't move!" another agent shouted.

The warning proved superfluous—John Dillinger was dead.

CHAPTER FOURTEEN

This marks the end of the trail for John Dillinger

Seconds after John Dillinger was gunned down, many of the women in the immediate area began screaming and crying. Bystander, Etta Natalsky, who had been struck in the left upper thigh by a ricocheting bullet wailed loudly: "I'm shot!" Another woman, Theresa Paulus, shot in the hip, was crying. Unlike the disaster at Little Bohemia, neither of the accidental shooting victims was seriously wounded.

Drawn to the sound of gunfire, a small crowd immediately congregated, enabling Polly Hamilton and Anna Sage to flee the scene of the shooting. Hamilton was understandably traumatized: "I jumped in fright. Then, I looked to see what happened, and there was *Jimmy* lying there shot..." Panic-stricken, Hamilton hurried away: "I ran to the doorway of the grocery store next door and bumped right into a gun in the hands of one of the officers, a government man, I suppose. He didn't pay any attention to me, so I ran on to the corner. There in all that crowd, I bumped into a woman who turned out to be Anna, who was running away, too. Then, a policeman stopped me. I guess he lost his head or something, for he let me go."

Both women soon made their way back to Sage's apartment. Hamilton's ready abandonment of her dead boyfriend would eventually lead many to question the truthfulness of her self-proclaimed ignorance about *Jimmy Lawrence's* true identity.

A police van, christened the "Black Maria" was summoned to the scene. After Dillinger's body was placed on a stretcher and loaded into the van, five

239

Bureau agents climbed inside to serve as an escort. The Black Maria was driven to Alexian Brothers Hospital, located at 1200 Belden Avenue. At 10:33 p.m., Doctor Walter Prusaig climbed into the back of the van, and after placing his stethoscope to Dillinger's chest, proclaimed: "This man is dead."

Sam Cowley and Melvin Purvis telephoned Washington D.C. with the news J. Edgar Hoover had yearned to hear. When informed that Dillinger was dead, the Director congratulated both men: "Fine work!" Hoover was not the only one who was delighted to learn of Dillinger's demise. When Sargent Frank Reynolds of the Chicago Police Department's Get Dillinger Squad first saw the body, he excitedly shook the corpse's hand.

The corpse was transported from the hospital to the Cook County Morgue. Pathologist, Dr. J. J. Kearns, assisted by Dr. David Fisher, performed the autopsy on Dillinger's body. In addition to the two gunshot wounds, the pathologist noted cosmetic surgery scars on his face, acid burns on his fingertips, and scars from bullet wounds on his leg, neck, and shoulder. The powder burns at the point of entry indicated the fatal shot to the base of the skull occurred at point blank range. While Dillinger's brain was removed and preserved in a formaldehyde-filled jar, the organ was later lost or stolen.

Dillinger's brain was not the only thing that went missing. At some point, Dillinger's pants were rifled; all but $7.70 of the $3,300 he had stuffed in his wallet and pockets went missing. The most likely culprits were thought to be two men, posing as Chicago Police detectives. The inventory of the dead man's possessions included: a pair of size 9D Nunn-Bush buckskin shoes, a pair of black silk socks, a pair of red garters, a pair of size 34 Hanes undershorts, a black belt, a white Kenilworth broadcloth shirt, a necktie, a pair of gray pants, a gold ruby ring (inscribed WITH ALL MY LOVE, POLLY), a gold, 17-jewel Hamilton pocket watch with a photograph inside its protective cover, a small knife attached to the watch, a white handkerchief, an extra pistol magazine, and two keys tied together with string (one of which fit the door lock on Anna Sage's apartment).

In spite of the fugitive's attempts to obliterate his fingerprints, Bureau agent, Max Chaffetz, was able to obtain a positive match. Chaffetz soon called Sam Cowley: "It's Dillinger. There's no question in my mind, at all."

After completion of the autopsy, the coroner allowed Dillinger's body to be placed on public display. From a line that stretched one-quarter-mile-long, nearly 15,000 people passed through the morgue to view the outlaw's corpse. A majority of the onlookers were women; one of them explained her reason for being there: "I wouldn't have wanted to see him except that I think it is a moral lesson." Another female observer confessed her prurient interest: "I'm disappointed—(he) looks like any other dead man. But, I guess I'll go through once more." A few of the morgue's employees managed to turn a fast buck; numerous toe tags, briefly hung on Dillinger's corpse, were sold to souvenir hunters.

Two groups were allowed to make plaster death masks for museum exhibits. Concerned that Dillinger's death was being exploited, the Chicago Police Department later confiscated several of the masks.

A coroner's inquest was held at 11:30, the following morning. Chicago police officials, angry that the Bureau had taken down Dillinger on their home turf, without notifying them, boycotted the hearing. The absence of the local cops made no difference in the outcome of the inquest, which ruled that Bureau agents had acted in appropriate fashion.

The news about Dillinger's death rapidly disseminated. Within an hour of the shooting, Chicago-area radio stations were issuing news bulletins. As a result, people immediately flocked to the scene of the shooting. Before dawn, "extra" editions of newspapers had been delivered to customers' doorsteps. One newspaper reporter's account was filled with dramatic prose: "John Dillinger died tonight as he lived, in a hail of lead and swelter of blood. He died with a smile on his lips and a woman on each arm."

In the early morning hours, a handful of morbid curiosity seekers dipped their extra-edition newspapers in the pools of Dillinger's blood. One ghoulish entrepreneur stained 12 separate handkerchiefs with the outlaw's blood, and immediately sold them as souvenirs. A street artist used chalk to compose a poem on a brick wall in an alleyway near the Biograph Theater: "Stranger, stop and wish me well; Just say a prayer for my soul in hell; I was a good fellow, most people said; Betrayed by a woman all dressed in red."

In Mooresville, Indiana, a reporter notified a stunned John Dillinger, Sr. about his son's death: "Is it really true? Are you sure there is no mistake?" After the newsman confirmed the accuracy of the report, the elder Dillinger continued: "Well, John is dead. At last, it has happened—the thing I have prayed and prayed would not happen. I want the body brought back here. I'm so sick, I can hardly think." During an interview with the *Indianapolis News*, a tearful John Sr. shared his grief: "I thought this time had to come, and I've been expecting it any time. You know, I can't think John was bad all the way through. There are lots of things he did that I don't think he should have done..."

The press flocked to Mooresville from all over the country, seeking to interview the deceased outlaw's family, friends, and acquaintances. Dillinger's sister, Audrey, who had long been his most steadfast defender, told a reporter: "John wasn't a bad boy. I reared him and I know. They got him. That's what they wanted to do, and there isn't anything more to say about it."

Inmates Harry Pierpont, Russell Clark, and Charles Makley received the news of Dillinger's death in their prison cells. When asked by a reporter for his comments, an angry Pierpont tersely replied: "You got a brother? Then you just write about your own brother and you'll have the right dope on Johnnie Dillinger." Makley also evoked fraternal images: "He was the kind of guy anyone would be glad to have for a brother." From her new home at the federal penitentiary in Milan, Michigan, a teary-eyed Billie Frechette was nearly speechless: "That's too bad."

When Baby Face Nelson learned that Dillinger had been gunned down, he seemed unfazed, as John Paul Chase later recalled: "This changes nothing. We can go ahead with the men we got. Nelson attempted to establish contact with Van Meter, hoping to patch up their differences. However, when he learned that Van Meter had immediately fled Chicago for the St. Paul area, Nelson castigated him as a "yellow dog."

As expected, law enforcement officials expressed no regrets about Dillinger's death. Attorney General Homer Cummings described the news as "gratifying, as well as reassuring," while giving notice to those outlaws still at large: "This marks the end of the trail for John Dillinger, but it is not the end of the trail for the Department of Justice. For us, this is but one more episode in the carefully planned campaign against organized crime, which we have been conducting for more than a year."

Late on Sunday evening, after learning that Dillinger had been gunned down, J. Edgar Hoover summoned his driver to take him to Bureau headquarters. There, he greeted reporters, and expressed satisfaction that Dillinger "was taken dead." The Director, however, spent more time focusing on what was yet to be done: "This does not mean the end of the Dillinger case. Anyone who ever gave any of the Dillinger mob any aid, comfort, or assistance will be vigorously prosecuted."

In the days following Dillinger's death, the story was repeatedly headlined across the country. The American press largely praised the Bureau's efforts. At least one foreign newspaper, Germany's pro-Nazi *Voelkisher Bedbachter*, criticized American justice: "Is a cop calling a man by his first name before shooting him down a sufficient trial? Does a country in which this happens still deserve the name of a country of law and order?"

The media championed the much-beleaguered Melvin Purvis as the hero of the Dillinger case. Purvis' picture was featured on the front page of the *Chicago Daily Times*, accompanied by the caption: *HE GOT HIS MAN.*

Much to the displeasure of J. Edgar Hoover, who expected his agents to be unassuming team players that directed all credit to the Bureau and its Director, Purvis seemingly basked in the spotlight. Purvis spoke about Anna Sage as "my informant," and delighted in retelling how he came face-to-face with Dillinger: "...Once I spotted him, I knew him at once, because of those killer eyes of his."

Two days after Dillinger's death, Purvis flew to Washington D.C. to meet with Hoover and other Department of Justice officials. As the pair stood in front of motion picture and still cameras, the Director quietly seethed as Purvis was referred to as "the man who got Dillinger." When *Time* magazine featured a picture of the Chicago SAC shaking Attorney General Cummings' hand, captioning the photograph, *MELVIN PURVIS AND FRIEND*, Hoover was incensed.

At the same time, Hoover appreciated the long-overdue accolades awarded the Bureau. In a formal letter to Purvis, the Director joined in the chorus of praise: "The shooting and killing of John Dillinger by the Agents under your admirable direction and planning are but another indication of your ability and capacity as a leader and an executive..." For a short time to come, Purvis would remain, just barely, in Hoover's good graces.

While Purvis acted as the show horse, Sam Cowley, who the *Chicago Tribune* described as "Purvis' chief assistant," remained the work horse. When Purvis traveled to Washington D.C. to shake Hoover's hand and have his picture taken, Cowley declined, and indicated there was work yet to be done.

Unlike Purvis, Cowley was a self-effacing, team player, who never sought credit for Dillinger's demise, which pleased the Bureau Director. In August of 1934, Cowley told the *American Detective* magazine: "One man, alone, is responsible for the end of John Dillinger, and that man is J. Edgar Hoover."

Among Cowley's first tasks was to locate Polly Hamilton and Anna Sage, both of whom had immediately fled the scene of the shooting. Two days after Dillinger was killed, a submachine gun and bulletproof vest were discovered in the shallow waters of Lake Michigan, adjacent to a pier. Bureau agents suspected the items had belonged to Dillinger and were likely disposed of by Sage.

The day after Dillinger's death, Detective Zarkovich drove Sage, who the press had already christened as *The Lady in Red*, to the Bureau's Chicago field office. Fearful that the Dillinger gang members, still at large, would hunt down and kill her for betraying their leader, Sage begged Cowley to find her a place to hide. After she was taken into Bureau custody, Sage was ordered to telephone Polly Hamilton, who was hiding out at a friend's house.

Both Sage and Hamilton were interrogated by Bureau agents. Hamilton reiterated that she only knew her deceased boyfriend as *Jimmy Lawrence*. While Sage was certain that her former roommate was lying about her knowledge of *Lawrence's* true identity, Cowley apparently accepted Hamilton's story at face value. Cowley soon made arrangements for Hamilton and Sage to be placed in protective custody, and the pair was whisked away to a hotel in Detroit.

When the two were eventually released from custody, Hamilton sought refuge at her parent's house in South Dakota. In October of that same year, Sage, who was residing in California, received her $5,000 share of the reward money related to the Dillinger case.

Cowley was focused on locating those who had provided assistance to America's Most Wanted: "In the removal of Dillinger let a somber warning be spread among all denizens, big and little, of the underworld. Let it be noted the *Federal Army of Justice* is upraised in protection of the law. It is only a fresh beginning."

On Tuesday morning, July 24th, Bureau agents broke down Dr. William Loeser's front door and arrested him. Loeser confessed that he had performed cosmetic surgery on both Dillinger and Van Meter, while they were living at Jimmy Probasco's residence. The following night, Bureau agents arrested Probasco at his house. Having discovered what they believed was a suicide note written by Probasco, Cowley ordered the arrestee placed under around-the-clock supervision. The morning after his arrest, Probasco was fingerprinted by Agent Max Chaffetz. After obtaining his fingerprints, Chaffetz left Probasco unattended in one of the field office's 19th-floor conference rooms. During that brief interval, Probasco leapt to his death from one of the windows.

Probasco's suicide was sensationalized, when unsubstantiated rumors arose that Bureau agents had earlier hung the arrestee out of the window by his feet during a contentious interrogation session. Within weeks, Probasco's girlfriend, Peggy Doyle, unsuccessfully attempted suicide by jumping from her third-story apartment, during a break from an exhaustive interrogation by Bureau agents.

Hoover was apoplectic when he was informed about Probasco's suicide, reprimanding the Chicago field office for "extreme carelessness." Ever the loyal soldier, Cowley recommended that both he and Chaffetz be suspended. Hoover, however, elected only to punish the fingerprint specialist, ordering a two-week suspension.

Another controversy erupted when Indiana State Police Captain, Matt Leach, informed Sam Cowley that a reliable informant told him that Detective Martin Zarkovich, who played a major role in setting up Dillinger's ambush, had actually been helping the fugitive hide out for several weeks prior to his death. Leach's informant also claimed that Zarkovich was responsible for the May 24th murder of the two East Chicago police detectives, and had stolen the money reported missing from Dillinger's personal belongings.

Relations between the Bureau and the Indiana State Police were already so strained that Cowley concluded Leach's allegations were unsubstantiated. After he passed along Leach's accusations to Hoover, the Director wrote: "Mr. Cowley stated he believes this is a frame-up. I stated I am of the same opinion; that I believe they are jealous because they didn't get him themselves..."

From the Cook County Morgue, John Dillinger's body was taken to Chicago's McCready Mortuary, located at 4506 Sheridan Road. On Tuesday, July 24th, the proprietor of the E. F. Harvey Funeral Parlor in Mooresville,

Indiana drove his 1923 Cadillac hearse to Chicago and returned the fugitive's body home in a wicker body basket lined with oil cloth. Nearly 5,000 people gathered outside the McCready Mortuary to witness Dillinger's body being loaded into Harvey's hearse.

Thousands of people lined the highways between Chicago and Mooresville to watch the passing hearse. Outside the Harvey Funeral Parlor, some 500 local citizens greeted the arrival of Dillinger's body. Once the corpse was taken inside the funeral home, the crowd swelled to 4,000. After the mortuary's screen door was torn off by an eager bystander, the public was allowed to come inside and view Dillinger's body.

Dillinger's body was eventually taken to his sister Audrey's house, where it lay in repose inside a $100 casket. A photograph of Dillinger when he was 16 years old hung above the casket. Morbid curiosity seekers, who parked their cars as far as a mile away from Audrey's house, began forming a long line, hoping for the chance to eyeball Dillinger's casket. Aggravated by triple digit temperatures and high humidity, a fight eventually broke out between newspaper and newsreel photographers and club-wielding private guards hired by Dillinger's family, forcing the police to intervene and put an end to the melee. The situation became so disruptive that only a few of the spectators were actually allowed to pass by the casket.

Funeral services were held in Audrey's house. Reverend Charles Fillmore, who had conducted Dillinger's step-mother's funeral 14 months earlier, appealed to the mourners' social consciousness: "We should eliminate the cause of these gangsters in our schools and home life by educational processes. Given the proper encouragement, who knows but that today John could have been a great preacher?"

Dillinger was buried on Wednesday July 25th in Indianapolis' Crown Hill Cemetery. In hopes of limiting attendance, the date of the interment was announced as July 26th. However, when more than 100 police officers began gathering at the cemetery on the 25th, the ruse was exposed. By the time the hearse arrived at 3:00 p.m., nearly 5,000 spectators had gathered on the grounds of the 560-acre cemetery.

John Dillinger was buried next to his mother in the family plot. During the graveside services, a fierce afternoon thunderstorm raged—perhaps a fitting metaphor for the tumultuous life of one of the 20th century's most infamous outlaws.

EPILOGUE

Soon after John Dillinger was killed, Baby Face Nelson left Chicago and headed for the west coast. After reaching the Cal-Nevada Lodge at Lake Tahoe, Nelson asked his long-time friend and renowned gambler, Tex Hall, to provide him with a hide-out. Hall's response surprised Nelson: "Can't do it, Jimmy—you're too hot."

On August 9, 1934, Nelson purchased camping equipment and provisions at a mercantile in the town of Fallon, Nevada. The next day, Nelson, along with his wife, John Paul Chase, and newly-recruited gang member, Jack Perkins, settled in for a lengthy stay at the Grant Lodge on the shores of Nevada's Lake Walker.

Homer Van Meter and his girlfriend, Mickey Conforti, fled Chicago immediately after Dillinger was gunned down. For the next month, the couple moved between various tourist camps in northern Minnesota. Van Meter was eventually done in by an informant; unlike Anna Sage, who would become well known as Dillinger's betrayer, the person who ratted out Van Meter remained anonymous.

At 5:00 p.m., on Thursday August 23, 1934, Van Meter arrived at St. Paul Motors to have his automobile serviced, where he was confronted by the Chief of Police and three detectives, who had been alerted to his pending arrival by the unknown informant. The group of lawmen from the notoriously corrupt St. Paul Police Department included Detective Tom Brown, who had previously accepted bribes from gangsters, including Baby Face Nelson.

"Stick 'em up!" one of the detectives ordered.

Instead, Van Meter jerked a pistol from his waistband and ran down the street, firing blindly over his shoulder. When the fugitive darted into an alleyway, he discovered, much to his dismay, that it was a dead end. By the time Van Meter could reverse his course, the cops had blocked the alley. Standing only 40 feet away, one of the detectives blasted the fugitive with a sawed-off shotgun, knocking him against the brick wall. The other lawmen also opened fire with their revolvers, riddling Van Meter's body with bullets. Someone, perhaps Detective Brown, rifled Van Meter's pockets, stealing all but $923 of the $6,000 the outlaw was carrying.

In Washington D.C., J. Edgar Hoover was informed of Van Meter's death, just an hour after the fugitive was gunned down. A Bureau agent assigned to the local office recalled Hoover's extreme displeasure: "The Director is very upset over the fact that that thing could take place in St. Paul without our knowing about it." Hoover, unable to abide the Bureau's exclusion from high-profile cases, shared his frustration in a memorandum: "I think our St. Paul office has shown an utter lack of aggressiveness."

Van Meter's girlfriend, Mickey Conforti, who was arrested by the Bureau three days after he was killed, complained about the harsh interrogation sessions that followed. In particular, she cited Sam Cowley's abusiveness: "He chained me to a chair, and every few minutes, he would ask, 'Where is Nelson?' Every time I said I didn't know, he slapped and punched me."

Baby Face Nelson, who remained out west, was less than grief stricken when he learned about Van Meter's death. While the two men had once been close, Nelson had long since soured on his fellow gang member, and coldly remarked that he regretted having not been the one who killed Van Meter.

A day after the shooting, Van Meter's body was shipped to his hometown of Fort Wayne, Indiana. There, without much notice, he was buried in Lindenwood Cemetery.

After Homer Van Meter's death, the Dillinger Gang, with the exception of Baby Face Nelson, who had drifted in and out of Dillinger's sphere, no longer existed. The Bureau, however, continued to actively pursue a handful of other so-called *Public Enemies*, including Nelson, Pretty Boy Floyd, Alvin Karpis, and the Barker family. The fugitives, whose mug shot photographs were repeatedly circulated to newspaper readers throughout the country, found it increasingly difficult to locate safe havens.

By now, J. Edgar Hoover had promoted Sam Cowley to serve as the point man in the search for those high-profile outlaws still at large. At the same time, the Director marginalized Melvin Purvis's involvement, seeking every opportunity to harass his one-time golden boy. On at least two occasions, Purvis received testy letters from the Director complaining about his unavailability to answer phone calls from the Washington headquarters. Hoover directly criticized Purvis for his slack office management skills, frequent late arrivals to work, speaking too softly over the telephone, and failure to complete paperwork. No longer able to charm the Director, Purvis was forced to endure the demeaning role of desk jockey.

Purvis, however, was able to seize another opportunity to bask in the limelight. In late October of 1934, while investigating a kidnapping in Cincinatti, Purvis received a tip that local authorities had Charles "Pretty Boy" Floyd on the run, near East Liverpool, Ohio. After receiving the begrudging blessings of Hoover, Purvis, accompanied by a team of agents, chartered a plane and flew to the East Liverpool area.

On October 22nd, Purvis was among the cadre of local and federal lawmen who cornered Floyd in a farmer's corn crib. When the outlaw made a desperate attempt to escape, running across a barren field, Purvis ordered the Bureau agents under his command, who were armed with pistols, shotguns, and a single submachine, to open fire. While Purvis was standing over Floyd's body, a local police officer recalled the Bureau agent's bloodthirsty comment: "Mr. Hoover, my boss, told me to bring him in dead." Purvis, however, denied ever making any such statement.

When Purvis notified Hoover about Floyd's death, the Director made it clear that the Chicago SAC was to issue no statements to the press. Hoover considered his directive to be unambiguous: "Mr. Purvis is also to leave tonight and the curtain is to be pulled down on the publicity there." The Bureau's official press release cited the "thorough cooperative efforts" involved in bringing Floyd to justice, and cautioned against designating a "so-called hero" in the successful operation.

Dubbed by the press as "America's Number One G-man," Purvis apparently could not resist the temptation to be interviewed by eager reporters. The *Chicago American* immediately headlined: *PURVIS'S STORY OF U.S. TRAP.*

The *Chicago Tribune* praised the "youthful attorney, who turned sleuth," noting that Purvis had "marked another notch on his gun."

Hoover was enraged; yet again, credit had been given to a single man, rather than the Bureau as a whole. Purvis' willing complicity as a media darling completely severed his once-intimate bond with the Director. Within days of Floyd's death, Purvis was instructed by a Bureau supervisor to stay away from the Chicago field office. When he foolishly inquired as to whether he should travel to Washington D.C. for another joint interview and photograph session with Hoover, Purvis was coldly rebuffed.

Now that Dillinger, Van Meter, and Floyd were dead, Sam Cowley took direct aim at Baby Face Nelson. The day after Dillinger's death, Nelson ascended to the position of *Public Enemy Number One*, where he would remain for the final four months of his life.

On Tuesday November 27, 1934, two days before Thanksgiving, John Paul Chase's girlfriend, Sally Blackman, confidentially informed the Bureau that Nelson, his wife, and Chase were returning from the west coast to a familiar winter hide-out—the Lake Como Inn, located in Lake Geneva, Wisconsin. That same day, Bureau agents staked out the inn, but were somehow caught off guard by Nelson's arrival. When the fugitive spotted the G-Men, he immediately sped away, before any gunshots were exchanged. To their credit, agents were able to provide a clear description of Nelson's black Ford and also recorded the vehicle's license plate number.

After learning Nelson had been sighted in Wisconsin, Sam Cowley and Agent Ed Hollis departed Chicago by automobile, bound for the Lake Geneva area. In another vehicle, Agents Thomas McDade and William Ryan were also en route to Wisconsin, ten minutes ahead of Cowley and Hollis. As they sped down the highway, McDade and Ryan were on the lookout for a black Ford with Illinois license plate number *639-578*.

After fleeing the Lake Como Inn, Nelson, Helen, and Chase sped toward Chicago on Highway 14. At 3:30 p.m., 35 miles from the Windy City, just outside the town of Barrington, Illinois, Nelson encountered Agents McDade and Ryan, who were headed in the opposite direction.

"Five-seven-eight!" Agent McDade exclaimed, after capturing a brief glimpse of the last three digits of the vehicle's license plate.

"There's two men and a woman inside," Agent Ryan informed his partner.

"Keep going to that curve and turn around here," Ryan told McDade, who was driving.

Nelson noticed the startled reactions of the two men in the passing car: "What the hell are those guys looking at?"

Glaring into the rearview mirror, Nelson realized the blue Hudson was executing a U-turn: "They're coming after us."

Instead of accelerating, Nelson pulled to the shoulder of the road and turned his own car around: "Let's see who those birds are."

"They've turned back," a surprised Agent Ryan said aloud.

After the two vehicles engaged in another passing encounter, Nelson executed an abrupt U-turn: "Get ready, I'm going to take them."

"You think they're government boys?" Chase asked.

"Who else would they be?" Nelson replied, before addressing Helen, "I don't know what's going to happen. Be ready to get your head down, if I tell you."

Agent Ryan, who was staring out the back window, could hardly believe his eyes: "They've turned again. They're right behind us."

In the rearview mirror, McDade anxiously eyed the approaching Ford: "I think we ought to stay ahead of them."

"No, no—let them catch up to us, so we can get a look at them," Ryan, who was the ranking agent, ordered his partner.

After veering in the opposite lane and pulling even with the agents' vehicle, Nelson honked the horn and waved his arms: "Pull over!"

At the same time, the Bureau agents spied Chase in the backseat of the Ford, armed with a Monitor automatic rifle. Ryan's anxiety escalated: "We've got to get out of here!"

When McDade accelerated, Nelson shouted: "Let 'em have it!"

Chase opened fire with his automatic rifle, shattering the Hudson's rear windshield. While steering with one hand, Nelson used the other to fire his .38 caliber pistol at the agent's vehicle. In response, Agent Ryan fired back with his own automatic rifle.

The 75-mile-per-hour gun battle proceeded only a short distance before Nelson gave up pursuit. Decelerating as he rounded a sharp curve, McDade briefly lost control of the car, which left the highway and bounded into a neighboring field. Once the Hudson came to a stop, McDade and Ryan took cover behind it. Waiting and watching, the agents were shocked when the pursuing Ford failed to round the curve.

"You know, this isn't going to look too good. We're federal officers. Weren't we supposed to be chasing them?" McDade asked his partner.

By now, Cowley and Agent Hollis had caught up with their colleagues, just in time to witness the running gun battle in the opposite lane of the highway. Cowley immediately executed a U-turn and pursued the other vehicles.

Much to Nelson's dismay, one of the bullets fired from Agent Ryan's rifle had punctured the Ford's radiator, causing steam to rise from under the hood: "I can't get any speed. Those guys must've hit the motor."

"We can't stay around here. We gotta get off the highway," Chase declared.

Eyeing the rearview mirror, Nelson saw the vehicle with Cowley and Hollis rapidly approaching: "There's a Hudson back there. It's gaining on us."

When Chase looked out the back window, he spied Agent Hollis leaning out of the passenger's side window, armed with a submachine gun: "One of them has a sprayer!"

"What are you waiting for? Blast 'em!" Nelson shouted.

As Nelson nursed the Ford's failing engine, Helen crouched in the front floor board, outside the line of fire. At the same time, Chase began firing his automatic rifle at the pursuing vehicle.

At 4:00 p.m. the two vehicles were nearing the outskirts of Barrington, Illinois. Determined to find a defensive, stationary position, Nelson eyed three gas stations (Standard, Shell, and Sinclair) to the north of highway. On the opposite side, he spied a gravel road, surrounded on either side by open fields, leading to a municipal park.

When Nelson unexpectedly swerved onto the gravel road, Hollis slammed on the Hudson's brakes, skidding to a stop nearly 100 feet from the fugitive's automobile. After Nelson sent Helen scampering into of the fields to hide among the waist-high weeds, he positioned himself behind the rear end of the Ford, armed with a Tommy gun. Chase, still wielding his automatic rifle, crouched behind the hood of the vehicle. Cowley, armed with a submachine gun, and Hollis, carrying a sawed-off shotgun, took positions behind their own car.

For the next three minutes, more than 30 bystanders witnessed a bloody gun battle. During the course of the shoot-out, Cowley managed to shoot Nelson several times in the chest and abdomen with his Tommy gun. Nelson somehow managed to keep his feet and kept advancing on the agents, even after Agent Hollis blasted him in the legs with his shotgun. Cowley, who had neglected to don a bulletproof vest, was shot twice by Nelson, once in the chest and the other in the abdomen, before collapsing in a ditch. Though gravely wounded, Nelson also managed to shoot Hollis three times.

Once Cowley and Hollis were incapacitated, Nelson summoned Helen from her hiding place, and the fugitives boarded the agent's now-empty car. Nelson instructed Chase, the only participant in the gun battle who had not been wounded, to take the wheel: "I've been hit. You'll have to drive." As the trio sped away, Nelson informed Helen: "I'm done for."

Still conscious, but critically wounded, Cowley gave a local police officer, William Gallagher, a telephone number—*Randolph 6226*: "That's the Chicago Division Office. Call them and let them know what happened here. Then, get in touch with my wife and tell here I won't be home for supper; (you'd) better just tell her I was called out of town."

Agent Hollis, who had been hit in the abdomen, lower back, and forehead, was rushed by ambulance to Barrington Central Hospital. Ten minutes after arriving at the hospital, he suffered cardiac arrest and died.

Cowley was taken by ambulance to Sherman Hospital in Elgin, 14 miles from the scene of the shooting. Melvin Purvis, without obtaining authorization from Washington D.C., rushed from Chicago to Cowley's bedside.

"I'm glad you made it," a bloodied Cowley greeted Purvis.

"You just rest and everything will be fine," Purvis comforted him. "What happened, Sam?"

"I emptied a Tommy at him," Cowley replied.

"Who was it?" Purvis inquired.

"It was Nelson and Chase," Cowley answered, and then told Purvis that even though Nelson "wouldn't go down," he was certain that "we got him."

Much to Hoover's chagrin, Purvis went directly to the press. Interviewed by a *Chicago American* reporter, Purvis vowed: "If it's the last thing I do, I'll get Baby Face Nelson—dead or alive!"

Purvis never had the opportunity to fulfill his dramatic vendetta. While Cowley lay gravely wounded in the hospital, Chase was speeding Helen and the mortally-wounded Nelson to a safe house in Winnetka, Illinois. Suffering from multiple gunshot wounds, Nelson died at 7:35 that night. Early the next morning, Chase wrapped Nelson's naked body in a blanket and deposited the corpse near St. Peter's Catholic Church in Skokie, Illinois.

Later that same day, the undertaker at Sadowski Funeral Home received an anonymous phone call telling him where a body could be found. The corpse, riddled with nine gunshot wounds was examined by four Bureau agents at the mortuary, who were able to verify Nelson's identity from his fingerprints. That night, Nelson's body was taken to the Cook County Morgue, where it was displayed on the same slab previously occupied by John Dillinger's corpse; more than 2,000 people visited the morgue to view Nelson's body.

Helen Gillis (Nelson) was in a state of shock after her husband's death. For a day and a night, she roamed the streets of Chicago, pausing to sleep in the doorway of an abandoned building. A hunted fugitive, the *Herald Examiner* characterized Nelson's widow as the "nation's first woman public enemy." *United Press* labeled her as "the tiger woman."

J. Edgar Hoover instructed the agents searching for Nelson's widow to "find the woman and give her no quarter." At least one of the agents took the Director's message to heart: "I'd hate to shoot a woman, but I'm not following Cowley and Hollis because of ideas over a woman like that." After a day and a half of aimlessly wandering, Helen contacted her sister-in-law, who telephoned the Bureau and made arrangements for the widow's surrender.

Nelson's funeral service, attended by 200 people, was held at the Sadowski Funeral Home. Six unidentified men, perhaps Nelson's relatives or childhood friends, served as pallbearers. In the absence of a priest, funeral home proprietor, Phillip Sadowski, recited six short prayers. Nelson's casket was taken by hearse to St. Joseph's Cemetery in River Grove, Illinois, where he was buried next to his father. Nelson's wife and mother were among the mourners who watched his casket lowered into the ground.

Sam Cowley died at 2:18 a.m., the day after he was shot. Cowley's body was returned to his home state of Utah, where his body lay in state in the rotunda of the state capital. With less ceremony, Agent Herman "Ed" Hollis was buried in his hometown of Des Moines, Iowa.

Harold "Pop" Nathan, the Bureau's Assistant Director, delivered Cowley's eulogy, remembering the fallen agent as "a national martyred hero." Nathan offered a solemn tribute: "The columns of the press are replete with his exploits, and men, women, and children in all parts of the country know him now. He is famous and justly so. And yet, Sam Cowley was one of the simplest men I ever knew. He was greatly simple. His was the simplicity of the saints, seers, and heroes of the ages, the simplicity of true worth, of true dignity, of true honor. We of the Division are very proud of him. As generations of new agents come into our service, they will be told of the life and death of Sam Cowley. He will become a tradition. He will have attained earthly immortality."

At the age of 35, Cowley was, and still is, the oldest federal agent killed in the line of duty. In sharp contrast to Melvin Purvis, J. Edgar Hoover would always regard Cowley as the ideal Bureau agent—self-effacing and loyal—the ideal team player.

After its early struggles to corral the Dillinger Gang, the Bureau proved ruthlessly efficient in killing or capturing the remaining infamous bank robbers of the Depression-era. On January 16, 1935, Bureau agents led an assault on a residence in Lake Weir, Florida, shooting to death the infamous Ma Barker and her son Fred.

On May 1st of that year, Alvin "Creepy" Karpis was arrested by Bureau agents in New Orleans. Once Karpis was cornered in the back seat of his car and discovered to be unarmed, J. Edgar Hoover, who been waiting a safe distance away, was brought on the scene and allowed to make the formal arrest. After absorbing criticism from a handful of enemies in Congress that he had never actually made an arrest, Hoover had insisted upon being present when the next high profile gangster was brought down.

Even though he was already dead, John Hamilton briefly occupied the position of *Public Enemy Number One*, based upon bogus sightings of the fugitive in various parts of the country. On August 28, 1935, Hamilton's badly decomposed, one-handed remains were discovered in the shallow grave John Dillinger had dug for him near Aurora, Illinois; Hamilton's body was positively identified through dental records.

The culprits responsible for the Kansas City Massacre, which had precipitated the Bureau's entrance into the War on Crime, proved elusive to pin down. Hoover fixated on Charles "Pretty Boy" Floyd, who had been killed by Bureau agents in October of 1934, as one of the perpetrators, even though he was neither a known associate of Frank Nash, nor a murderer by reputation. Adam Richetti, a crony of Pretty Boy Floyd's, was eventually convicted of the murder of Officer Hermanson. The G-Men who testified against Richetti, however, failed to mention that some of those killed and wounded may have been casualties of friendly fire from Bureau agents.

Richetti, who maintained his innocence until the very end, was executed on October 7, 1938. Hoover, who could finally claim retribution for the Kansas City Massacre, ignored the likelihood of perjured testimony in Richetti's trial, and offered a typical self-serving benediction: "Justice has been done."

By the end of 1935, the War on Crime had come to an end. While the Bureau had not been responsible for the arrests or killings of every high profile outlaw, Hoover made sure the federal agency claimed the bulk of the credit. Hoover proved to be a master at public relations and carefully orchestrated the beginning of the Bureau's triumphant legacy. To facilitate this process, the Director gave select reporters, writers, directors, and producers access to Bureau case files, such that they could craft the heroic stories Hoover wanted told.

Courtney Riley Cooper, a free-lance reporter from Kansas City, wrote 24 separate stories spotlighting the crime-fighting expertise of the Bureau; 23 of those stories appeared in *American* magazine. In May 1935, a revised compilation of Cooper's stories was published as a hard cover book, entitled *Ten Thousand Public Enemies*. The book quickly rose to the top of the bestseller's list. For the less literary-minded, in 1936, a syndicated comic strip (*Secret Agent X-9*) debuted, chronicling the exploits of a heroic detective-turned-Bureau agent.

In 1935, Warner Brothers' *G-Men* appeared in movie theaters throughout the country, touted as "the first great story of the men who waged America's war on crime." The popular film starred James Cagney as a dedicated federal agent, who successfully battled a gang of kidnappers, all of whom were caricatures of real-life outlaws, like John Dillinger and Baby Face Nelson. The popularity of the movie spawned seven additional big screen productions about the crime-fighting exploits of federal of agents, including *Public Hero Number One, Public Enemy's Wife, Whipsaw, Mary Burns, Fugitive, Let 'Em Have It,* and *Show Them No Mercy.*

While Hoover made a token protest against Hollywood's glorification of the Bureau, he was immensely pleased by heroic, clean-cut images of the G-Men as presented on the big screen. Hoover took time to sit for interviews with reporters eager to learn more about the Bureau, and posed for publicity photographs with actor, Pat O'Brian, who starred in *Public Enemy's Wife.*

By virtue of movies, comic strips, and the written word, the Bureau became the standard of heroism in the epic battle of good versus evil. Much to Hoover's delight, the Bureau established its own loyal cadre of followers, who inundated headquarters with fan letters. Once the legend of the Bureau was launched, it continued to fly high for decades to come.

The successful prosecution of the War on Crime reinforced J. Edgar Hoover's determination that all glory was to be directed at the Bureau, and perhaps more importantly, the Bureau's Director. Hoover's one-time golden boy, Melvin Purvis, who had grown accustomed to being interviewed by reporters and having his picture taken, soon paid the price for running afoul of the Director's edict.

As the Bureau was rounding up the last of the infamous bank robbers, Hoover reassigned Purvis from high profile cases. The Director also dispatched inspectors to the Chicago field office to fulfill a pre-determined agenda. In their official report, the inspectors described Purvis as "extremely temperamental" and "egotistical," while documenting enough failures in his management style to warrant his being transferred to a smaller field office.

In March of 1935, Hoover wrote Purvis, demanding an explanation for rumors that he (Purvis) had been intoxicated at a party. Purvis immediately repudiated the allegation as an "unmitigated and unadulterated lie." Purvis' secretary, Doris Lockerman, who believed that Hoover was merely "jealous," saw the handwriting on the wall: "Unless you continue to please the king, you didn't continue as a favorite very long..." Lockerman deplored Hoover's successful attempts to humiliate Purvis: "...Every effort was made to denigrate him, to embarrass him. He was terribly hurt."

On July 10, 1935, Purvis submitted his resignation to Hoover via telegram. Unrestrained by Bureau regulations, Purvis was now free to engage in unlimited self-promotion. He soon penned a series of articles for Redbook magazine, entitled *The Inside Story of America's Most Famous Man-Hunting Organization*. In 1936, Purvis authored a full-length book, *American Agent*; as a measure of pay back, Purvis's tome about the War on Crime failed to mention either Hoover or Sam Cowley.

Gillette hired Purvis to appear in advertisements for razor blades, while Dodge used his heroic image to sell automobiles. When Post Toasties cereal contracted with Purvis to serve as a national spokesperson, an angry Hoover wrote General Foods, demanding the company identify Purvis as an "ex-agent" of the Bureau. Parker Brothers joined the crime-fighting craze, developing a board game called *Melvin Purvis G-Man*. Purvis also served as the announcer for a children's' radio show, *Junior G-Men*.

Once the Bureau's most-favored agent, Purvis soon found himself at the top of Hoover's voluminous list of enemies. Hoover not only refused to mention Purvis' name publicly, but also made every effort to excise the former agent from the Bureau's annals.

On July 20, 1935, the serialized program, *Radio Crime Busters*, debuted over the country's airways. The 13 episodes, produced and directed by Phillips H. Lord, highlighted the Bureau's famous cases, including those involving John Dillinger, Baby Face Nelson, Pretty Boy Floyd, and Machine Gun Kelly. With Hoover's apparent blessing, the story of Dillinger's demise was rewritten, eliminating any mention of Melvin Purvis and Anna Sage. In the revised version, Dillinger was ultimately tracked down by a nameless Bureau fingerprint technician, and Sam Cowley was given full credit for orchestrating the ambush of the fugitive; the lone, indirect reference to Purvis came in the form of a character name *Nellis*, who was the agent that lit his cigar in front of the Biograph Theater. Of greater historical note, in Hoover's authorized history of the Bureau, *The FBI Story*, Purvis' name was never mentioned.

Hoover maintained an ever-growing confidential file on Purvis, filled with malicious rumors and unflattering innuendo. Hoover leaked to the press that Purvis was far more interested in making money than serving as a Bureau agent. More than once, the Director falsely claimed that Purvis had been fired, rather than tendering his resignation.

On multiple occasions, Hoover directly interfered with Purvis' attempts to seek employment. After learning that the Motion Picture Producers and Distribution of America planned to hire Purvis, Hoover quickly intervened. After the agency agreed not to employ Purvis, the Director provided the services of active Bureau agents, "free of charge," to function as technical advisors. When the Santa Anita horse-racing track offered Purvis a job as a security officer, Hoover informed the facility's management that the ex-agent was "persona non grata," and threatened to withhold any further cooperation from the Bureau.

Even after Purvis served with distinction in the Army during World II and was promoted to the rank of Colonel with the Judge Advocate General (JAG), Hoover refused to abandon his smear campaign and erected roadblocks in front of the ex-agent's attempts at career advancement. When the Senate Civil Service Committee expressed interest in hiring Purvis as its Director, Hoover confidentially informed lawmakers that he was a "publicity seeker," who "didn't have a gut in his body," and "would louse up any job he got into."

Purvis apparently believed that Hoover's demonization of him would not last forever and made efforts at reconciliation. On more than one occasion, when he was in Washington D.C., Purvis visited Bureau head-quarters. Each time, Hoover made it clear that he was "not available" to meet with Purvis.

On February 29, 1960, 56-year-old Melvin Purvis committed suicide, shooting himself in the head with the handgun given to him by fellow agents at the time of his resignation from the Bureau. Hoover seemed unmoved by Purvis' death, and made no efforts to comfort the grieving family by letter, telegram, or telephone call. Purvis's widow eventually wrote the Director a terse letter: "We are honored that you ignored Melvin's death. Your jealousy hurt him very much, but until the end, I think he loved you."

If the widow's missive evoked guilt or remorse, Hoover's response betrayed neither: "It was well we didn't write, as she no doubt would have distorted it." In the case of Melvin Purvis, the Director was unable to forgive or forget. A high-ranking Bureau employee remembered that the mere mention of Purvis's name in front of Hoover was "like dropping a bomb in Mount Vesuvius."

At least one other major player in the Dillinger saga fell into disfavor with Hoover. Captain Matt Leach, angered by the Bureau's exclusion of the Indiana State Police from Dillinger's ambush, attempted to extract a measure of revenge. Leach began circulating false rumors that Dillinger was unarmed at the time of his death, and had actually been shot to death by an East Chicago Police officer rather than a Bureau agent. Leach's ill-advised rumor mongering placed him squarely in Hoover's crosshairs; in 1937, the Bureau Director pressured the Indiana State Police into firing Leach.

After losing his job in law enforcement, Leach returned to the military, serving in the Army Air Corps, and was eventually promoted to the rank of major. In 1955, after meeting with a publisher in New York City about writing his own account of the Dillinger case, Leach was killed in a car accident (along with his wife), while returning home to Indiana.

John Dillinger's associates and family members moved on with their lives, with varying degrees of success. John Paul Chase, who had been a member of the Second Dillinger Gang and participated in the shoot-out that left Sam Cowley, Ed Hollis, and Baby Face Nelson dead, was arrested in Mount Shasta, California on December 26, 1934. After the local police turned him over to the Bureau, Chase was taken to San Francisco for several days of intense interrogation. Chase confessed to traveling with Nelson for nearly a year, but denied participating in any bank robberies. While admitting to taking part in the shoot-out with Agents Cowley and Harris, Chase claimed that he fired only in "self-defense," and denied shooting either of the G-Men.

Chase's trial began on March 18, 1935 and lasted for one week; the first murder trial held in a federal court since 1893. Chase was ultimately convicted for murdering a Bureau agent in the line of duty. After the jury recommended leniency, Chase served a 31-year prison sentence, first at Alcatraz Island, and then at Fort Leavenworth. In spite of protests from an aging J. Edgar Hoover,

Chase was paroled in 1966. He worked the last years of his life as a janitor in Palo Alto, California. Chased died in 1973, at the age of 71.

Early on the morning of December 6, 1934, Helen Gillis (Nelson) was escorted to the Dane County Jail in Madison, Wisconsin. The following day, she was interviewed in Judge Patrick T. Stone's chambers, at which time the jurist asked her why she had violated her probation.

When her response was less than forthcoming, Stone inquired: "What about your two children? You love them, don't you?"

"Yes, very much," she replied.

"Your husband was an outlaw who was certain to be caught. If you loved your children, how could you leave them behind with relatives and follow your husband around?" Stone asked.

"I knew Les didn't have long to live, and I wanted to be with him as long as I could," she answered.

Later that same day, a formal hearing, witnessed by 150 spectators, was held in Judge Stone's courtroom. When Helen confessed to violating her parole, Stone congratulated her for finally exhibiting a sense of responsibility: "I believe you have a little more respect for the Department of Justice, now, than when you were placed on probation in May."

After praising the actions of the Bureau, Stone revoked the defendant's probation and sentenced her to 366 days at the Women's Correctional Farm in Milan, Michigan. After completing her full prison sentence, Helen was ordered to serve one year's probation. Helen returned to live in Chicago, working in a factory and raising her two children.

Helen Gillis outlived Baby Face Nelson by over a half-century, dying from a cerebral hemorrhage in July of 1987, at the age of 76, and was buried next to her husband. Later in life, Helen tried to explain her tumultuous life with the notorious outlaw: "When you love a guy, you love him. That's all there is to it."

Russell Clark, a member of the First Dillinger Gang, served a 34-year prison sentence. In August of 1968, he was granted a "dying prisoner release." He succumbed to cancer four months later, at the age of 70.

Harry Pierpont and Charles Makley, also members of the First Dillinger Gang, attempted to escape from the Ohio Penitentiary's death row in September of 1934, using fake pistols constructed from soap, wire, and other materials. Makley was shot and killed during the failed prison break. Pierpont was captured and executed on October 17th of that same year.

Dillinger's attorney, Louis Piquett, was acquitted of charges of *harboring a fugitive*, after successfully arguing that his actions were a justifiable protection of the rights of his infamous client. However, he was successfully prosecuted for harboring Homer Van Meter, who *was not* his client, and was sentenced to a two-year term at Fort Leavenworth. After Piquett unsuccessfully appealed the unconstitutionality of his conviction all the way to the U.S. Supreme Court, he was eventually issued a pardon by President Truman, just prior to his death in 1951. Piquett's investigator, Art O'Leary received a one year suspended sentence for his role in *harboring* Dillinger and Van Meter. A bitter O'Leary later claimed that Bureau agents broke a half-dozen of his ribs while interrogating him.

On August 2, 1935, Hyman Lebman, the San Antonio gunsmith who sold weapons to Baby Face Nelson (including specially-modified machine gun pistols, one of which ultimately made its way to John Dillinger), was convicted of violating the state of Texas' Machine Gun Law. A week later, he was sentenced to a five-year term at the state penitentiary in Huntsville. On appeal, his conviction was overturned. Six months later, after a second trial ended in a hung jury, the indictment was dismissed. Lebman returned to his gunsmith business without further legal difficulties.

While Anna Sage, the infamous *Lady in Red*, secured her share of the reward money ($5,000) for leading the Bureau to John Dillinger, she was unable to avoid deportation. J. Edgar Hoover, perhaps as a rebuke to Melvin Purvis, made no efforts to halt Sage's deportation. In 1936, she was forced to return to her native land of Rumania. Later in life, Sage also lived in Hungary, Italy, and Egypt. She died of liver failure in Rumania in 1947, at the age of 58.

Polly Hamilton, Dillinger's last love interest, eventually married a salesman and settled in the Chicago area. Hamilton outlived Dillinger by 35 years, dying in 1969, at the age of 59.

After she was released from prison, Billie Frechette, who many regard as the great love of Dillinger's life, spent a brief period of time on the travel circuit, sharing stories about her experiences with the infamous outlaw. Twice wed after Dillinger was killed, Frechette died in 1969, at the age of 62.

Beryl Hovious, the only woman who was known to have actually married Dillinger, outlived his other romantic interests. Hovious died in 1993, at age of 87, in Mooresville, Indiana, not more than a mile from the Dillinger's farmhouse.

John Dillinger, Sr. travelled for a time, giving lectures about his infamous son, both on the stage and as a featured attraction at carnivals. At one point, the elder Dillinger addressed an audience at the Little Bohemia lodge, which Emil Wanatka had transformed into a *Terror Gang Museum*. John, Sr. died in 1943, at the age of 79, and was buried next to his first born son.

Hubert Dillinger continued to work as an automobile mechanic. Ironically, he was later employed by one of his notorious half-brother's long-time nemeses, the Indiana State Police. Hubert Dillinger died in 1974, at the age of 61.

Audrey Dillinger Hancock, who remained her younger brother's staunchest defender, lived to the ripe old age of 98. After her death in 1987, Audrey was buried in the family plot at Indianapolis' Crown Hill Cemetery.

John Dillinger's family waited for two years before placing a headstone over his grave, hoping the passage of time would lessen the public's obsession with the infamous outlaw. Vandals and souvenir-hunters later chipped away pieces of several tomb stones, forcing the Dillinger family to purchase replacements. John Dillinger, Sr. turned down $10,000 from parties interested in purchasing his son's body. When conspiracy theorists alleged that the body buried in the Dillinger family plot was an imposter, John Sr. grew wary of grave robbers. Consequently, he arranged for three feet of scrap iron-reinforced concrete to be poured atop his sons' burial vault. In section 44, lot 94 of Crown Hill cemetery, a four-feet-tall obelisk, engraved with the name *Dillinger* marks the final resting place of the notorious bank robber.

John Dillinger generated more newsprint and newsreel footage than any of his outlaw contemporaries, including Baby Face Nelson, the Barker/Karpis Gang, Bonnie and Clyde, Machine Gun Kelly, and Pretty Boy Floyd. His dramatic career as a bank robber, about which millions of words have been written, lasted for only13 months.

During that brief interval, however, Dillinger's exploits captivated the interest of Americans suffering from the economic oppression brought on by the

Great Depression. While law enforcement agents regarded him as nothing more than a high profile outlaw, Dillinger was romanticized as a modern-day Robin Hood by many of his fellow citizens.

The felonious acts of Dillinger and his peers forced law enforcement agencies, prisons, and banking institutions to change how they conducted business. Police cars were soon routinely equipped with two-way radios, facilitating improved communications during the pursuit of law-breakers. Local, state, and federal police forces upgraded their transportation fleets, purchasing swifter automobiles powered by V-8 engines. Lawmen were soon equipped with more powerful weaponry and better protective body armor; an eventual outgrowth of these changes would be the development of *Special Weapons and Tactics (SWAT)* teams.

The challenge of keeping felons like Dillinger behind bars led jails and prisons to reinforce their walls with steel. Armed guards, occupying protective cages at the entrances and exits of jails and correctional institutions, became more commonplace. Nearly every penitentiary in America eventually erected machine gun towers overlooking the prison grounds.

During Dillinger's reign as a bank robber, financial institutions began improving their security features. Many banks started employing 24-hour security guards. The physical structure and layouts of banks were also modified, to include stronger walls, bulletproof glass windows and partitions, and electronically-timed vaults.

To combat the Dillinger-era criminals, the federal government was mandated a greater role in law enforcement. For the first time, federal agents were authorized to carry firearms and make arrests. A number of offenses were added to the federal crime code, including robbery of federally-insured banks, interstate transportation of stolen vehicles, and escape from prisons.

Overcoming a series of early blunders during the pursuit of the Dillinger Gang, the Bureau finally proved successful at "getting its man." While chasing the "bad guys," the Bureau broadened its powers and adopted a new name. In 1935, the Bureau of Investigation was officially renamed as the *Federal Bureau of Investigation (FBI)*. Assistant Director Edward Tramm coined what would soon become a household name. The now familiar acronym embodied the characteristics J. Edgar Hoover found most honorable—*fidelity, bravery,* and *integrity*. At the FBI Academy, each of the initials is accompanied by a quote: **Fidelity:** *Prosperity asks for fidelity; Adversity exacts it* (Seneca); **Bravery:** *Courage is the resistance to fear; Mastery of fear is not the absence of it.* (Mark Twain); **Integrity:** *Integrity without knowledge is weak and useless, and knowledge without integrity is dangerous and dreadful* (Samuel Johnson).

From its inauguration in 1935 until May 2, 1972, spanning nearly 37 years, the FBI would have only one Director—J. Edgar Hoover. It is more than mere coincidence that the transformation of the Bureau of Investigation into the Federal Bureau of Investigation occurred less than a year after John Dillinger was gunned down.

Hoover's masterful public relations coup in the wake of Dillinger's death enabled the Bureau to establish itself as the nation's foremost crime fighting agency. Addressing a youth group in 1936, Hoover used the Bureau's most famous case to illustrate the evils of lawlessness: "John Dillinger was nothing but a beer-drinking, pug-ugly, who bought his way from hide-out to hide-out, being brave only when he had a machine gun trained upon a victim and the victim was at his mercy. When Dillinger was finally brought to bay, he was not a hero, he was not a Robin Hood, he was not a romantic motion picture figure, but only a coward, who did not know how to shoot, except from ambush."

For the remainder of his life, in the anteroom of his office, Hoover displayed the artifacts preserved from the night of Dillinger's demise—the outlaw's death mask with its clearly demarcated exit bullet wound beneath his eye, Dillinger's straw hat, the photograph of a girl found in the outlaw's pants pocket, Dillinger's shattered-lens eyeglasses, and the La Corona Belvedere cigar the fugitive was carrying in his shirt pocket. Such was the importance of the Biograph Theater that it was recreated at the FBI Academy, to be used in training exercises, emphasizing the need for teamwork.

Hoover's focus on gangsters largely ended after the notorious Depression-era bank robbers were killed or imprisoned. For the most part, he ignored organized crime and the mafia's vice rackets, including drugs, prostitution, and extortion. On more than one occasion, Hoover denied the existence of an entity known as *organized crime*. In 1957, when local and state law enforcement agencies launched their historic raid on a meeting of major mafia families in Apalachin, New York, the FBI was publicly embarrassed. Hoover was finally forced to devote a measure of FBI resources toward fighting organized crime. Even then, the Director made a token effort; in 1959, two years after the Apalachin raid, the FBI had 489 agents assigned to investigations involving alleged communists, but only four assigned to organized crime.

William C. Sullivan, one-time head of the FBI's Domestic Intelligence Division, explained that Hoover was aware of organized crime's corrupting influences on local and state law enforcement agencies, as well as politicians. Sullivan believed Hoover was fearful that federal agents would also succumb to bribery, which proved to be the major motivator in the image-conscious Director's denial of the significance of the organized crime: "... That's why Hoover was afraid to let us tackle it—he was afraid that we'd show up poorly..."

Beginning in the 1940s and continuing for the remainder of his life, Hoover's primary obsession was the threat of communism. During the administration of President Harry S. Truman, Hoover grew concerned that the executive branch was not taking the FBI's reports about communist infiltration in federal government seriously. Consequently, Hoover began leaking investigative reports to the House of Representatives Un-American Committee (HUAC). Testifying before the committee in March of 1947, Hoover outlined the history of communist infiltration, dating back to his early days as a Department of Justice employee: "The communist movement in the United States began to manifest itself in 1919. Since then, it has changed its name and its party line whenever expedient and tactical. But, it always comes back to fundamentals and bills itself as the party of Marxism-Leninism. As such, it stands for the destruction of our American form of government; it stands for the destruction of free enterprise; and it stands for the creation of a 'Soviet of the United States,' and ultimately world revolution."

While Hoover forever claimed that he was apolitical, to the point of never voting in presidential elections, his philosophies were decidedly conservative. During that same 1947 HUAC hearing, Hoover directly linked communism with left-wing political ideology: "Communist propaganda is always slanted in the hope that the communist may be aligned with liberal progressive causes. The honest liberal and progressive should be alert to this, and I believe the communists' most effective foes can be the real liberals and progressives who understand their devious machinations."

Early on, civil libertarians were convinced that Hoover's preoccupation with communism manifested itself through witch hunts. President Truman largely disregarded Hoover's investigations during the so-called "Red Scare" era, and ignored the salacious tidbits forwarded from the Director's secret files. During a private conversation with an aide, Truman explained his reasons for intentionally distancing his administration from Hoover, complaining that the FBI was "dabbling in sex life scandals and plain blackmail, when they should be catching criminals." In spite of their distrust of Hoover, Truman and the Presidents who followed him, most notably John F. Kennedy, were unwilling to risk the political fall-out from firing Hoover, particularly among powerful conservatives. In Kennedy's case, Hoover had accumulated far too much damaging information about the President's extramarital sexual affairs in his secret files.

In 1950, shortly after the outbreak of the Korean War, Hoover proposed suspending the writ of habeas corpus by detaining some 12,000 Americans that the FBI suspected of disloyalty. President Truman, however, refused to consider such a drastic plan.

By the mid-1950s, Hoover had grown frustrated by U.S. Supreme Court rulings which limited the Justice Department's ability to prosecute and/or deport alleged subversives based solely on their radical political philosophies. In 1956, Hoover established the FBI's *Counter Intelligence Program* (*COINTELPRO*), designed to discredit radical organizations. The covert actions of agents assigned to COINTELPRO involved not only the infiltration of supposed left wing groups and the spreading of false rumors, but also included *black bag operations* that were clearly illegal, including phone and wiretapping, burglaries, and planting of forged documents.

While COINTELPRO mainly targeted suspected communist groups, it later took aim at civil rights groups and their leaders, as well as the more radical African-American organizations. Among those investigated were the NAACP, the Southern Christian Leadership Conference, and the Black Panther Party.

Like many hard-core conservatives of his generation, Hoover would go to his grave believing that the civil rights movement was communist-inspired. Hoover took great effort to single out Martin Luther King, Jr. who he repeatedly denigrated as a "demagogue and faker." In 1964, Hoover contacted officials at Marquette University, and convinced them not to award King and honorary degree, alleging that the civil rights leader and his Southern Christian Leadership Conference were directly link to communist subversives. His sense of morality offended by King's repeated extramarital affairs, Hoover castigated him as a "tom cat," with "degenerate sexual urges." Using COINTELPRO wiretaps of hotel rooms occupied by the civil rights leader, the FBI sent a tape recording of King having sex with another woman to his office in Atlanta, accompanied by a note suggesting that he should commit suicide. When the package was opened and the tape was listened to by King's wife, it proved highly embarrassing to the famed civil rights leader.

COINTELPRO remained in operation until 1971, just one year before Hoover's death. While the FBI's invasive and often illegal activities would later be widely condemned in the court of public opinion, many conservatives lauded Hoover's war against communist subversives. Hoover's tome on the threats of communism, *Masters of Deceit: The Story of the FBI*, published in 1958, sold more than 250,000 hardback copies and more than 2,000,000 paperback editions. *Masters of Deceit* remained on the best-seller list for 31 weeks, including three weeks as the number one non-fiction book.

Hoover continued his masterful promotion of the FBI's heroic public image. He served as consultant to the 1959 Warner Brothers big screen movie, *The FBI Story*. Beginning in 1965, he adopted a similar role for the popular network television series, *The FBI*.

Hoover made sure field agents throughout the country established cordial relationships with local citizens and newspaper publishers. Smaller newspapers, thrilled to get "scoops" from the FBI, eagerly ran articles lauding the accomplishments of the federal agency.

Hoover's extensive secret files on individuals and organizations were the foundation of his immense, if not unprecedented power. Among the individuals whose unflattering and career-damaging secrets were catalogued in the Director's files included Presidents, Vice-Presidents, Cabinet officers, Senators, Congressmen, Governors, and popular entertainers.

In April of 1962, Arizona Senator, Carl Hayden, Chairman of the Rules and Administrative Committee and President Pro Tempore of the Senate, was reportedly influenced to support a 60 million dollar appropriation for construction of a free-standing FBI building, after learning Hoover was in possession of information about his alleged extra-marital affairs. Hayden later recalled the pressure applied on him by the FBI: "I interpreted it as attempted blackmail." Among the files that were later released via the Freedom of Information Act, is a report on a lawmaker, whose name is redacted: "The other night, we picked up a situation where this Senator was seen drunk, in a hit-and-run accident, and some good-looking broad who was with him. We got the information, reported it in a memorandum, and by noon the next day, the Senator was aware that we had the information, and we never had trouble with him on appropriations since."

J. Edgar Hoover was found dead on the bedroom floor of his Washington D.C. home on the morning of May 2, 1972, the apparent victim of a heart attack. A day later, President Richard Nixon named L. Patrick Gray as the Acting Director of the FBI—only the *second* person in history to occupy the position Hoover referred to as the *Seat of Government*. The President's official statement, prepared by speechwriter Pat Buchanan, was overflowing with praise: "All Americans today mourn the death of J. Edgar Hoover. He served his nation for 48 years under eight American Presidents with total loyalty, unparalleled ability, and supreme dedication. It can be truly said of him that he was a legend in his own lifetime."

Privately, Nixon was happy to be rid of the aging FBI Director. In his diary, the President shared his private thoughts: "He died at the right time; fortunately, he died in office. It would have killed him had he been forced out of office or resigned even voluntarily...I am particularly glad that I did not force him at the end of last year." Hoover and Nixon had long been allies in the fight against Communism, but the relationship grew strained when the President tried to use the FBI as a personal and political police force.

Hoover's dogged refusal to investigate Nixon's political enemies led the President to form his own investigative group, now infamously known as the *White House Plumbers*. The illegal activities of the Plumbers, most notably the botched 1972 break-in at Democratic National Committee headquarters at the Watergate Hotel, set in motion the chain of events that culminated in Nixon's resignation in 1974.

Nixon, however, could scarcely afford to alienate ardent conservatives, and afforded Hoover a full state funeral. Hoover's body lay in state in the Capitol Rotunda atop the same catafalque used by Abraham Lincoln. Chief Justice of the Supreme Court, Warren Burger, delivered Hoover's eulogy during a private service in the Capitol Building attended by Senators, Congressmen, Supreme Court Justices, and Cabinet officers. Burger remembered Hoover for his ability to create the FBI "without impending on the liberties guaranteed by the Constitution and by our traditions," an assertion that civil libertarians would find difficult to stomach. On a rain-soaked day, 25,000 mourners stood in a long line for the opportunity to pass by the flag-draped coffin and pay their respects to the man known as *The Director*.

Approximately 2,000 mourners attended Hoover's nationally televised funeral at the capitol city's National Presbyterian Church, including the President, First Lady Pat Nixon, and former First Lady, Mamie Eisenhower. The two people who remained most loyal to Hoover, Associate FBI Director, Clyde Tolson (who submitted his resignation the day of Hoover's death) and his personal secretary, Helen Gandy (who, by pre-arrangement, shredded many of the Director's most confidential secret files on the day of his death), watched the services from side pews, hidden from the crowd. President Nixon was among those who eulogized Hoover: "He personified integrity; he personified honor; he personified principle; he personified courage; he personified discipline; he personified dedication; he personified loyalty; he personified patriotism..."

President Nixon ordered the flags atop all government buildings to fly at half-staff, with the exception of the one at FBI headquarters—a symbolic gesture of Hoover's resolve and courage "in resisting the vicious attacks on his organization." Many government leaders, whose relations with Hoover had long been frosty, praised him in death, including Massachusetts Senator, Edward Kennedy: "Even those who differed with him always had the highest respect for his honesty, integrity, and his desire to do what he thought was best for the country."

Others were unforgiving. Martin Luther King's widow, Coretta, focused on Hoover's long-standing abuse of power: "We are left with a deplorable and dangerous circumstance. The files of the FBI gathered under Mr. Hoover's supervision are replete with lies and are reported to contain sordid material on some of the highest people in government, including Presidents of the United States. Such explosive material has to be dealt with in a responsible way.

Black people and the black freedom movement have been particular targets of this dishonorable kind of activity." Pediatrician and New Left activist, Dr. Benjamin Spock, also shed no tears for Hoover: "It was a relief to have this man (gone), who had no understanding of the underlying philosophy of our government or our Bill of Rights; a man who had such enormous power, and used it to harass individuals with whom he disagreed politically and who had done so much as anyone to intimidate millions of Americans out of their right to hear and judge for themselves all political opinions."

Hoover was buried in range 20, site 117 of Washington D.C.'s Congressional Cemetery, next to his parents and a sister (who died as a small child). Fearing potential desecration of the gravesite, Helen Gandy and John Mohr, the FBI's Assistant to the Director for Administrative Services, saw to it that Hoover was buried in a $3,000, brass, lead-lined casket that weighed more than 1,000 pounds.

Hoover's loyal companion, Clyde Tolson, was presented the American flag that adorned the Director's casket. In his will, Hoover left the bulk of his estate to his long-time friend. When Tolson died in April of 1975, he was buried in Congressional Cemetery, not far from Hoover's grave.

In the early years after his death, Hoover's memory was actively honored. In 1974, FBI headquarters in Washington D.C. was renamed the *J. Edgar Hoover Building*. That same year, Congress voted to publish a memorial book, *J. Edgar Hoover: Memorial Tributes in the Congress of the United States and Various Articles and Editorials Relating to His Life and Work*.

With the passage of time, as previously classified documents were released to the public, Hoover's shining star was tarnished. A closer examination of Hoover's tenure as Bureau Director uncovered his repeated abuses of power, including the pursuit of personal vendettas, employment of illegal surveillance (both telephone bugs and wiretaps), agent-instigated burglaries, planting of evidence, and the use of government employees to perform personal duties on his behalf.

In 1975, COINTELPRO was revealed to the public during hearings before the Senate Selective Committee to Study Government Operations (also known as the Church Committee, named for the Chairman, Idaho's Frank Church). The committee concluded that many of COINTELPRO's activities were illegal and unconstitutional. A year earlier, Attorney General Laurence Silberman had been incensed when he learned about the full extent of the former FBI Director's secret files: "J. Edgar Hoover was like a sewer that collected dirt. I now believe he was the worst public servant in our history."

Since that time, the backlash against Hoover has often been harsh. Many biographies, magazine articles, documentaries, and movies detailing Hoover's life and career have focused on the unflattering aspects of his personality, his often-questioned sexual orientation, and his vindictive nature, sometimes to the extent of blatant sensationalism.

In 1994, a grade school in Schaumburg, Illinois, which bore the name of the former FBI Director, was renamed to honor of President *Herbert Hoover*. Seven years later, Nevada Senator, Harry Reid, submitted an unsuccessful proposal to remove Hoover's name from the FBI Building, describing it as a "stain."

Once revealed to the public, Hoover's glaring faults largely overshadowed his accomplishments. Under Hoover's leadership, the Bureau was transformed into a first-rate law enforcement agency, with a widely-acclaimed training program, arguably the world's foremost crime laboratory, and an invaluable centralized index of finger prints.

The War on Crime: J. Edgar Hoover versus the John Dillinger Gang is not only a dual biography of sorts, but also a study of cops and robbers, the stereotypical images of good versus evil, how America dealt with its first great crime wave, political adroitness, and the origins of power. J. Edgar Hoover's grasp on power was solidified after the Bureau overcame its share of pitfalls and claimed victory over the Depression-era bank robbers, most notably John Dillinger and his gang. Once firmly entrenched in his self-proclaimed Seat of Government, Hoover's self-righteousness and unwillingness to tolerate opposing viewpoints left him vulnerable to critical analysis by historians, as succinctly reflected in the words of author, Bryan Burrough: "The War on Crime bestowed upon Hoover's FBI something close to absolute power, and the day eventually came when Hoover's FBI was corrupted absolutely by it. The Bureau wrestles with its legacy to this day." Relying solely upon the Bureau's rendition of the War on Crime deprives the reader or listener from understanding the real story, as succinctly summarized by Baby Face Nelson co-biographers, Steven Nickel and William J. Helmer: "We now know that the good guys weren't always so good, and bad guys were not quite the personi-fication of evil..."

Hoover's world was black and white, right and wrong, and good versus evil, devoid of gray zones. Ramsey Clark, who served as Attorney General from 1967 to 1969, offered an apt appraisal of Hoover: "I think he had to have bad guys, and he specialized not in creating them, but illuminating them." John Dillinger proved to be the prototypical bad guy.

Would Hoover occupy such a major role in American history had the Bureau not been reluctantly drawn into the pursuit of the John Dillinger gang? Or, would he have exploited another readily-identifiable force of evil, like Communism, as the springboard to unprecedented power? Perhaps Hoover himself answered those questions, when he said the "greatest thrill" of his career was "the night we got Dillinger."

BIBLIOGRAPHY

Books:

Ackerman, Kenneth D. *Young J. Edgar: Hoover, the Red Scare, and the Assault on Civil Liberties.* Carroll & Graf, 2007

Aronson, Marc. *Master of Deceit: J. Edgar Hoover and America in the Age of Lies.* Candlewick Press, 2012.

Beverly, William. *On the Lam: Narratives of Flight in J. Edgar Hoover's America.* University Press of Mississippi, 2003.

Burrough, Bryan. *Public Enemies: America's Greatest Crime Wave and the Birth of the FBI, 1933-34.* Penguin Books, 2004.

Cox, John Stuart and Athan G. Theoharis. *The Boss: J. Edgar Hoover and the Great American Inquisition.* Temple University Press, 1988.

Felt, W. Mark and John D. O'Connor. *A G-Man's Life: The FBI, Being 'Deep Throat,' and the Struggle for Honor in Washington.* Public Affairs, 2006.

Garrow, David J. *The FBI and Martin Luther King, Jr. from 'Solo' to Memphis.* W. W. Norton, 1981.

Gentry, Curt. *J., Edgar Hoover: The Man and the Secrets.* Plume, 1991.

Gorn, Elliott J. *Dillinger's Wild Ride: The Year That Made America's Public Enemy Number One.* Oxford University Press, 2009.

Guin, Jeff. *Go Down Together: The True, Untold Story of Bonnie and Clyde.* Simon & Schuster, 2009.

Hack, Richard. *Puppetmaster: The Secret Life of J. Edgar Hoover.* Phoenix Books, 2007.

Holden, Henry M. *FBI 100 Years: An Unofficial History.* Zenith Imprint, 2008.

Hoover, J. Edgar. *Persons in Hiding.* Gaunt Publishing, 1938.

Hoover, J. Edgar. *Masters of Deceit: The Story of Communism in America and How to Fight It.* Holt Rinehart and Winston, 1958.

Hoover, J. Edgar. *A Study of Communism.* Holt Rinehart and Winston, 1962.

Jeffreys-Jones, Rhodri. *The FBI: A History.* Yale University Press, 2007.

Kessler, Ronald. *The Bureau: The Secret History of the FBI.* St. Martin's Press, 2002.

Matera, Dary. *John Dillinger: The Life and Death of America's First Criminal Celebrity.* Carroll & Graff Publishers, 2004.

Nickel, Steven and William J. Helmer. *Baby Face Nelson: Portrait of a Public Enemy.* Cumberland House, 2002.

Porter, Darwin. *J. Edgar and Clyde Tolson: Investigating the Sexual Secrets of America's Most Famous Men and Women.* Blood Moon Productions, 2012.

Powers, Richard Gid. *Secrecy and Power: The Life of J. Edgar Hoover.* Free Press, 1987.

Powers, Richard Gid. *Broken: The Troubled Past and Uncertain Future of the FBI.* Free Press, 2004.

Schott, Joseph L. *No Left Turns: The FBI in Peace and War.* Praeger, 1975.

Stove, Robert J. *The Unsleeping Eye: Secret Police and Their Victims.* Encounter Books, 2003.

Summers, Anthony. *Official and Confidential: The Secret Life of J. Edgar Hoover.* G. P. Putnam's Sons, 1993.

Theoharis, Athan G. *From the Secret Files of J. Edgar Hoover.* Ivan R. Dee, 1993.

Theoharis, Athan G. *The FBI: A Comprehensive Reference Guide.* Oryx Press, 1998.

Toland, John. *The Dillinger Days.* Da Capo Press, 1995.

Weiner, John. *Enemies: A History of the FBI.* Random House, 2012.

Web Resources:

www.biography.com
www.abcnews.go.com
www.washingtonpost.com
www.zpub.com
www.findagrave.com
www.johnedgarhoover.com
www.alumni.gwu.edu
www.guardian.co.uk
www.nytimes.com
www.time.com
www.nypost.com
www.archives.gov
www.polkonline.com
www.salon.com
www.worldcat.org
www.nasonline.org
www.presidency.ucsb.edu
www.chicagotribune.com
www.imdb.com
www.opinionjournal.com
www.fas.org
www.tucsoncitizen.com
www.fbi.gov
www.johndillingerhistoricalmuseum.com
www.johndillinger.com
www.itnsource.com

Acknowledgements

As always, it has been an entertaining and informative endeavor to write another in my series of *Bringing History Alive* books. I am indebted to the writers, living and dead, who have researched and written about the FBI, J. Edgar Hoover, John Dillinger, and the other Depression-era gangsters, whose names are listed in the bibliography.

I owe a great deal to my wife, Anne, who patiently endures my focus on the writing project at hand—I love her very much. My sons, Andy and Ben, who are now young adults, continue to make it all worthwhile—I love them more that I can put into words. Jim Fulmer once again unselfishly gave of his time to edit this manuscript, making my words more readable—I am honored to call him my friend.

I sincerely hope you found *The War on Crime: J. Edgar Hoover versus the John Dillinger Gang* both entertaining and informative. Thank you for taking time to read my book.

About The Author

Jeffrey K. Smith is a physician and writer. A native of Enterprise, Alabama, he earned his undergraduate and medical degrees from the University of Alabama. After completing his residency at the William S. Hall Psychiatric Institute, he entered private practice in upstate South Carolina.

Dr. Smith is the author of three murder-mystery novels and nine works of non-fiction. He and his wife, Anne, reside in Greer, South Carolina. They are the proud parents of two sons, Andy and Ben.

OTHER BOOKS BY JEFFREY K. SMITH

Fiction:
Sudden Despair
Two Down, Two to Go
A Phantom Killer

Non-fiction:
Rendezvous in Dallas: The Assassination of John F. Kennedy
The Fighting Little Judge: The Life and Times of George C. Wallace
Fire in the Sky: The Story of the Atomic Bomb
Bad Blood: Lyndon B. Johnson, Robert F. Kennedy, and the Tumultuous 1960s
Dixiecrat: The Life and Times of Strom Thurmond
The Loyalist: The Life and Times of Andrew Johnson
The Eagle Has Landed: The Story of Apollo 11
The Presidential Assassins: John Wilkes Booth, Charles Julius Guiteau, Leon Frank Czolgosz, and Lee Harvey Oswald

Made in the USA
Lexington, KY
26 April 2015